UNEXPECTED RETURNS

Understanding Secular Stock Market Cycles

ED EASTERLING

Cypress House

UNEXPECTED RETURNS:
Understanding Secular Stock Market Cycles

Cypress House
155 Cypress Street
Fort Bragg, CA 95437
(800) 773-7782
www.cypresshouse.com

This publication is designed to provide accurate and authoritative information in regard to the subject matter covered. It is sold with the understanding that the publisher is not engaged in rendering professional services. If professional advice or other expert assistance is required, the services of a competent professional person should be sought.

Book and cover design: Cypress House
Clippings cover illustration © Getty Images
Puzzle cover illustration © Cypress House

Library of Congress Cataloging-in-Publication Data

Easterling, Ed, 1959-
    Unexpected returns : understanding secular stock market cycles / Ed Easterling.
        p. cm.
Includes index.
    ISBN 1-879384-62-0 (case : alk. paper)
1. Stock exchanges. 2. Business cycles. 3. Investments. I. Title.

    HG4551.E37 2005
    332.63'22--dc22   2004030470

 This book is printed on recycled, acid-free paper containing a minimum of 10% post-consumer waste recycled fiber.

First Edition

Printed in Canada

4 6 8 9 7 5

CONTENTS

FIGURES

ACKNOWLEDGMENTS

First and foremost, I would like to express the highest appreciation to you, the reader, for your interest in *Unexpected Returns: Understanding Secular Stock Market Cycles.* In publishing, as well as the financial markets, supply has no value without demand. I hope you will enjoy your time with the book and will prosper from the experience.

The earliest catalyst for the book was John Mauldin. Several years ago, John expressed an interest in the research that I had developed during 2001 and 2002. He then asked if he could reference some of it in his weekly letters. Before long, the Crestmont Research website was created to make a library of Crestmont's research available to the public. By 2003, John's book, *Bull's Eye Investing,* was in full development. When he asked to include some of Crestmont's research in his book, I was honored that John, an internationally recognized market sage, would include the research and graphs in his book. Before long, draft notes became a chapter, and then one co-authored chapter expanded into two.

Co-authoring chapters in John's book was an inspiration. There have been kind comments from *Bull's Eye* readers about the co-authored chapters, and inquiries about the additional information that many people have found on the Crestmont website. *Unexpected Returns* is dedicated to those who have asked for its publication and those who will, I hope, benefit from its information and perspectives.

Through their writings and presentations, many bright minds have indirectly contributed to the development of the concepts in *Unexpected Returns*. Although there are too many to name individually, many are included in the bibliography. Throughout the process, my loving wife, Kelly, has been an encouraging partner, strong supporter, and detailed reviewer. Toward achieving the final result, I would like to express appreciation to Eric Troseth, whose journalistic expertise was a valuable resource. Special thanks are extended to Lori Bensing, Fritz Hager, Brent Haggard, Rob Holmes, Phil McKee, John Peavy, Brad Reifler, Chris Sorrow, Stan Swim, Andrew Thorby, and Marshall Yount for their detailed reviews and many insights, comments, and suggestions. Accolades to Cynthia Frank and the staff at Cypress House for their extraordinary efforts, which were invaluable in providing you with the book you hold in your hands. If I have inadvertently forgotten anyone, please let me know and I'll try to include you in the book-related section of the website.

INTRODUCTION

The next decade can be expected to be one of prosperity, economic growth, and continued gains in the standard of living. There are many good reasons for optimism. History demonstrates that economic growth has strong forward momentum and limited periods of recession.

Solid economic growth, however, does not always drive financial market returns—the returns in the markets are primarily driven by the trend in inflation. The main driver for bond returns is recognized by economists and investors to be the level of interest rates, which is closely tied to the expected level of inflation. For the stock market, too, inflation is the main driver of valuation levels as reflected in price/earnings ratios.

Returns from the stock market are likely to be well below average for some time, since current market valuations remain relatively high. The average returns of the past reflect a combination of above-average periods and below-average periods. It is highly likely that the recent bull market, one of the longest in history, will be followed by an extended period of below-average performance. Clearly, financial markets have gone through seasons of high returns combined with seasons of low returns or losses over the past century. Investors who choose to see the stock market through the lens of reality can expect the cycles to continue in the future.

Are you frustrated that the above-average period from 1982–1999 has yielded to the choppy and unrewarding period since 2000? You may be asking if this is a temporary lull or the early stages of an extended secular bear market—a period of choppy, below-average or negative returns. The answers to these questions lie in the pages that follow. You will see that historical evidence and market fundamentals indicate that returns will very likely be below average for the decade 2000–2010, and possibly for the next decade as well. A period of below-average returns should not be surprising after a period of such extraordinary gains in the 1980s and 1990s.

Markets experience long cycles that move from periods of relatively high valuations to periods of relatively low valuations. The periods that start with relatively low levels of valuation produce high subsequent returns; the periods starting with relatively high valuations result in low returns. While it is true that historically the long-term average return for stocks has exceeded the average return for bonds, stocks have not always returned more than bonds. A number of times, stocks have gone through long periods of under-performance relative to bonds. The good news is, you need not suffer through droughts as you wait for better weather. If you know that it is currently a drought period in the markets, move your investments to more fertile areas. *Unexpected Returns* will help you to recognize the conditions of the financial markets, to understand the key drivers for the markets, and to identify some of the ways to profit in all market environments.

The following chapters are packed with extensive facts and details about the financial markets, their dynamic history, and the prospects for the future. Using a geological metaphor, the book's journey explores the sharp cliffs of annual stock market movements and the rolling mountains of interest rate cycles. The terrain will be explained as financial formations that are caused by specific factors in the economy and the markets.

The journey will weave throughout the fundamental relationships that drive stock market gains and bond market returns. Crestmont's model for the markets, known as *Financial Physics*, succinctly defines the relationships between the principles of economics and the tenets of stock market valuation. The model identifies the trend in inflation as the key driver for interest rates and the stock market.

You will find that the journey toward investment truth includes an exploration of two highly different approaches to investing: one produces returns based on the prevailing winds of the markets; the other generates returns from the skill of the investment manager.

The first, the traditional approach to investment management, relies on the direction of the markets. It is a patient, relative return approach that enjoys gains when they occur and suffers losses during market declines. Historically, over long periods of time, the gains have exceeded the losses. In this approach, risk is your friend; based on the principles of Modern Portfolio Theory and the Capital Asset Pricing Model, it is the driver of your returns. This is the Draconian philosophy of investment management: no pain, no gain.

Conversely, the progressive approach to investment management derives its results from the skills of the investment manager, rather than predominantly from the intermittent runs of bull markets. This absolute return approach seeks gains regardless of the prevailing market winds; its objective is consistent profitability. Here, risk is generally the enemy, and you seek to mitigate it. This is the esteem-oriented philosophy of investment management: reward achievements and learn from failures.

The investment world is awakening to a new dawn. Risk tools are becoming readily available. Investors no longer need to toil under the sweat and pain of volatility to achieve gains; currently, risk management enables sophisticated investors to manage an enhanced relationship between returns and risk—the ability to profit with reduced risk. A convergence between the relative return approach and the absolute return approach is underway. Over the next couple of decades, investors will come to expect and use the disciplines of risk-managed investing and controlled returns.

For now, investors are boaters on the high seas of investing. Wise investors will generate profits from sailing with the prevailing winds, by using buy-and-hold strategies when the winds are favorable, and rowing in still seas by using progressive strategies. The decades of the 1980s and 1990s provided strong tailwinds, prompting some of the best buy-and-hold returns of the past century. A bubble in the latter years of the 1990s propelled typical secular bull market valuations into the stratosphere. When the bubble burst in 2000, the days of smooth sailing ended, at least for some years. Now, active rowing strategies are the order of the day for investors who wish to succeed.

Today's investors find themselves in an environment of valuation that investment pioneers have seen, but generally are not around to explain. The wisdom from those who experienced similar conditions many decades ago is squelched by the mantra of those preaching a new era and hope. When the last set of hopeful investors experienced the current level of valuation, the storms of reality soon followed. The reality is that above-average valuations in financial securities subsequently result in below-average returns.

This book is organized into six sections. The first, entitled "Getting Started," provides concepts and principles that will serve as background for the details and discussions that follow in the later sections. Section II, entitled "Market History," contains information about the past returns, volatility, and relationships in the stock and bond markets.

Section III, "Secular Cycles," organizes the history that was explored in section II into patterns called secular cycles, explains the elements of secular cycles, and identifies the state of the current cycle. Section IV is titled "Financial Physics." Whereas prior sections have provided an historical perspective of the financial markets and explained the nature of secular cycles, section IV presents a framework that not only explains the factors that drive the stock market, but also enables investors to better understand the conflicting information that market pundits present. This section concludes with a rational series of projections for stock market returns over the remainder of the decade.

Following the background of history and explanations for the current environment, section V, "Investment Philosophy," explores the differences between the skill-based absolute return approach and the risk-based relative return approach to investing. This section explains the need for different investment approaches based on the general market climate. Section VI, "Investment Strategy," provides specific examples of techniques that can be used in more challenging market conditions. This section concludes with discussion of the continuing evolution in the area of investment management, and the current process of convergence between the traditional relative return and the progressive absolute return approaches.

It is quite fitting that the metaphor for seeking knowledge involves climbing to reach a guru on a mountain. Just as a climber succeeds by overcoming the forces of gravity, so those who pursue insight by overcoming the forces of tradition will gain a clearer view of reality. The key to investment success, then, is to apply today's investment strategies, tools, and technology in a way that is consistent with the enduring principles of the markets. The goal of investing is profits, and hope is not a strategy for profits.

The following pages present a road map to understanding the markets' topography, the path to future returns, and examples of techniques for navigating the current terrain. There are many roads investors can travel—some based on rational methods and others derived from random chance. To more closely control your investment destiny, seek the rational principles.

For ongoing insights and periodic updates to the charts and material discussed in this book, please visit Crestmont's website at www. CrestmontResearch.com.

SECTION I

GETTING STARTED

Chapter 1

Planning the Journey

"I'm about ready to give up." Exasperated, he finally uttered those words at dinner one evening. As with many investors today, he had become increasingly frustrated with his investment performance over the past several years. After accumulating enough capital during the 1990s to play the markets on his own; ultimately, the markets played him. Exciting gains in one position evaporated into a lesson that he swore would never happen again. Another approach worked very well for many months; but it was the market's fault when it failed. And then there was the advice of professionals in some of the most recognized firms: "Buy and hold. Invest for the long term. You have to take more risk to get higher returns."

The conventional wisdom of the past two decades has not worked for the first five years of this decade. There are clear reasons why it has not worked and will not work in the foreseeable future. Once you understand the fundamentals that drive the markets, there are positive ways to enhance your investment strategy. The following chapters represent a journey for those who seek to understand the basics of market environments and want to feel empowered to be more effective investors and advisors.

The Long-term View

The value of history rests in the insights that it can provide about the many shorter-term periods that comprise the long term. Conventional wisdom often takes a long-term view, however, and ignores the underlying details, thus missing the opportunity to learn from history. The research presented in the chapters that follow will unpack uncommon insights about stocks and the financial markets by looking at the trees that create the forest. Further, the book will provide you the tools and understanding to more accurately interpret the wide range of information streaming from investment sources.

During the 1980s and 1990s, the brawn of the bull market enabled every investor to generate gains in his or her portfolio. The stock market environment changed in 2000 when the bubble of the late 1990s burst. Over the past several years, the market has deflated back toward reality. Many investors now are hopeful that the market can resume its historical ascension and again provide average returns. In reality, the fundamental market conditions are positioned for returns to be below the historical average for some years to come.

If the past several years have caused you to feel disoriented and to believe the pundits who either sell hope or blame the markets, the journey will provide you several key insights for your investment strategy. These include: (1) The financial markets are more volatile that most investors realize; (2) Market volatility can be either your friend or your foe; (3) The general trend in the stock and bond markets is driven by the direction and level of inflation; and (4) Financial returns from stocks and bonds are heavily dependent on the conditions that exist when you invest. For example, the conventional wisdom of investing for the long term would include an assumption that an investor who buys stocks at top of the market in 2000 could expect the same long-term returns as an investor who entered the market at the lows of 2002. In fact, reality differs from that assumption; the starting point makes a significant difference in your ultimate returns. Additionally, though you cannot affect the market conditions that will exist during your investment lifetime, you can adjust your strategy to the conditions.

The scenery along the journey includes analyses, concepts, and graphics that start with lessons of history and conclude with visions of the future. The objective of *Unexpected Returns* is to provide you practical knowledge about investing in the financial markets. The book is based on the research advanced by the author's firm, Crestmont Research. Its focus on intermediate-term time frames—periods that are relevant for most investors—differs from the longer-term approach taken by many investment manuals and much scholarly research. While traditional investment philosophy mutes the details of highly relevant five- to twenty-year periods of market action by focusing on long-term average returns, Crestmont's research highlights the topography of the markets and assesses the conditions associated with its highs and lows. To dress for success as an investor, you need to wear what is appropriate for the climate and conditions. In the following pages, you will find the facts that too often get lost when the markets are viewed only from the vantage point of long-term averages.

The Right Frame of Mind

The traditional investment strategies that worked so well for two decades have not worked for several years. Many investors are frustrated and want to understand what is reasonable to expect in the current environment. This is where the journey begins: a journey to the land of truth. The goal is to find the insights that explain the current environment in the stock market and the bond market.

Fork in the Road

The land of truth is not easy to find. As you begin, your first stop will be at a fork in the road. One of the trails will lead to the land of truth, and the other to the land of lies. In the land of truth, everyone always answers questions truthfully; in the land of lies, everyone always answers questions with lies. There is a troll camping at the fork—sometimes a troll from the land of truth and other times a troll from the land of lies. You do not know which troll will be there, but you can ask him one question to determine which trail to take to be sure that you go toward the land of truth. What is the question? The answer to the puzzle will come later.

Basics of Navigation

When you embark on a trip toward a desired destination, it is important to know your starting point and the path that you will take. For every investor, the destination is financial success. During the past two decades, the path seemed obvious. The conventional wisdom of "buy-and-hold" worked quite well—not because it is a timeless strategy, but because it was the right strategy for the market environment over those two decades. By contrast, the conventional wisdom of buy-and-hold was devastating to investors during the 1960s and 1970s; it simply does not work in all environments. The following chapters will identify the drivers of broad trends in the financial markets and show how you can adjust your investment strategy to achieve financial success.

The journey starts almost 2000 years ago with Ptolemy, a famous cartographer and astronomer. Unlike some in his era, Ptolemy believed that the world was round. To better define his world, he drew horizontal rings around his globe, rings that started at the equator and were spaced equally upward and downward toward the poles. Intersecting the horizontal lines, Ptolemy drew vertical lines, each starting at the North Pole and arching across the equator to the South Pole. His lines were the early forerunners of the coordinates we know as latitude and longitude.

For mariners at the time, as for anyone on a journey, successful navigation depends on accurately measuring where you are in relation to your starting point and your destination. Early travelers used sightings of stars and constellations to determine their latitude, their distance north or south of the equator. But seafarers faced the challenge of determining their horizontal position on a map while at sea; they needed to know how far east or west they needed to travel. As ships ran aground or became lost at sea, determining horizontal distance or location became such a problem that the British Parliament enacted the Longitude Act of 1714, which offered a substantial bounty to the inventor who could devise an accurate measure of horizontal location on the globe.

Forty-five years later, an English clock maker named John Harrison developed the means to accurately navigate the globe, and he ultimately collected the prize. Mr. Harrison developed a clock that would accurately measure time despite the adverse conditions of high seas, temperature, and humidity.

Time was the key to solving the problem of horizontal distance. We experience this effect today in the form of time zones. The constant rotation of the earth moves time at a steady pace around the world. For example, the sun reaches noon in New York three hours before it does in California. Mr. Harrison solved the problem by recognizing that the difference in time between any unknown location and any known location could be used to determine the horizontal distance between those two points based on the rotation of the earth. For the unknown location, a sundial could be used to determine the time. His challenge was to develop a clock that maintained accurate time for the point of origin under the conditions of sea travel. Once it was developed, mariners had both latitude and longitude, and could identify their exact location on the map, ensuring that they stayed on course.

For investors, a financial plan represents the map, and a strategy represents the route, to investment success. Understanding secular stock market cycles and identifying the current point in the cycle is crucial to reaching your destination. As you navigate the following chapters, it may be helpful to know where you are headed and what you can expect along the way. This first section, chapters 1 and 2, is designed to point you in the right direction and help to identify a few of the sights along the way. Chapters 3–7 examine market history, interest rates and inflation, secular bull and secular bear market cycles, the current cycle, and *Financial Physics*. Chapters 8–12 present a formula for future stock market returns and the reasons behind a natural upper limit for price/earnings ratios (P/Es). In addition, they examine absolute return and relative return investing, "rowing" and "sailing" investment strategies, investment techniques for traditional investors, and a perspective on the future of investment management.

The journey will reveal a series of insights that every investor should know to *avoid failure* and to *achieve success*. Avoiding failure and achieving success are entirely different concepts—as different as risk and return.

On the first element, risk, avoiding failure is the first objective of prudent investing. As Omaha's Oracle, Warren Buffett, has many times repeated, "Rule number one, never lose money. Rule number two, never forget rule number one." Upcoming chapters provide specific insights that will enable you to sort through the clutter of misinformation, make better investment decisions, and avoid irrational mistakes.

Toward the second element, return, achieving success is the ultimate objective of investing. *Unexpected Returns* explains the rules of the game for investing in financial markets. Understanding the rules, you can make the appropriate decisions to be successful. The market's rules are found primarily in the rich history of the market's actions, rather than in the history of people or events. Subsequent chapters will seek to present key insights to arm investors with the knowledge to make better investment decisions.

The body of market history that will be explored focuses primarily on the modern period, starting at the turn of the twentieth century. Only five years later, George Santayana published *Life of Reason*, in which he so wisely noted, "Those who cannot remember the past are condemned to repeat it."

For those who seek rational explanations for the empirically based presentations, Section III details the fundamental drivers of market movements and cycles. And for those who want a few examples of how to apply the new wisdom, as well as examples of the specific tools and techniques for playing the game, the later chapters include tangible tactics.

Background on the Matrix

One of Crestmont's most recognized presentations is the Stock Market Matrix ("Matrix"), the multicolored mosaic of investment returns over the past century. A university professor who includes it in his course work at Duke's Fuqua School of Business, Dr. Campbell R. Harvey refers to it as Crestmont's stock market "heatmap." Some have asked how it was created.

The Stock Market Matrix was one of Crestmont's first research initiatives. The objective, in the summer of 2001, was to determine whether the stock market had completed its retreat from recent highs and would soon return to new heights, or whether the pullback was far from complete. In a discussion with an experienced investor, debate raged about long-term returns in the stock market and whether the trend had made its way back to the level that would allow average returns in the future. The crux of the discussion focused on the returns that are typically presented, the long-term return series of seventy-five years or more that is often used by investors and investment advisors.

Some of the most popular presentations of long-term stock market returns arbitrarily start in the 1920s and determine the returns through a recent date. Is that starting date reasonable, or does it distort the analysis due to its single-point risk? If the starting level in the stock market is the high in 1929, the returns are quite different than if the starting level is the low that occurred after the crash in 1929. An analysis of returns that is dependent on a single starting point has the risk of providing invalid information.

After many long hours, a detailed presentation was developed. Rather than looking at one date in the distant past, every decade was chosen as a starting point, and eleven sets of analyses were laid out for consideration. Almost conclusively, they reflected that the market remained overvalued to various degrees. The astute investor, however, struck like a lightning bolt when he asked, "But isn't the analysis still subject to single-point risk? What if the start of every decade distorts the results for some reason?"

Responding to the challenge, the Stock Market Matrix was developed as a method to present every annual return scenario since 1900. The Matrix, presented in chapter 3, provides every starting year and every ending year, and then calculates the annualized return for the periods. As well, the Matrix uses modes of coloration and ancillary information to enhance its effectiveness as a communication tool. Returns are denoted in shades of red, blue, and green to reflect the level of returns. Further, information about economic growth, inflation, and historical events over the past century are included to add depth to the chart's messages. Today, more than 100,000 copies are in use around the world.

Investment Insights and Advertising

In the advertising business, it is often said that half of all advertising is effective—it is just hard to determine which half. Thus advertisers are destined to pursue hopeful strategies with as much diligence as is possible in an imprecise situation. Some investment books and market pundits present a similar dilemma; they provide great insights, ambiguous information, and poor information, which sometimes can be challenging to differentiate.

The journey that follows will provide the tools and background to help you to decipher and extract investment wisdom from the investment guides as well as from the investment pros. It is filled with rational insights about stock and bond market history as well as perspectives about the financial markets going forward. Specific techniques for enhancing your own investment management are included as well.

Beginning with the End in Mind

Throughout the following chapters, ten key concepts will tie together the message of Unexpected Returns. These points help to frame into perspective the information described in the text and displayed in the graphics; they also offer a glimpse of the messages that will be forthcoming.

Ten Key Concepts

1. Valuation matters. Over periods of decades, the average rarely happens; above-average returns occur when P/E ratios start low and rise; below-average returns occur when P/E ratios start high and decline.

2. The financial markets are much more volatile than most investors realize! Volatility matters. Two gremlins can devastate the returns that are actually realized: negative numbers and the dispersion of returns.

3. The stock market experiences extended periods of secular bull markets and secular bear markets based on the trend in P/E ratios, which is driven by the trend in inflation.

4. The Y-Curve Effect reflects the strong relationship between P/E ratios and inflation or deflation.

5. The current financial conditions indicate relatively low or negative returns from stocks and bonds.

6. Crestmont's *Financial Physics* model aligns the interconnected relationships between the economy and the financial markets that determine the stock market's overall direction.

7. P/E ratios for the market have a sustainable peak or limit in the range of 20–25 when inflation is near price stability—very close to where P/Es were in 2004.

8. The progressive strategies of absolute return investing rely on skill for seeking consistent returns, and the traditional strategies of relative return investing rely on taking a long-term view of market risk for return.

9. During secular bull markets, the investment strategy of "sailing" by buying and holding stocks and bonds can be very effective; during secular bear markets, the investment strategy of "rowing" with absolute return strategies can be very effective.

10. Evolution in the financial markets and investment management is expanding the concept of risk management from use in absolute return strategies to use in traditional portfolio management.

CHAPTER 2

THE PRINCIPLES

At this point, your backpack is full of concepts for the journey through the coming chapters. The importance of these will become clear at points along the way. The following discussion of principles will raise significant investment insights to help you prepare for the upcoming exploration of financial market history and investment management.

Final Preparation

The following principles provide perspectives about conventional wisdom in investment management. Many of the mantras that pepper investment presentations and financial market commentaries do not take into account the realities of the markets. Further, some concepts accepted as conventional wisdom claim relationships that do not truly exist. In some instances, the thought process about primary principles gets reversed. In other words, if A sometimes causes B, it is not necessarily true that if B occurs it was caused by A. Likewise, if A occurs, B is not always the result. For example, investors are told that if they take more risk, they can achieve higher returns. Higher risk also means a greater chance of a loss, and not necessarily higher returns.

Risk Is Not a Knob

First and foremost, risk is not a knob that one turns to automatically receive higher returns. Too often, investors believe that higher returns are available simply by taking more risk. They naively approach investments with a mistaken confidence in future returns by assuming that higher risk means only near-term volatility rather than permanent losses to their account. The conventional wisdom about long-term returns provides a false sense of security, promoting an unwarranted complacency that wrongly assumes that interim losses always blossom, at some point, into future gains.

Traditional financial logic argues that since stocks are riskier than bonds—in that they have a greater potential for loss than bonds—an efficient market will price stocks to deliver higher returns than bonds over the long term. Therefore, the logic goes, investors should increase their allocations to stocks in order to generate higher returns in their portfolios.

The flaw in the logic is that market fundamentals can drive stocks to high levels of valuation, prices that make it difficult to earn good returns in the future. From those high levels, the expected return for stocks can be very low or even negative for years. Thus in those circumstances, stocks are priced at levels that ultimately provide a lower return than bonds. An investor who then adopts the traditional logic that higher risk leads to higher returns—and who acts on this advice by increasing his stock allocation at a time of high stock valuations—ends up lowering his expected return rather than increasing it. The investor is simultaneously increasing his risk and lowering his expected return for years into the future.

Overall, stocks are riskier than bonds. History and the operation of rational markets have shown that stocks should return more than bonds over the very long run, but the degree of risk in stocks varies greatly depending on market valuations. Stocks are most risky when valuations, reflected in relatively high prices, are high; that is when the risks of decline and loss are greatest.

Higher risk in financial markets can lead to higher losses, when it is not addressed with the tools of risk management. The chapters that follow explain when and why stocks are a risky and vulnerable investment, and when they are a high-potential investment.

Peanut Butter Cups

Many years ago, a TV advertisement relating to Reese's Peanut Butter Cups appeared. The ad featured a person eating a bar of chocolate bumping into a person eating from a jar of peanut butter. The result of the crash was a combination of chocolate and peanut butter that neither person had previously considered. Chapters 7 and 8 are dedicated to exploring the concept that emerges through a combination of economics and stock market finance, a model that many experts have never considered.

Economics is the study of how goods and services are produced and consumed. Stock market finance relates to the valuation of companies, the overall value of equity securities, and investments in those securities and markets. Crestmont has titled the concept that combines the two *Financial Physics.* It links the principles of economics and the components of stock market finance into a simple pragmatic model. The *Financial Physics* model is a tool enabling investors to reconcile much of the financial and market information that can often be confusing or contradictory.

The Reconciliation Principle

Many factors in the economy and the financial markets are interrelated. As a result, a change in one variable directly or indirectly affects other variables. Applied to the subjects in this book, the reconciliation principle states that an analysis or discussion about economic and financial market issues should be internally consistent. In other words, assumptions should be consistently applied to all variables in the analysis. If an experienced fishing guide indicates to you that the most fish can be caught in the coolest parts of the day, yet schedules your trip in the midday sun, you may question whether there is an inconsistency in his planning, as it does not reconcile with what you know about the other variables.

In the financial world, inflation and interest rates are strongly related. Higher inflation leads to higher long-term interest rates. As interest rates rise, the return that investors require from stocks increases as well. Generally, this results in lower prices on stocks, to make them less expensive and to provide for the expected higher future returns. If you hear bullish stock market pundits espouse that bonds are risky due to potentially higher inflation, yet they promote stocks as a good investment, you may want to challenge their logic. The condition of increasing inflation that increases interest rates and adversely affects the bond market also adversely affects the stock market. They may have other assumptions that will reconcile the apparent inconsistency, or their opinions may be affected by illogical biases. The reconciliation principle requires that assumptions be consistently applied rationally and logically across all markets and the economy.

One way that Crestmont's research uses this approach is by looking at multiple analyses about the same subject and observing any logical inconsistencies across the group. Further, each analysis is reviewed for its internal consistency. Using multiple observation points about the same information can improve the credibility of analysis and research. Crestmont's research looks for confirming or conflicting signals to increase the validity of the work. A clear objective is to develop credible analyses. It is often said, "The devil is in the details." A critical eye is needed to focus on the underlying assumptions to ensure logically consistent and internally reconciled research analyses.

Hope, Fear, and Greed

For those who remember the original Star Trek TV series, the characters included a highly logical character named Mr. Spock, who was from the planet Vulcan and was the son of a Vulcan father and a human mother. Spock was raised on Vulcan, and was influenced by the logical environment on his planet. As a Vulcan, Spock fought hard to suppress his human emotions and approach the world from a very logical perspective.

The financial markets are structured to be driven by logic. Whether in the trading pits of Chicago or the cyberspace of Internet markets, buyers and sellers meet to battle over the values of securities. Although moments may be filled with excitement and enthusiasm, actions are driven by focusing on the logical objective of making a profit. Good traders will say that emotions are the source of most bad decisions by investors; human nature raises the desire to buy securities that have gone up, and to sell after prices have fallen. Presumably, Spock would have been a great trader—deciding to buy securities that were rationally positioned to increase in value and to sell securities that were overvalued. As long as his emotional instincts were controlled, his investment decisions would have been logical.

Most of the mistakes that investors make are the result of three emotions: *hope, fear, and greed.* An investor who buys a stock at $10 per share might see the price fall to $9 upon the release of unfavorable news. Though it is often said that the first loss is the best loss, the investor is likely to *hope* that the price will rise again to $10. There is no better feeling than coming from behind to break even. As a result, investors make their first emotional mistake when they hold on to losing positions, hoping for them to recover. Unfortunately, losing positions often fail to recover, and simply become greater losses. The illogical reasoning that investors often invoke says, "A loss is not a loss until you take it."

On the other hand, the price might rise to $11. For some, the second emotional mistake occurs when investors *fear* that the gain will get away, and as a result, they sell too soon. Many investors have a higher proportion of small winners and a couple of big losers each year—the result of fear and hope.

If the investor hold the stock and it rises to $20, the third emotional mistake occurs when, succumbing to greed, the investor does not sell when the stock price exceeds its value. Experienced traders say that many dollars have been lost because investors try to get the last dime.

The combination of emotional decision making and contradictory opinions about the values of securities drives the markets on a wild and volatile ride. Both factors also create a significant amount of inefficiency in the markets. Later chapters will highlight the high levels of volatility in the markets, and the ways that skill-based investing takes advantage of having better information and capitalizes on mispriced securities.

Markets are an efficiency process, not an efficient condition. One of the roles of the markets is to bring together a wide variety of information and insights to vet prices toward fair value. This is noted as Warren Buffett quotes the investment wisdom of Benjamin

Graham: "In the short run, the market is a voting machine; but in the long run, it is a weighing machine." Over longer periods of time, prices tend to reflect the values of securities. In the short run, prices can vary significantly from the underlying value based upon the daily battle between buyers and sellers.

One can only wonder about the financial markets on the planet Vulcan. If all buyers and sellers were logical and diligent, would the markets achieve the state of an efficient condition—methodically adjusting to new information and quietly reflecting fair value?

Convergence and Divergence

Do you believe that markets have a centerline of fair value and that they fluctuate around that centerline, from a condition of being overvalued to a condition of being undervalued? Or do you believe that markets move in trends until the trend changes? Probably, you believe a bit of both.

Convergent markets are those that fluctuate around a centerline from states of mispricing to states of fair pricing. When assets become mispriced, either too high or too low, the markets operate to bring prices back into line with fair value. This philosophy reflects the convergent view of the world.

Divergent markets are those that trend in a particular direction due to factors in the market, or momentum, until the trend changes. The securities in the market have a fair value trend, irrespective of a fair value centerline, and tend to move in a certain direction until the trend changes. Markets that move in one direction until the trend diverges toward another direction reflect the divergent philosophy of the world.

To illustrate the difference between convergent and divergent views, consider the example of a coin toss. The likelihood of tossing heads or tails on a fair coin is 50 percent. Imagine the instance in which tails has been tossed three times in a row. What is the probability of another tails? The statistical answer remains 50 percent, since each coin toss is independent, unrelated to the prior toss. Nonetheless, the convergent investor expects that heads is more likely, since at some point heads and tails will need to be equally represented. If tails has a lead of 3-0, then heads will need to catch up. On the other hand, the divergent investor expects that another tails is more likely. Obviously, the trend is biased toward tails, and whatever factors are driving tails are not expected to stop suddenly. If you were to guess the next flip of the coin, would you say heads or tails?

As you consider your portfolio allocation strategy and your investment alternatives, it may be helpful to assess them in the context of a convergent or divergent view of the markets. Additionally, some of the research in the coming chapters is based on long-term trends in the economy and the financial markets. You will see that these long-term trends have short-term swings that ultimately converge to the base trendline. For example, the long-term trend in economic growth has been relatively consistent over time. Periods of above-average growth were followed by periods of below-average growth, producing an average trend of growth over time. The concept of trends fluctuating around a centerline is often called "reversion to the mean" or "regression to the mean." This reflects the propensity for an economic variable or a stock price to cycle around a centerline value, returning to the average after having drifted away.

Farsightedness

In the field of ophthalmology, farsightedness is the ability to see distant objects better than objects that are nearby. It is probably fair to say that most stock market optimists suffer from investment farsightedness. A long-term perspective is quite relevant for scholarly studies and for the assessment of long-term relationships, but is not a good idea for developing assumptions that are to be used for investment planning. Most investors do not have such long-term horizons in their real lives; further, their investment performance can be improved by including assumptions that take into account the likely effects of shorter-term conditions.

Interestingly, farsightedness is more often experienced with stocks than with bonds. The conventional wisdom on stocks is that you should invest with a long-term perspective and can expect the long-term return over time. Keep in mind that such advice held the same long-term return outlook for the investor in stocks in early 2000 as it does for an investor today—according to conventional wisdom, both investors can expect the same long-term return. Understandably, you know that such thinking is not logical or reasonable, yet that reasoning has become mainstream thinking by many investors and is reflected in the advice of many professionals.

Further, have you ever noticed the incongruity of the advice about individual stocks and the stock market? Consider a great company's stock price, which has risen to the point of being highly valued. Often, the advice from market professionals is to sell the stock and find a better value. Even though the company is expected to generate good profits in the future, the current high valuation is expected to result in relatively lower returns. By contrast, when the stock market as a whole is highly valued, the most common advice is to hold for the long term. Also, there is an underlying message that returns will be average from that point forward. Such advice suffers from farsightedness as well as logical inconsistency. Even though the economy may perform well in the future, above-average valuations generally result in below-average returns. If the reasoning works with individual stocks that become overpriced, it should likewise apply when the overall stock market is priced highly in relation to its historical or underlying value.

Consider farsightedness in the context of investing in bonds. The historical average return from high-quality bonds is close to 7%. As of late 2004, long-term interest rates are less than 5%. Some people expect that interest rates may rise back to the historically average level of interest rates. Although it may be reasonable to assume that over several cycles your average return from bonds may increase to 7%, it is not reasonable to assume that you will achieve 7% over the next few years or even the next decade. And using the reconciliation principle, the only way to achieve an average of 7% starting from 5% would be for interest rates to rise to well more than 7%. As interest rates rise, the value of existing bonds declines. If you invest in longer-term bonds today with a long-term perspective, you may experience a significant loss over the next few years while waiting for the long-term to get you back to average.

In the chapters that follow, you will see that current interest rates are relatively low and stock market valuations relatively high. The concepts of the previous chapter and the principles in this chapter will be used to explain the fundamentals that drive the financial markets. In addition, you will gain insights regarding the implications for the next few years as well as for the coming decades. This increased understanding will position you to make better investment decisions and to develop realistic assumptions about future investment returns. *Unexpected Returns* does not provide all the techniques and programs you will need; it complements the investment books written to give advice. Once you have the information and perspectives this text provides, you should be able to distinguish between rational content and misinformation throughout your readings and discussions about investing in the financial markets. The journey resumes in the next section with a realistic view of the performance history of the financial markets, starting with stock market history and concluding with the history of the bond market and interest rates.

SECTION II

MARKET HISTORY

CHAPTER 3

STOCK MARKET HISTORY

The conventional wisdom for investing in the stock market is reflected in the traditional approach of buying and holding for the long term. The next two chapters explore stock market history and interest rate history for insights about the shorter-term periods that comprise the long term. The information in these chapters will challenge many of the traditional assumptions about stocks, bonds, and investment management.

The Stock Market Matrix: Taking the Red Pill

In the film *The Matrix,* Morpheus, the group leader, discusses truth with the ultimate hero, Neo. In their world, most people are wired into a machine that feeds their minds images of a false existence. Morpheus and his group have escaped the machine and live in reality. Neo, though still wired into the machine, has begun to question this digital dream. Morpheus tells Neo about the world that has been pulled over his eyes to blind him to the truth. The world is a prison for his mind—he does not have the senses of touch, taste, or smell; he lives in a dream created by the machine to control him. Morpheus holds out two pills: the blue one will eliminate Neo's doubts and enable him to enjoy the machine's pleasant program; the red one will free him from the machine and irrevocably enlighten him to the truth of reality.

The graph titled Stock Market Matrix provides a "red pill" insight into the realities of the stock market. It exposes the myths of a system that seeks to corral investors into a mindset of smooth long-term returns and investment security. As Morpheus later explains to Neo about their world, most of the people believe what the machine feeds into their brains, and most are not ready to be unplugged—they are hopelessly dependent on the system.

The Stock Market Matrix dispels popular myths associated with "thinking long-term," and reveals a surprisingly volatile market in which highly-rewarding, multiyear seasons for investment are followed by periods of high risk and disappointing returns. Let's unplug and see stock market reality.

The Big Picture

Soar into space, and the earth loses its distinctive features: the Himalayas flatten; the Grand Canyon appears no deeper than a ditch; and details fade from view. The long view from space reveals the beautiful blue planet, but it gives few, if any, clues to the harsh geographical and financial realities that you would face walking across the earth's surface.

If you take a long-term view of the stock market, perhaps fifty or seventy-five years, it becomes the beautiful blue chip market. But the long-term rise in the market obscures the realities that affect almost every investor. Investors need to pay for college. They buy houses, they take early retirement, and they sometimes lose their jobs. In each case, they need money immediately and may not have the luxury of waiting for good long-term results in the stock market. They are greatly affected by the market's intermediate-term moves, which last five to twenty years.

While a 75-year chart of stock market performance provides a pretty picture, most investors are not in a position to participate for the full 75-year ride. Even long-term-oriented pension funds and endowments have obligations and expectations that preclude them from successfully employing a Rip Van Winkle approach to investment management. Most individual investors are forced by the realities of life to work with a shorter investment time frame of about twenty years. They do not accumulate substantial assets until they are in their forties, and need to begin drawing on those assets in their sixties. Those who have retired depend on their investment portfolios for their livelihoods.

Further, long-term declining and choppy markets significantly affect the returns achievable by average investors. As you will see in the pages that follow, market cycles include extended periods of charging upward followed by extended periods of idling in choppy waters. Some studies include only the richest periods, while others include a longer-term mix. Even those that use long-term horizons sometimes start at a low point, thus distorting the returns that were typically available at most other times. So, what returns should investors realistically expect from the stock market?

Issues with Averages

RETIRE IN THE LAND OF ETERNAL SUNSHINE — AVERAGE TEMPERATURE 76 DEGREES!

So proclaims a sales brochure eagerly read by shivering Minnesotans huddled indoors during a February blizzard. Unfortunately, those who responded would have found themselves living out their retirement dreams next door to a Gila monster in Death Valley, where winter mornings approach freezing and summer days are hot enough to fry a rattlesnake. Nonetheless, it is a land of sunshine with an average temperature of 76, just like Hawaii.

Similarly, average stock market returns do not tell the entire story. No investor earns, let alone spends, average returns. Each investment yields, and each investor receives, a compounded return. Average returns represent the simple average for the periods (i.e., the sum of the returns divided by the number of periods). Compounded returns represent the single rate of return applied to each period, which produces the same end result as the actual series of returns.

For example, if the returns for stocks over three years were +10%, –15%, and +25%, the simple average return would be 6.67% (10% minus 15% plus 25%, divided by 3). If you had invested $10,000, the account would be $11,688 at the end of the three years. The compounded return is the single rate that would be earned annually to produce the gain of $1,688. In this example, the compounded rate is 5.34%. In other words, $10,000 invested in an account at approximately 5.34% per year for three years would grow to $11,688, while $10,000 invested in stocks at +10%, –15%, and

+25% (reflecting a simple average of 6.67%) would grow to the same $11,688.

Compounded returns can be far lower than simple average returns, particularly in the stock market. In fact, in the past 104 years ending 2003, the average annual return in the Dow Jones Industrials Average, excluding dividends and transaction costs, was 7.4%, compared to a compounded annual change of 5%.

In addition, averaging stock market returns over time masks the annual volatility of the market. An average number can lead to a feeling, perhaps even an expectation, of stable or consistent returns. The actual market ride, however, might more closely resemble snowboarding down an avalanche or climbing a cliff. In fact, the stock market, as reflected by the Dow Jones Industrial Average, has raced ahead by as much as +82% in a single year, and fallen by as much as –34%, –53%, and –23% in consecutive years. If the average moves in the market do not tell its real story, what does?

The Matrix

The chart titled Stock Market Matrix offers realistic perspectives of the stock market over more than a century. It shows clearly that some periods are far more rewarding for investors than other periods. It also reveals that returns are highly dependent on the starting point and ending point. Investors who buy into expensive markets risk large declines; also, they risk disappointing returns over long periods of time. Investors who buy into the stock market when valuations are low take less downside risk and have a much higher probability of satisfactory returns or even exceptional returns. This is an intuitive result, yet one that has historically gone unheeded by investors.

One version of the Matrix is presented in figure 3.1 as a two-page spread on the next pages. That version and others with alternative assumptions are available at www.CrestmontResearch.com. The website also enables readers to access updated versions of both the Matrix and other charts in this book.

The power of the Matrix is that it presents the facts and does not pre-select starting and ending points for the reader. You may start in any year since 1900 and end whenever you choose. The starting and ending points are yours, and the conclusions become inescapable.

The matrix mosaic of over 5,000 possible scenarios over more than a century also provides illuminating insights into the big picture of the market. While the big picture can be described by a long-term average return for the market, that average is the result of a significant number of shorter-term periods with a high amount of variability. The Matrix enables the reader to plunge below the superficiality of average returns as it reveals market waves, seasons, and cycles over periods of many years.

Explaining the Matrix Layout

The chart can be explained in terms of time, return, valuation, and reference information. The Matrix reveals much information about the stock market over the past century. This tool was developed to help viewers gain a realistic perspective about various aspects of the market. First, it presents returns over time. Unlike most long-term return presentations, the Matrix provides every scenario for periods since 1900. Secondly, beyond providing the annual returns for all periods, it categorizes the returns by magnitude in vivid colors. Thirdly, beyond listing the price/earnings ratio (P/E) by year, the chart incorporates the concept of valuation into every scenario. Lastly, the Matrix includes reference values for each year, and historical snippets to help the reader travel through the timeline of the past century.

Time

There are three columns on the left-hand side of the page and three rows on the top of the page. The column and row closest to the main chart reflect every year from 1900 through 2003. The column on the left side will serve as the starting year, and the row on the top represents the ending year. The top row has been abbreviated to the last two numbers of the year. Therefore, if you want to know the annual compounded return from 1950 to 1974, look for the row represented by the year 1950 on the left and look for the intersecting column designated by 74 (1974). The result on the version titled "S&P Index Only" is 6, reflecting an annual compounded return of 6% over that twenty-four-year period.

Figure 3.1. Stock Market Matrix

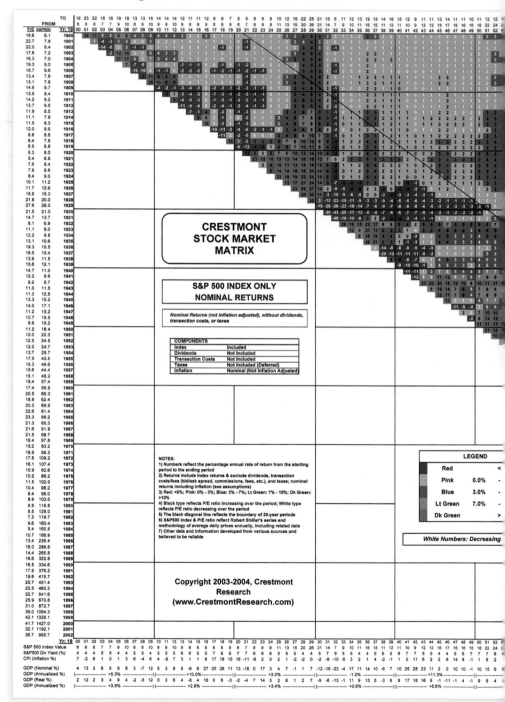

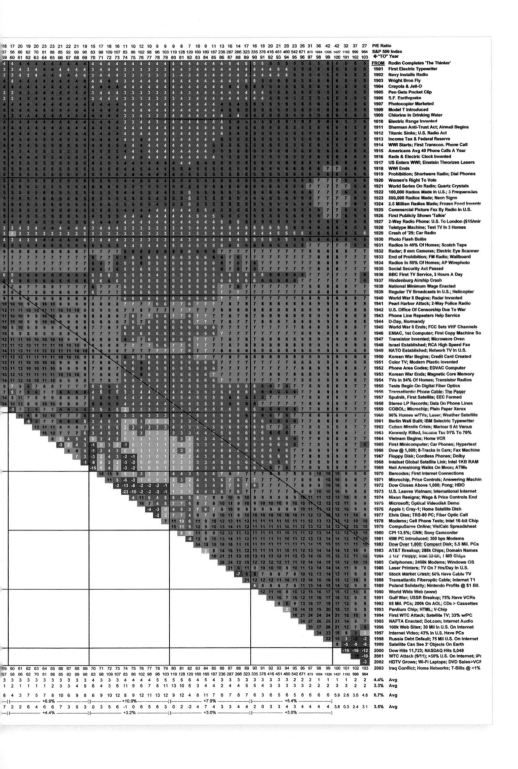

Return

Also note that the return number resides in a cell that has been shaded blue. The color of the cell represents the level of the return. If the annual return is less than 0%, the cell is shaded red. When the return is between 0% and 3%, the shading is pink. Blue is used when the range is 3% to 7%; light green when the returns are between 7% and 10%, and dark green indicates annual returns in excess of 10%. This enables you to look at the big picture, long-term periods as well as shorter periods of time. Where long-term returns tend to be shaded blue, shorter-term periods reflect all shades of returns.

Valuation

Note additionally that the original number 6, mentioned above, was presented in a black-colored font. Some of the numbers are presented in black, while others are white. This feature is used to designate the direction of the market's level of valuation. The most common method of expressing valuation levels in the stock market is to divide the price of a stock by the underlying earnings of the stock, to produce a ratio known as the stock's price/earnings ratio, also known as the "P/E" or "P/E ratio." For example, if the S&P 500 Index is 1,000 and earnings total $40 per share, the P/E ratio for the market is calculated to be 25 (i.e., 1,000 divided by 40).

The P/E ratio approach can be used to express the valuation of an index as well as individual stocks. Note that when the P/E ratio is rising, it increases stock market gains beyond the growth in earnings. Similarly, when the P/E ratio is declining, stock market gains are reduced below the level of earnings growth as the multiplying factor declines. The effect of declining P/Es can reduce the level of market gains below the level of earnings growth, and it can cause losses despite significant increases in earnings. Using the example above, if earnings per share increase by 20% from $40 to $48, but the P/E ratio declines from 25 to 20, the S&P 500 Index would fall to 960 — significantly higher earnings were more than offset by a decline in the P/E ratio.

In the Matrix, if the P/E ratio for the ending year is higher than the P/E ratio for the starting year — representing rising P/E ratios — the number is black; for declining P/E ratios, the color is white. In general, red and pink most often have white numbers, and the greens share space with black numbers. The P/E ratio for each year is presented along the left side of the page and along the top of the chart. The use of white and black numbers emphasizes the multiplier effect, both up and down, of P/E ratios on the market.

Reference Information

The chart includes additional data. On the left side of the page, note the middle column; likewise, on the top of the page, note the middle row. Both series represent the index values for each year. This is used to calculate the compounded return from the start period to the end period. Along the bottom of the page, you will find the market index, dividend yield, inflation (Consumer Price Index), real gross domestic product (GDP-Real), nominal gross domestic product (GDP-Nominal), and the ten-year annual compounded average for both GDP measures. For the market index, keep in mind that the S&P 500 Index value for each year represents the average across all trading days of the year. Along the right, there is an arbitrary list of developments for each of the past 104 years. In reviewing the list of historical milestones, it can be humbling to reflect upon the past century and see the great number of revolutionary developments and innovations. It also casts doubt on the claims of the gurus of the 1990s who asserted that we were in a "New Economy" era.

Message of the Matrix

The Matrix shows that if you look at longer periods of time, the compounded returns are indeed what investors typically hear: high single digits. But the real story is that most investors do not invest over 75-year periods. Shorter periods of time—a decade or two—are more relevant for most investors. Therefore, the market conditions during your investment period will determine whether the traditional approach to investing in the stock market will be financially successful.

If the reader moves diagonally down the alternating red (negative return) and green (positive return) choppy edge in the center of the Matrix, it becomes apparent that the market's long-term return is produced by a series of distinct shorter periods of time. These somewhat shorter periods of a decade or two are called "secular bull cycles" and "secular bear cycles." The cycles that occur during an individual's period of investment will dramatically influence the returns that investor realizes.

Since many people accumulate assets into their forties and then begin to harvest out of the stock market in their sixties, the Matrix includes a black diagonal line that shows returns for twenty-year periods. What quickly becomes clear from following the line is that a twenty-year holding period can produce substantial returns, poor returns, or even negative returns. The investor can establish his or her own definition of "satisfactory returns" and then look on the Matrix to see how long a holding period would be required to have a strong likelihood of obtaining those returns. For most investors, a holding period far longer than twenty years would be required.

Making Returns and Assumptions Relevant

This book seeks to present analyses that relate to the monies that finally go into your pocket, rather than to gross returns before all the related costs. That enables you to make relevant comparisons. For example, when you buy a bond, its price and yield are quoted on a net basis, so the return on bonds is a net return, unless you also have the costs of a bond manager or mutual fund.

In a stock portfolio, however, the commissions are paid *in addition to* the quoted price. Further, since most investors have turnover in their stock portfolios, there are bid/ask spreads (the difference between the price at which you can buy a stock and the price at which it can be sold); execution slippage (when stock managers and mutual funds place larger orders, the size of the order often affects the average price they pay or receive beyond the quoted price for smaller market orders); and other transaction-related charges. Also, transaction costs tend to balance out across the size range of investors: though smaller investors pay more in commissions and asset management fees, they have lower slippage costs. Larger investors pay lower commissions and asset management fees, yet have higher slippage costs.

Why is it relevant to consider these costs? The stock market returns that are most often presented by the pundits are the gross returns of an index (for example, the S&P 500 or the Dow Jones

Industrials Average). Sometimes, the quoted returns will include dividends and as a result will be referred to by the term "total returns." These measures of gross returns do not include commissions, slippage, or other transaction expenses that significantly affect realized returns. Therefore, neither the index return nor the total return is truly representative of the total net return that results in the monies in your pocket.

Some of the returns that are presented in the media and in investment publications do not include the yield from dividends—thus they have excluded a component that can offset some of the transaction-related deductions. A conservative estimate of the aggregate transaction costs is generally 2% or more. For example, a 10-cent bid/ask spread on a $20 stock is 0.5%. In addition, commissions can be approximately 1% ($20 for a $4,000 order is 0.5% to buy and again to sell). Other investment expenses and mutual fund fees can average more than 1%, while asset management charges are often 0.5% or more. For larger portfolios, the slippage of executing large orders can cause the final price to vary by more than 1%. Slippage occurs when an investor buys or sells a large quantity of securities and realizes an average price that is beyond the initially quoted price.

In recent years, and likely for some time, the average dividend yield for the major stock indexes has been and should be around 2%. Therefore, when the index is used without dividends to discuss volatility or annual changes, it is probably also a reasonable estimate for future expected returns that can be realized in your pocket. Some of the analyses that follow will adopt that convention. That helps make them comparable to other investments (i.e., bonds and alternative investments, etc.), which generally have transaction costs included in their reported returns. This also will better provide the reader a rational perspective on net returns from the financial markets. One noteworthy exception is the Matrix. It was developed with intricate detail and includes assumptions for each year that consider the historical dividend yield, transaction costs, taxes (in the taxable investor version), and inflation (in the real-return version), etc. The next analysis will examine generational returns: returns covering twenty-year periods—the time frame of a generation.

Generational Returns – Twenty-Year Returns

Consider an extended period of twenty years, a reasonable investment time horizon for most people. Despite conventional wisdom
about average stock market returns, there are twenty-year periods
that barely have positive cumulative returns in the stock market. A
closer look at individual periods of time will show why some periods
produce staggering returns while others produce dismal results.

Investors who began investing near the beginning of the 1982–1999
bull market with $100,000 and sold out of the market near the top
became millionaires simply by riding a market trend that increased
more than tenfold. By contrast, in figure 3.2, an investor who bought
the stocks in the Dow Jones Industrial Average when the average was
at 874.13 at the start of 1965 could have joined Rip Van Winkle for
almost seventeen years and awakened at the end of 1981 to find the
Dow almost exactly where he had left it — at 875.00. Had the same
investor awakened at odd points during the interim, though, he might
have found his portfolio down as much as 40% or more.

Clearly, the stock market offers more favorable and less favorable
periods or seasons for investing, periods that can last decades. The
more favorable seasons are known as secular bull markets, periods
of generally rising stock values; the less favorable seasons are secular bear markets, periods of generally choppy and low or negative
returns from stocks. The term "secular" means an era or an extended period of time. Just as successful farmers know to do their planting during the season that promises the best results, so can investors
learn to identify those stock market seasons that hold the promise of
the most abundant harvest. Investors can also learn to invest more
effectively in those seasons that appear to hold less promise.

One of the most common methods of determining valuation levels
in the stock market is to divide the price of a stock by the earnings
of the stock to produce a ratio known as the stock's price/earnings
ratio (i.e., P/E = stock price ÷ earnings per share). The same approach can be used to express the valuation of a stock market index
or basket of stocks.

As reflected in figure 3.3, total returns including dividends and
transaction costs for twenty-year periods vary widely. The twenty-year

Figure 3.2. DJIA: 1964 to 1981 & 1982 to 1999

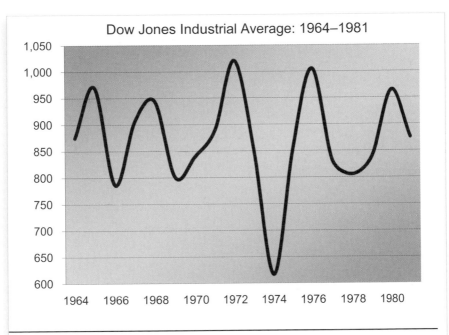

Dow Jones Industrial Average: 1964–1981

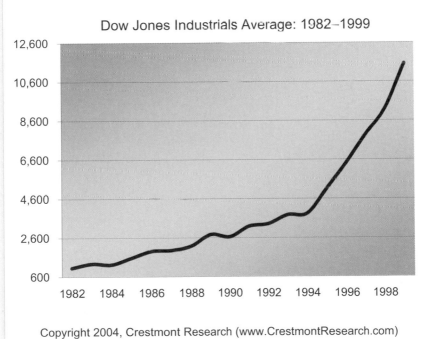

Dow Jones Industrials Average: 1982–1999

Figure 3.3. Generational Returns: Twenty-year Periods

Twenty-Year Periods Ending 1919–2003 (85 periods)
S&P 500 Stock Index: Total Net Return

TEN DECILE GROUPS	DECILE RANGE TOTAL RETURNS FROM	TO	DECILE AVG	AVG BEGIN P/E	AVG END P/E
Bottom 10%	1.2%	4.5%	3.2%	19	9
9th 10%	4.5%	5.2%	4.9%	18	9
8th 10%	5.2%	5.4%	5.3%	13	12
7th 10%	5.4%	5.8%	5.5%	12	12
6th 10%	5.9%	7.2%	6.5%	15	14
5th 10%	7.2%	8.8%	8.1%	16	18
4th 10%	9.0%	9.3%	9.2%	16	17
3rd 10%	9.4%	10.8%	10.2%	12	18
2nd 10%	11.0%	11.9%	11.7%	12	22
Top 10%	11.9%	15.0%	13.4%	10	29

*Note: Net total returns including market gains, dividends,
and transaction costs of 2%*

Copyright 2004, Crestmont Research (www.CrestmontResearch.com)

periods starting in 1900 have been sorted based on the compounded annual total returns and then grouped into ten sets. Each set, since it represents a tenth of all periods, is called "a decile." Note that the returns for each decile generally appear to be dependent on the starting level of P/E ratios as well as the change in P/E ratios over the twenty-year period. The twenty-year periods with the highest returns generally start from times of low P/E ratios and reflect periods of P/E expansion. Further emphasizing the significance of starting with low P/Es, you can see that all periods with returns of greater than 10% started with low P/Es. Finally, the highest-return twenty-year periods peaked during the late 1990s bubble and contributed to the currently popular, and misguided, notion that stocks are always a

Figure 3.4. Returns Based Upon Starting P/E Ratio (1900–2003)

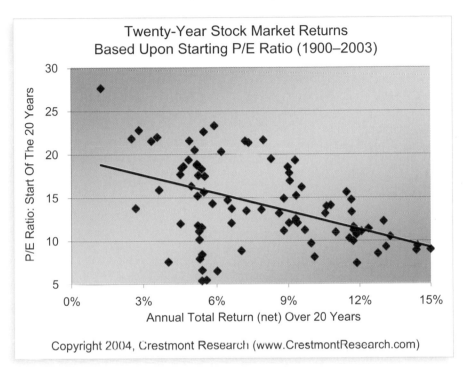

Copyright 2004, Crestmont Research (www.CrestmontResearch.com)

good investment, regardless of price. Over half of the periods in the top decile in figure 3.3 occurred from 1997 to 2002, reflecting that the period of the late 1990s and early 2000s provided unusually high returns.

Looking further into the details of every twenty-year period since 1900, figure 3.4 reflects the scatter plot of total annual returns in the S&P 500 based on the P/E ratio at the start of the twenty years. A distinct trend appears that reflects the relationship between starting valuations and future returns. Periods that start with lower valuations tend to have higher returns, while periods that start with higher valuations tend to have lower returns.

P/E Warning

The level and trend in P/Es greatly influence the level of returns that can be and will be realized by investors over multiyear periods.

Periods that start with above-average P/Es produce below-average returns, and periods that start with below-average P/Es produce above-average returns. As of late 2004, the P/E on the S&P 500 was nearly 23, historically one of its highest levels. High valuation levels trumpet a warning to investors: the price that you pay matters, and high valuations often carry high risks of disappointing returns over periods of many years.

Prudent investors recognize the potential for P/Es to decline from their current levels. Figure 3.5 presents the returns for the series of twenty-year periods since 1900. There have been 85 twenty-year periods since 1900; the first was from 1900–1919, the second was from 1901–1920, and the last was 1984–2003. The blue bars represent the compounded average annual return for each of the twenty-year periods. As reflected in figure 3.5, there has been a wide range in returns over the past century. Almost half of the twenty-year periods have provided investors with annualized total net returns of less than 6%, far less than the commonly accepted notion that the stock market will almost certainly generate average annual returns of 10% or more for holding periods of more than a few years.

Figure 3.5 provides another insight into the returns from the past 85 twenty-year periods. In addition to the bars that represent double-decade investment periods, there is a red line strolling through the graph that represents the change in the P/E ratio over the twenty-year period. When the P/E ratio increased to end higher than it began, the change is positive; a declining P/E over the twenty years is reflected as a negative number. Note the relationship between positive increases in the P/E ratio and tall-bar high returns. Further, note the depressing effect to returns of decreases in the P/E ratio, when the red line sinks below the zero waterline. From current levels in the P/E ratio of almost 23, the prospects of an above-average bar for the next twenty years are unlikely. Even if the current high P/E can be sustained at its lofty level, thus reflecting no change over time, the red line of P/E changes will decline to the zero waterline, while the blue bar settles in at a point somewhat below average. Later chapters discuss the empirical and fundamental reasons that high P/Es result in below-average returns.

Figure 3.5. Twenty-year Rolling Return & Change in P/E Ratio

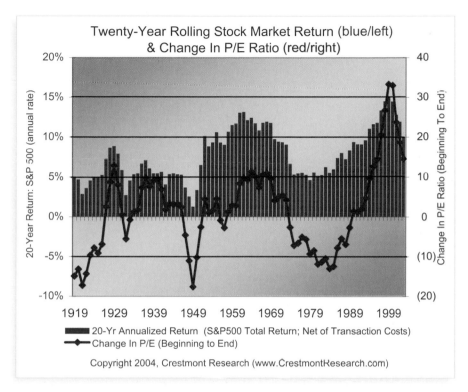

Significant Swings

Seen from 30,000 feet, a rough ocean seems almost calm, and even a battleship would be barely visible. Onboard the ship, however, sailors struggle to save the vessel. Crossing the North Atlantic, with its crashing thirty-five-foot waves, tests the mettle of the best sailors, and the ride is anything but smooth. Similarly, the stock market seen from a distance reflects a placid 7% annual return over the past century. Yet the range of annual returns is dramatic, and the ride for investors sometimes feels like a North Atlantic crossing.

The stock market is much more volatile than most investors realize. One measure of volatility is the range of annual moves in the market from year-end to subsequent year-end. The market moves dramatically both positively and negatively to ultimately produce its modest long-term average return.

The average annual change for the Dow Jones Industrials Average stock market index, as a simple average, is just over 7% over the past century, 1901–2003. Over that period, in what percentage of the years would you expect that the annual change would occur in the range of –10% to +10%? Most investors seem to guess a number between 60 and 70 percent—that a clear majority of the years would be inside the range. What range would be required to include half of the years inside that range? As reflected in figure 3.6, it is very surprising to most investors that the yearly change in the stock market has been inside the range of –10% to +10% only 30 percent of the years. Remarkably, to include half the years inside the range, it has to be expanded to –16% to +16%. The profile is not affected by years early in the century; the percentages are very similar over the past fifty years and the past twenty years.

Figure 3.6. Significant Swings (Dispersion of Annual Changes)

Dow Jones Industrial Average
DISPERSION OF ANNUAL STOCK MARKET CHANGES
Percent Of Years
(1901–2003)

RANGE	103 Yrs FREQUENCY
<-10%	21%
-10% to +10%	30%
>+10%	49%

RANGE	103 Yrs FREQUENCY
<-16%	16%
-16% to +16%	50%
>+16%	35%

Yes, when you awaken on New Year's Day and contemplate the coming year's impact on your investment portfolio, there is a 70 percent chance that it is going to be a double-digit year—up or down. In addition, there is a 50 percent chance that the change up or down will be in the high teens or greater! If New Year's Eve did not give you a headache, the level of volatility certainly should.

Why Volatility Matters

Just as huge crashing waves can affect the well-being of sailors in the North Atlantic, stock market volatility can affect the success of investors. But why should volatility, the choppiness of returns over time, matter to an investor who plans to hold stocks for the long term?

First, volatility diminishes compounded returns in comparison to average returns. Secondly, the quality of the ride does make a difference. Sharp downdrafts and roller coaster volatility can drive many investors out of their stock holdings. As a result, investors would experience the decline, but not be invested during the recovery.

Volatility Gremlins

Investors cannot spend average returns, the returns that are often cited to promote stocks as consistently good investments. Investors can only spend compounded returns. The distinction between the two is important to the returns that you actually realize to your account. A brief discussion with an example will highlight the differences.

A simple return is the mathematical average of a set of numbers. For example, the simple average of 10% and 20% is 15%. A compounded return is the single annual percentage that provides the cumulative effect of a series of returns. From the example above, if an investment grew by 10% and then again by 20%, its cumulative increase would be 32%—a number greater than the sum of 10% and 20%, due to the power of compounding. But, the single percentage that would grow to 32% over two periods is 14.9%—slightly less than the simple average of 15%.

In figure 3.7, the simple average of the annual changes for the stock market was 7.4% during the period from 1900–2003. The compounded

Figure 3.7. Volatility Gremlins (DJIA: 1900–2003)

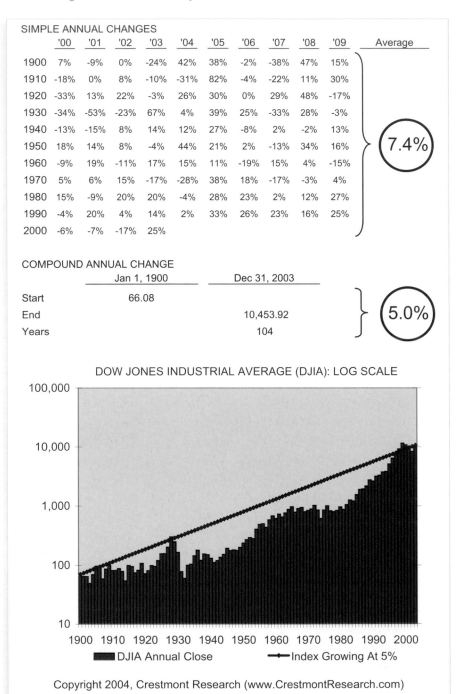

SIMPLE ANNUAL CHANGES

	'00	'01	'02	'03	'04	'05	'06	'07	'08	'09	Average
1900	7%	-9%	0%	-24%	42%	38%	-2%	-38%	47%	15%	
1910	-18%	0%	8%	-10%	-31%	82%	-4%	-22%	11%	30%	
1920	-33%	13%	22%	-3%	26%	30%	0%	29%	48%	-17%	
1930	-34%	-53%	-23%	67%	4%	39%	25%	-33%	28%	-3%	
1940	-13%	-15%	8%	14%	12%	27%	-8%	2%	-2%	13%	
1950	18%	14%	8%	-4%	44%	21%	2%	-13%	34%	16%	7.4%
1960	-9%	19%	-11%	17%	15%	11%	-19%	15%	4%	-15%	
1970	5%	6%	15%	-17%	-28%	38%	18%	-17%	-3%	4%	
1980	15%	-9%	20%	20%	-4%	28%	23%	2%	12%	27%	
1990	-4%	20%	4%	14%	2%	33%	26%	23%	16%	25%	
2000	-6%	-7%	-17%	25%							

COMPOUND ANNUAL CHANGE

	Jan 1, 1900	Dec 31, 2003	
Start	66.08		
End		10,453.92	5.0%
Years		104	

DOW JONES INDUSTRIAL AVERAGE (DJIA): LOG SCALE

◼ DJIA Annual Close   ◆ Index Growing At 5%

Copyright 2004, Crestmont Research (www.CrestmontResearch.com)

annual change, reflecting a more accurate view of realized annual returns, was only 5% for the same 104 years. Although total returns were slightly higher, since dividends generally were greater than transaction costs over that period, the difference between simple returns and compounded returns is dramatic.

In other words, excluding dividends, transaction costs, and taxes, the use of the simple average change of 7.4% would provide the illusion that had you invested $1,000 in the market in 1900, you would have $1,676,661 by the end of 2003—$1,000 compounding at 7.4% annually over 104 years grows to $1,676,661. An investor in the stock market over that same period, however, ended with $159,841. The investment of $1,000 that is increased repeatedly by 5% annually over 104 years grows to only $159,841. The average return is quite different from the compounded return. Compounded returns are the relevant returns that generate cash in your account that can be spent.

Although you may be told that the average return was 7.4%, if your investments are only compounding at 5%, the financial results will be quite different. The difference between the average return and the compounded return is the result of two effects that will be called the "volatility gremlins." These volatility gremlins reduced the dollars you could actually receive by more than 90 percent!

Two volatility gremlins are at work eroding the average return into the compounded return, the simple return into the actual return. These two mathematical mites are negative numbers and the dispersion of returns around the average. Each of them has a significant effect on realized returns. By understanding their impact, investors can further appreciate the benefits of reducing volatility and increasing the consistency of investment returns. As a result, investors can realize higher compounded returns and experience a more enjoyable and less stressful investment ride.

The Impact of Negative Numbers

The first volatility gremlin is the impact of negative numbers on compounded returns. To illustrate the effect, consider an investment over two years. Make 20% the first year and lose 20% the second year. What is your average return? Zero! For the simple average return, when +20% is added to –20%, the sum is 0%. When 0% is divided by the number of years (i.e., 2), the simple average return is 0%.

$$20\% - 20\% = 0\%$$
$$0\% \div 2 = 0\%$$

What actually happens, though, to your investment account? Start with $100,000. Gain 20%. You now have $120,000. Next, look at the impact of losing 20% of $120,000. You lose $24,000 and end up with $96,000 rather than $100,000. Your average return is 0%, but your compounded return is negative, and you have lost money:

$100,000 + 20% ($20,000) = $120,000 (after year 1);

$120,000 – 20% ($24,000) = $96,000 (after year 2).

Wait, Mr. Market Magician, let's try that again. This time put the negative return first. Surely that might make a difference. Start again with $100,000. If you first lose 20%, you will have $80,000. Next, if you gain 20% on $80,000, you will make $16,000 and end up with $96,000. It remains equally less than your original $100,000. Your average return is again 0%, your compounded return is negative, and you have again lost money:

$100,000 – 20% ($20,000) = $80,000 (after year 1);

$80,000 + 20% ($16,000) = $96,000 (after year 2).

To break even, it takes a greater positive return than the offsetting negative loss. For –20%, the offset is +25%. It works the same, whether the positive or the negative occurs first.

$100,000 – 20% ($20,000) = $80,000 (after year 1)

$80,000 + 25% ($20,000) = $100,000 (after year 2)

The Impact of the Dispersion of Returns

The second volatility gremlin is the impact of the range of returns on the average. As the returns in a series become more dispersed from the average, the compounded return declines. This second dynamic is illustrated by another example. The compounded return from three periods of 5% returns is greater than any other sequence that averages 5%. Figure 3.8 illustrates this mathematical phenomenon. If you earn a return of 5% per year for three years in a row, your simple average return is 5%, and your compounded return is 5%.

If, however, you earn 6% the first year, 5% the second year, and 4% the third year, your simple average return remains 5%, but your compounded return drops to 4.997%. While this minor difference may be an interesting result, it may not yet seem to have great significance.

It turns out, though, that the greater the volatility of the returns, the greater the drop in the compounded return. Consider the third case, in which you earn 9% the first year, 5% the second year, and 1% the third year. Your simple average return remains 5%, but your compounded rate of return—the return that supplies you with dollars that can be spent—drops a good bit further to 4.949%. The actual volatility of the stock market is much greater than the example, and the impact on compounded returns is much more significant. Keep in mind that half of all years in the stock market occur outside of a 32 percent range from –16% to +16%. As the level of dispersion increases, the impact from the second volatility gremlin increases.

When the impact of the first gremlin, negative numbers, combines with the power of the second, dispersion of returns, the pair can be lethal to your portfolio. But, the weight of these gremlin foes can be used against them. The techniques to harness the volatility gremlins to make them work for you are discussed later in the book.

Returns and Volatility: An Uncanny Relationship

Figure 3.9 presents the historical relationship between stock market performance and the volatility of the market. There are many ways to measure market volatility. For this analysis, it is measured using the average range for each day, from the low index value to the high index value, expressed as a percentage of the starting value for the day. This analysis does not attempt to determine whether trends in the stock market drive volatility or whether volatility drives trends in the stock market. Rather, the analysis reflects that there is a strong relationship between stock market performance and volatility.

This is important because it indicates that many factors of risk actually compound in declining markets. Similarly, the reward-to-risk

Figure 3.8. Impact of Volatility and Negative Numbers

Impact Of The Volatility Gremlins: Dispersion & Negative Numbers

	CASE A	CASE B	CASE C	CASE D	CASE E	CASE F
Year 1	5.0%	4.0%	9.0%	15.0%	25.0%	30.0%
Year 2	5.0%	5.0%	5.0%	-10.0%	-15.0%	-25.0%
Year 3	5.0%	6.0%	1.0%	10.0%	5.0%	10.0%
Simple Average Return	**5.000%**	**5.000%**	**5.000%**	**5.000%**	**5.000%**	**5.000%**
Compounded Return	**5.000%**	**4.997%**	**4.949%**	**4.419%**	**3.714%**	**2.361%**

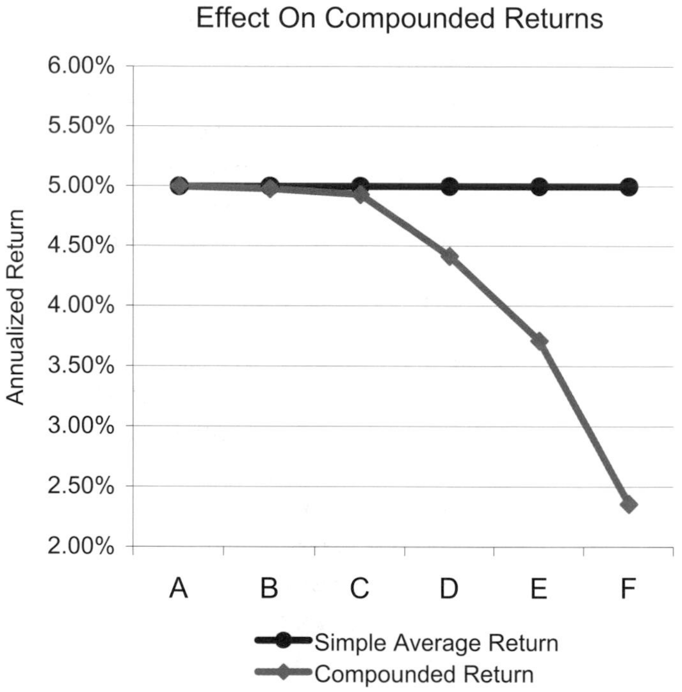

Effect On Compounded Returns

Simple Average Return
Compounded Return

relationship significantly improves in strong markets. In the context of secular bull and bear markets, this relationship further emphasizes the need to consider risk as well as reward in an investor's investment decisions.

Greater volatility relates to a higher probability of declining markets. Lesser volatility relates to a higher probability of a rising market. For example, when the average daily range in the S&P 500 Index is low—between 0% and 1.1%—the odds are high, about 90 percent, that investors in a market will enjoy a year of gains. On the other hand, there is almost a two-thirds probability of a losing year when the average daily price range based on annual data moves up to the highest quartile of 1.8%–2.6%. From the tables in the top of figure 3.9, you will note that effects of volatility affect monthly performance as well as annual performance. The relationship and effects of volatility on returns and risk are consistent and are not offsetting—when volatility increases, risk increases and returns decrease.

This is particularly important in secular bear markets. Unlike secular bull markets, when a strong rising trend in the markets masks the impact of volatility, secular bear markets are vulnerable to volatility. When the impact of the volatility gremlins is considered, it becomes even more important to seek investment strategies and approaches that control risk and enhance returns.

Other Considerations of Volatility

Interestingly, these volatility characteristics also contribute directly to investor psychology. The low volatility that characterizes bull markets contributes to the comfort and confidence many investors feel during those periods. As you might expect, the higher volatility that occurs during bear markets adds greatly to the discomfort and anxiety felt by investors who experience declining markets. This emotional roller coaster often causes investors to react irrationally, which can result in poor performance for their investment portfolios. As well, broad-based irrational behavior by investors due to the volatility of the markets may accentuate the irrational movements of the market and may create mispriced securities in the market.

Finally, the skew of volatility toward declining markets impacts portfolio strategy. For example, one portfolio management technique

Figure 3.9. Volatility and Market Returns

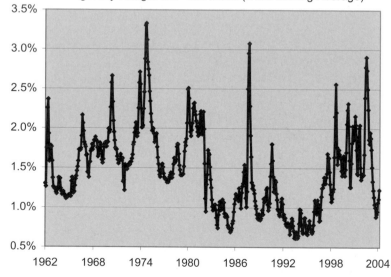

**Relationship Of Volatility & Market Returns
(S&P 500 Index: 1962–May 2004)**

MONTHLY DATA: S&P 500 INDEX AVERAGE DAILY RANGE

Quartile	Volatility Range	% Chance Up Month	% Chance Dn Month	If Up Avg Gain	If Down Avg Loss	Expected Gain/(Loss)
1st	0% - 1.1%	69%	31%	3.2%	-1.9%	1.5%
2nd	1.1% - 1.4%	63%	37%	2.8%	-2.2%	0.9%
3rd	1.4% - 1.8%	57%	43%	3.3%	-3.1%	0.6%
4th	1.8% - 4.8%	43%	57%	5.1%	-4.7%	-0.5%

ANNUAL DATA (1962–2003): S&P 500 INDEX AVERAGE DAILY RANGE

Quartile	Volatility Range	% Chance Up Month	% Chance Dn Month	If Up Avg Gain	If Down Avg Loss	Expected Gain/(Loss)
1st	0% - 1.1%	90%	10%	18.3%	-1.5%	16.3%
2nd	1.1% - 1.5%	80%	20%	15.7%	-9.0%	10.7%
3rd	1.5% - 1.8%	80%	20%	14.4%	-11.6%	9.2%
4th	1.8% - 2.6%	36%	64%	16.3%	-16.6%	-4.7%

Avg Daily Range: S&P 500 Index (3 Mo Moving Average)

is known as "rebalancing," the adjustment of the weighting in your portfolio based upon changes due to performance. An investor holding 60 percent stocks and 40 percent bonds would be holding, following a decline of 18% in the stock market, 55 percent stocks and 45 percent bonds. To rebalance, an investor would sell some of the bonds and buy stocks to return the ratio to 60 and 40 percent. In downward and volatile markets, there is a benefit to rebalancing more frequently. This will be discussed in greater detail in chapter 11.

Stock Market Yo-Yo

As you watch the evening news or read the newspaper, there is almost always a reason for the market's increase or decrease on any given day. Sometimes that reason is *"because of"* some events; other times it is *"in spite of"* something. It might be that "Yesterday the market rose *in spite of* high oil prices," only to be followed by "Today the market fell *because of* the same high oil prices." A review of the positive and negative days in the market explains that this yo-yo activity is a natural part of the market's processes, rather than a keen relationship to daily events. As presented in figure 3.10, almost 50 percent of days are up and 50 percent are down across a wide range of periods. The range may sway a bit to 45 or 55 percent, yet the relative consistency is significant.

The market seems to move higher one day and lower the next, only occasionally putting together a streak of higher days or a slump of multiple lower days. In fact, over the past five decades, through secular cycles, decades, and individual years, the range of up days versus down days is close to 50/50. More specifically, over the past five decades, 53 percent of the days have been up days, while 47 percent have been down days.

As you might expect, overall returns in the stock market are generally better when more of the days in the market are up compared to when there are more down days. Interestingly, though, the average net daily return tends to decline when the percentage of up days increases. The reason for this is not clear, yet it does show that returns occur slowly in the market with a great amount of volatility.

Figure 3.10. Almost 50/50: Up & Down Days in the Market

Percent of Days Positive And Negative Across Markets

50+ YEARS	**1950-2004**					
Up Days %	53%					
Down Days %	47%					

DECADES	1950s	1960s	1970s	1980s	1990s	2000s
Up Days %	57%	54%	51%	53%	54%	49%
Down Days %	43%	46%	49%	47%	46%	51%

SECULAR	BEAR 1966-1982	BULL 1983-1999
Up Days %	51%	54%
Down Days %	49%	46%

RECENT	1999	2000	2001	2002	2003
Up Days %	51%	48%	48%	44%	55%
Down Days %	49%	52%	52%	56%	45%

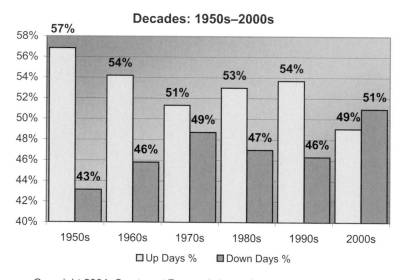

Copyright 2004, Crestmont Research (www.CrestmontResearch.com)

Figure 3.10. (continued)

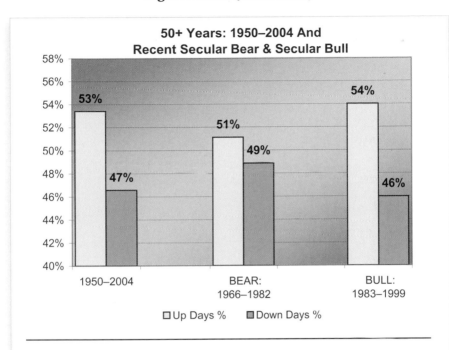

50+ Years: 1950–2004 And Recent Secular Bear & Secular Bull

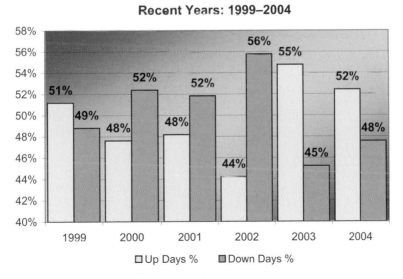

Recent Years: 1999–2004

Although investors may perceive bull markets as strings of good events that provide chains of positive days, the pattern is much more balanced. Likewise, investors may feel like the sun never shines a daily gain when the bears are roaming, yet historical evidence indicates a fair share of both winning and losing days across both bull and bear markets. This is significant for investors who want to make rational decisions in the market. Beware the sense that the market will follow the events of the day, or that strong trends are needed in either direction to make a winner or loser out of your portfolio.

Must Be Present to Win?

Wall Street's traditional advice has been, "Since you can't time the market, investors should remain invested in stocks at all times to avoid the risk of missing the opportunity for returns." Some pundits say, "You have to be in to win." One statistic often cited is that most of the market's return occurs on a few days and, if an investor is not invested on those days, the investor will under-perform the market.

This statistical fallacy relates to the selective use of the extreme numbers in a diverse series. An example will best illustrate: Over the course of a week, assume that the daily returns are +1%, −1.5%, +2%, −1%, and +1.5%. For the week, the cumulative market return would be up approximately +2%. Stock market advocates would say that the market's move occurred on the middle day, and since you could not know when the move would occur, you must stay invested to get the market's return. The fallacy of that statement is that in a series of alternating positive and negative days, the cumulative return will always be found in a few of the highest days of the year.

For the stock market, there are approximately 250 trading days each year. In both bull and bear markets over the past century, the up days represent between 45% and 55% of the days. As reflected in figure 3.11, 2002 and 2003 were on each end of the range. As a result, most of the days offset each other. So regardless of the total return for the year, a small number of the most extreme days can be added together to equal the net return for the year—whether positive or negative.

Figure 3.11. Profile of Best and Worst Days

EXAMPLES FROM 2002 & 2003	2002	2003	Combined
Percent of Days Up	44.2%	54.8%	49.5%
Annual Return (S&P 500 Index)	-24.2%	26.4%	-2.1%
Worst 10 Days (Total Return)	-28.4%	-20.5%	-24.6%
Return Without Worst 10 Days	5.9%	59.0%	29.8%
Best 10 Days (Total Return)	50.8%	29.6%	39.8%
Best 2 Days (Total Return)	11.5%	7.1%	9.3%

Copyright 2004, Crestmont Research (www.CrestmontResearch.com)

Similar to the fallacy of "staying invested," the following statements, derived from the same data, are also true, but are misleading. (1) A few days will represent all the losses in down years, so just get out of the market on those days to avoid down years; (2) In all years, the two or three best days will produce total returns of over 10%, so learn to time the market. Obviously, though, consistently picking the best or worst two or three days each year is unfeasible.

The appropriateness of staying invested should not be affected by the statistics of daily changes. Rather, it should be driven by the overall trend in the stock market. Staying invested over time subjects investors to the annual losses as well as the annual gains of the market. There have been extended periods of years that produced strong returns, known as secular bull markets, and extended periods of sideways or declining trends, known as secular bear markets. It is important to assess the overall market conditions and characteristics to determine which secular period is in force and adjust your allocations accordingly. The call by stock market advocates for investors to stay in the market drives a fear that the investor may miss out on the market's great gains. But, if the conditions are not favorable for solid gains, there may be little for investors to miss. Therefore, invest when and where good returns are most likely.

Summary

Conventional wisdom focuses investors away from the details of the stock market and encourages a patient, long-term perspective. As a result, many investors have lost the perspective that the market is volatile and has extended periods of relatively high returns and extended periods of relatively low returns. These high and low periods create a hypothetical average year that rarely occurs as an actual result. The trend in the level of valuation, as measured by the price/earnings ratio, has a greater impact than earnings growth on the performance of the stock market. In addition, the significant volatility of the market adversely affects realized returns in relation to average returns. These volatility gremlins reduce the effective returns that investors achieve. Therefore, investors should take into consideration the overall conditions in the market. An explanation of the fundamentals that drive the market will soon follow and will help you determine your perspective on the market and the appropriate investment strategy for your portfolio.

The following chapter will continue the journey through financial market history by reviewing the field of interest rates and the bond market. The review will also identify some of the common elements that affect both the stock and bond markets and address some of the myths about interest rates. The combination of stock market history and interest rate history in this section will provide insights and background for upcoming chapters.

CHAPTER 4

INTEREST RATES & THE INFLATION ROLLER COASTER

Money and Power

On December 5, 1996, the second most powerful saxophone player in the world leaned forward, uttered the words "irrational exuberance," and sent world markets into turmoil. Such is the influence of Alan Greenspan, chairman of the Federal Reserve Board and arguably the second most powerful man in the world. Among the most important of his powers is the ability to influence the cost and supply of money in the United States.

Money is the currency in your pocket, the funds in your checking and savings accounts, and the borrowings for your home, car, credit cards, and all other credit. Money is a tool for exchanging goods and services without having to barter every transaction. As a result, money facilitates economic growth.

As the U.S. economy has grown, the supply of money has expanded to accommodate the higher volume of goods and services. So the Federal Reserve Board, which influences or determines the cost of money, substantially impacts the country's future economic growth. In addition, the cost of money affects the cost of every house and every meal. As Sir Reginald McKenna, former president of the Midland Bank of England said, "Those who create and issue money and credit direct the policies of government and hold in the hollow of their hands the destiny of the people."

The discussion about the history and factors in the financial markets began in the previous chapter with the stock market. A sister security to stocks is the bond, an instrument that generally has a fixed principal value and pays interest over time. Bonds generally have an established date in the future when the bond matures and the principal is repaid. The amount of interest a bond pays and the value of existing bonds are driven by the level of interest rates in the market at a given time. The issues that affect the stock market also impact the bond market. This chapter introduces key concepts relating to bonds and interest rates. Further, it provides perspectives on the history and volatility of interest rates.

Overview of Interest Rates

Since debt forms much of the fabric of both the U.S. economy and the supply of money, an understanding of interest rates becomes vital. Interest rates reflect the level of annual return that lenders require from borrowers for the use of their money. Most people judge interest rates to be high or low in relation to recent experience. This chapter, though, will provide the reader a long-term perspective on interest rates. And the look at interest rate reality will challenge several widely held notions about the volatility of interest rates and the relationship of interest rates to inflation.

In *A History of Interest Rates,* Sidney Homer and Richard Sylla wrote:

> A comprehensive view of the history of interest rates will unsettle most preconceived ideas of what is a high rate or a low rate or an average rate. Each generation tends to consider as normal the range of interest rates with which it grew up; rates much higher suggest a crisis or seem extortionate, while rates much lower seem artificial or inadequate. Almost every generation is eventually shocked by the behavior of interest rates because, in fact, market rates of interest in modern times rarely have been stable for long. Usually they are

rising or falling to unexpected extremes. Students of the history of interest rates will not be surprised by volatility. Their backward-looking knowledge will not tell them where interest rates will be in the future, but it will permit them to distinguish a truly unusual level of rates from a mere change.

Interest rates are the compensation that debt holders receive for lending money (i.e., the "rent" that borrowers pay for the use of the money). Historically, interest rates were often arbitrarily set. Interest payments were structured as service charges for borrowed money or as a participation in the business venture that borrowed the funds. Over the past two centuries, financial markets have evolved, world economies have strengthened, and the concept of money is now much better understood. As a result, the concept of interest payments now represents protection against monetary inflation, and compensation for the risk of providing the loan or making the investment. Both of these concepts, inflation and risk, are explored further in this chapter. For now, the focus is the term structure of interest rates. These concepts are part of the foundation for understanding the financial markets and the *Financial Physics* model, which is explored in chapter 7.

The rate of interest for a loan depends on the length of time that the loan will be outstanding and the length of time that the interest rate will be fixed. Generally, the rate of interest for a loan that is fixed for ten years will be higher than the rate of interest for a one-year period. The rate of interest for shorter periods is often referred to as "short-term interest rates" and the rate of interest for longer periods is referred to as "long-term interest rates." Short term is typically recognized as less than one year, and long term is typically ten years or more. The periods between short term and long term are considered to be intermediate.

Short-term interest rates, however, move independently of long-term interest rates. The factors that affect each interest rate term are different. Generally, a country's monetary authorities drive its short-term interest rates. In the United States, the monetary authority is the Federal Reserve Bank, also known as "the Fed." Among the Fed's roles is the responsibility to ensure that sufficient money is in the economy to facilitate commerce. Since so many factors impact an economy, that job is not an easy one. If the money supply grows too quickly, a condition known as monetary inflation occurs, and the value of the currency is depreciated. If the money supply grows too slowly, then economic growth can be constrained or monetary deflation can occur. One of the ways that the Fed controls the money supply is to change its price by raising interest rates. Therefore, the short-term interest rate set by the Fed is based upon the objectives of promoting stable economic growth and managing appropriate money supply growth.

Long-term interest rates are not as objectively determined. They are dictated by the invisible hand of the financial markets, based on the expected monetary inflation rate and the other risks specific to the loan or investment. Since inflation is the bandit that depreciates the value of a currency, lenders demand protection against inflation in the form of an interest rate. Therefore, excluding issues of credit quality and structure, the core long-term interest rates are set by the market's expectation of future inflation.

As a result, financial market spectators often see a contorted show as short-term and long-term interest rates whip around, sometimes in the same direction and other times in opposite directions. It would be easier to understand their underlying characteristics and varying routes if the English language had more distinct words to reflect the differences in long-term and short-term rates. For example, the English word "love" relates to a concept that has many distinct meanings. The love between a husband and wife is quite different from the love between friends, yet the same word is used to describe the two distinct concepts. You can generally discern the meaning of "love" from the context of its use. For interest rates, one identifies the distinction by qualifying interest rates as either short-term or long-term. Keep in mind that the drivers for each are quite distinct, and the relationship between the two is indirectly determined. Of course, as will be presented later in this chapter, interest rates have only begun to follow the modern laws of finance within the past fifty years.

The discussion of interest rates continues with the topic of monetary value, the supply of money in relation to the economy. When the relative quantity of money changes, there is a change in the overall value of money known as inflation or deflation.

Overview of Inflation

Inflation is always and everywhere a monetary phenomenon.
—Milton Friedman (1968)

Once upon a time, money may have been invented on an island that needed a way for fishermen to exchange their food with the tailors for clothes. The barter system of trading fish for clothes worked well until an enterprising official suggested using coins to "denominate" goods and services across the island. As a result, fish that were sold one day could be exchanged the next week for clothing, shelter, other goods, or services. Additionally, profits and wealth could be accumulated and invested. Before long, someone was needed to manage this new phenomenon: the money supply. The island needed its own Alan Greenspan to control the money supply and monitor inflation.

Inflation is as two-faced as Dr. Jekyll and Mr. Hyde. Most consumers think of inflation as a rise in prices, but the wise Dr. Jekyll economists see price increases as the economy's way of regulating supply and demand. Rising prices during periods of limited supply or excessive demand restore balance between supply and demand, a fundamental law of economics. These swings in price are self-regulating over time. Higher prices encourage producers to create more supply to meet the rising demand. Likewise, price declines tend to purge excess capacity. This is the normal function of the markets, and does not affect the overall level of prices for goods on the island.

When Machiavellian Mr. Hyde, however, holds the reigns of the island's monetary authority (i.e., its Federal Reserve Bank), the supply of money can be manipulated. The version of inflation that financial markets fear occurs when extra coins are distributed beyond the level of goods in the economy. In other words, assume that the economy includes fish being traded for clothes at the rate of one coin per unit of fish or clothes. If Mr. Hyde distributes additional coins to everyone on the island to make them feel richer (so they can buy more goods), the eventual effect will be to raise the prices of all goods and services by the amount of money that was distributed. The additional coins dilute the value of the original coins. Just because everyone has twice as much money, for example, does not make them all twice as rich, if the result is that everyone has twice as much money with the same amount of goods to buy. Growing the money supply without growing the economy does not increase the population's wealth.

Throughout history, most civilizations have grown their economies through population growth (more people working and consuming) and through productivity (the same people producing greater amounts of goods). If the money in an economy grows at the same rate as the goods and services in it, generally there is no monetary inflation. The value of each coin will buy the same amount of goods. When the growth in coins exceeds the growth in goods, however, the value of each coin declines, and inflation results.

Financial assets in an economy fear the decline in value resulting from excess money supply growth, the coins in this example. If the supply of fish declines and the price increases, but people switch to chicken, financial assets do not care. They worry when extra coins are leaked into the economic system beyond the general economic growth.

Therefore, higher prices are not necessarily inflation — unless there is a broad-based increase in prices, due to an increase in the amount of money beyond the quantity of goods in the economy. In addition, there are factors of quantity and quality challenging the ability of economists to precisely quantify inflation.

Quantity and Quality

For many people, the perception is that the price of everything is rising. That is probably because rising prices catch your attention more than declining prices. Prices rise for many reasons: higher quality, increased demand, lower supply, substitution of goods, etc. Financial assets generally ignore these factors and focus instead on monetary inflation, which occurs when prices rise regardless of whether these issues are present. Higher prices across the economy, without the impact of quantity, quality, supply, or demand, are most often due to excess money supply growth. And financial assets want protection from monetary inflation!

Regarding quantity, consider that the average home price has risen over the past few decades, yet the average size of a home has more than doubled over the same period. Therefore, one must look closer to see if the same home from 1980, in terms of size and features, is more or less expensive today, ignoring the impact of its location or the effects of age. If it is more expensive today, there may have been monetary inflation. On the other hand, if the average home over the same time period has doubled in price as well as doubled in size, there probably has not been monetary inflation. If the price increase relates to increased size or quantity, then an increase in the average price of a new home does not necessarily mean that there has been monetary inflation.

Regarding quality, consider that the average car price has risen over the past few decades. In addition, the fuel efficiency and features have improved. Therefore, as it relates to inflation, it would be appropriate to look at whether the same car from 1980 would have increased in price today. If the price increase relates to increased quality, then an increase in the price of a car does not necessarily mean that there has been monetary inflation.

Demand, supply, substitution, and other micro-economic factors are the price-adjusting mechanisms that drive the efficiency process of the markets. If these are the factors affecting the price of your latte, monetary inflation is not necessarily the culprit. If freezing weather in Brazil results in a decline in the coffee-bean harvest and thus an increase in coffee-bean prices, the increased cost of a latte relates to micro-economic factors, not to monetary inflation. Over longer periods, however, if the general price of coffee beans rises along with most other products in the economy, monetary inflation may be the culprit.

Striking Gold!

A discussion of inflation would hardly be complete without striking gold. For many investors and financial market commentators, gold is a bellwether of inflation. At the least, gold is believed to be a hedge against inflation. This section does not attempt to fully vet the issues of gold, monetary policy, and inflation. It may be worth considering, however, whether gold is the traders' proxy for the sentiment of inflation, or an actual metric of inflation. Thus gold may behave as it does because investors and traders believe it to be inflation-protected wealth, not because it actually is an inflation-protected storehouse. At times and in various cultures, gold was recognized as the ultimate currency. Today, however, its role may be diminished as a result of a much more complex system of money supply and international trade.

In the past, when gold was used to support the value of a currency, gold held value at an exchange rate that was established by policy. The "gold standard," as it was known, required a physical supply of gold to back up the currency. This was an effective way to control the growth of money, since it required physical support. Today, the gold standard has been eliminated, and the value of a currency either floats in relation to other currencies or is pegged to a benchmark currency at a specific exchange rate.

One might ask, "Why does gold have value?" or "What is the true value of gold?" For most assets, investors look to the intrinsic value or productive value, the amount of cash that an asset returns to its holder over time. For many commodities, the intrinsic value is its value as a raw material used to produce goods. Gold's intrinsic value may be hard to directly relate to its market price. As long as gold is viewed as the emperor with clothes, it will hold a special place in the minds of many investors, but if intrinsic value relates to the value of its uses, then gold does not seem to possess an intrinsic value that justifies its current price. Rather, gold may now be the traders' proxy for the sentiment of inflation, at least as long as it holds its luster from the traditions of history. The effectiveness of using the price of gold as a measure for developing and operating monetary policy may deserve further research.

Financial Securities and Inflation

Financial securities are not always affected by the temporary factors that affect the prices of goods and services in the economy. They are primarily driven by the factors that affect the general prices of all products due to extra money in the system. This represents one of the challenges in assessing inflation. Over long periods of time, monetary inflation can be assessed, though still somewhat imprecisely. In the short run, markets rely upon the expectation of future inflation to value financial assets. All of these factors should be considered when trying to anticipate inflation and the trends in financial markets.

Since much of Crestmont's research is historically based and incorporates longer periods of time, readily available and accepted measures of inflation are used, including the gross domestic product deflator (GDP Deflator) and the consumer price index (CPI). The GDP Deflator is a measure of inflation that reflects the difference between real growth in the gross domestic product (GDP) and the nominal growth in the GDP. Gross domestic product is a measure of all goods and services in the economy. Real GDP is the growth in GDP without inflation, essentially unit growth. Nominal GDP includes real economic growth plus inflation. Thus, the GDP Deflator is the measure of inflation that is derived from estimating real and nominal economic growth.

The CPI is a measure of inflation based on an extensive basket of goods that are priced across the country by government analysts. During the process of preparing each month's value, analysts adjust the CPI using established procedures to minimize the biases caused by quality and quantity improvements. Although some advocates contend that this measure of inflation is understated, many economists and several reputable studies have shown that the CPI may overstate inflation slightly.

While the GDP Deflator, CPI, and other measures have their benefits and faults, the variances tend to mute over time, and increased levels of precision do not tend to change the conclusions. If you are preparing to do battle with a bully who is six feet, seven inches tall, a more precise yardstick that shows him as one inch taller or shorter will not change the probability that the punches will be coming downward at you. Most of the valid measures of inflation provide similar perspectives about periods when inflation was high, low, rising, or falling. As of 2004, monetary inflation is relatively low and around 1%–2%, but the opinions of many experts differ about the future direction of monetary inflation.

Interest Rates and Inflation

As reflected in figure 4.1, the fundamental relationship that is widely accepted today—that interest rates are directly affected by the rate of inflation—was not as consistent during the first two-thirds of the past century. In fact, interest rates, especially long-term rates, stayed relatively stable until the liberating 1960s, and largely ignored very significant swings of both inflation and deflation prior to that time. In figure 4.1, both short- and long-term interest rates initially reflect this inconsistency and later tie closely to the trends in inflation.

What accounts for the lack of significant correlation between interest rates and the rate of inflation during the first two-thirds of the twentieth century? Several factors play a role. First, interest rates were seen more as service charges for money loaned than as financial compensation for monetary devaluation of a currency's buying power. When there is monetary inflation, additional money is created in excess of the goods in the economy. The effect is that a dollar is worth less than it was prior to the inflation; the amount of goods that it can buy is less. Bond investors use interest payments in part as compensation for the loss in buying power that results from inflation. As inflation rises, and the loss of buying power increases, bond investors increase their required interest rates to cover the increased inflation.

Historically, inflationary periods often followed wars and thus were seen as temporary rather than long-term phenomena. Today, by contrast, inflation is virtually assumed to be a fact of economic life. Deflation, on the other hand, has not occurred in the U.S. in over half a century. When it reared its head repeatedly in the first half of the century, it was felt to be a short-term and temporary adjustment following economic downturns. There were times during 2003 that Fed officials expressed concern about the potential for, and risks of, deflation. By 2004, most of those fears had faded. As of late 2004, some recognized economists continued to see the potential for deflation, while more of them saw potentially increasing inflation.

During the 1960s, the dynamics of interest rate behavior began to change. Long-term rates, which had hovered roughly in the range of 3%–5% for decades, cut their ties to relative stability and became attached to the inflation roller coaster. By the early 1980s, long-term rates soared to over 13%. Then, following the path of declining inflation, they fell to near 4% in the first decade of the new millennium. Short-term rates took an even more dramatic ride, rising to 14% and then plunging to less than 1%.

Figure 4.1. Bond Yields and Inflation (20-year T-Bond vs. CPI)

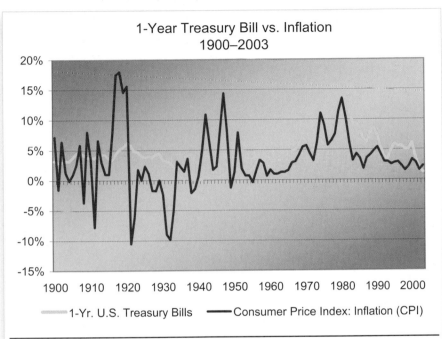

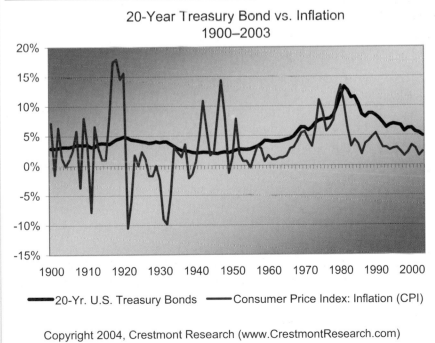

Copyright 2004, Crestmont Research (www.CrestmontResearch.com)

In the early 2000s, monetary policy principles and the Fed's job have changed. Dr. Harvey Rosenblum, Senior Vice President and Director of Research for the Federal Reserve Bank of Dallas, wrote, in an article published in *Business Economics* in January 2003:

> Throughout the 1980s and 1990s, the Fed's job has been to cap the rate of inflation from above. Put differently, the Fed attempted to and succeeded in putting an ever-lower ceiling on the inflation rate. As the economy approaches price stability, the Fed's job has shifted to one of maintaining a floor under the rate of inflation, probably at some very low, but positive inflation rate, on average.

Dr. Rosenblum has had a long career with the Fed, the focus of which has been to understand and tame inflation and help bring in an era of price stability. He also noted:

> In spite of the fact that inflation is such an important macroeconomic variable, I have come to the conclusion that economists don't fully understand the subject and have tried to oversimplify what turns out to be an extremely complex phenomenon … Strict monetarist ideology no longer works in the modern-day financial system. Money is difficult to define, its growth even harder to control, and its relationship to economic activity often uncertain.

Dynamic History

A high-level review of economic history and interest rates can be enlightening. It is presented in Crestmont's dynamic history of interest rates, a motion presentation that graphically displays interest rates annually since 1900 (available at www.CrestmontResearch.com). The interactive presentation takes you on a visual tour of interest rates, the yield curve, the stock market, and financial indicators such as the Consumer Price Index and Gross Domestic Product. The model dynamically presents the yield curve across each year of the past century. The yield curve, the graphical depiction of interest rates across maturities, shifts and pivots as it moves through the years. Clearly, some shifts have major implications for market performance.

In addition, the model illustrates that short-term rates differ from long-term rates, and that the level of interest rates has changed significantly over time. Further, it makes clear that the magnitude of changes in long- and short-term rates can differ dramatically. Finally, the model provides historical perspectives on inflation, economic growth, and stock market changes.

Interest Rate Reality

Interest rates and all of the factors that influence them are complex. For example, corporate, government, and mortgage-backed securities vary greatly in their rates, characteristics, and risks, yet pundits tend to discuss interest rates as though they were a unified whole marching in lockstep like West Point cadets. And while the appearance of military order can be appealing, reality in the interest rate world is messy and volatile. The image of marching drills should be replaced with a picture of the Marx Brothers in action—related entities often headed in a somewhat similar direction, but stumbling over each other along the way.

The desire to simplify the interest rate discussion also leads to misinformation. There is a tendency, for instance, to assume that changes in short-term rates drive changes in long-term rates and vice versa. Interest rate history shows that short- and long-term rates move independently and by different orders of magnitude. At the same time, the size of the moves can be both significant and surprising.

Many imagine that interest rates are set by respectable people gathered in a boardroom, surrounded by portraits of ancient and elegant financiers. They imagine conservative bankers seated at a mahogany table operating under the scrutiny of tradition. They picture their grandfather's banker—a man, who as a matter of principle, never wore stripes. In essence, they picture concerted effort, benevolence, and stability. And they are wrong.

Enter instead the world of interest rate volatility, where, ultimately, market participants set most interest rates. Much of fixed income trading has become a Wild-West world where bond vigilantes stampede prices lower at breakneck speed, where the relevant game is liar's poker, and where titanic leverage can create or evaporate fortunes in nanoseconds.

Trading in the financial markets is a fast-paced cutthroat activity. Prices are constantly changing as buyers and sellers of securities wager on the next change in price. Any tidbit of information or intuition that could impact the value of a security is used immediately. The market price of a security then changes as buyers increase or decrease their bids, or sellers step in or back away from the market. The financial markets are the ultimate battlefields of valuation and pricing, and the bastion of capitalism.

The 6/50 Rule

Interest rates move further and faster than most people imagine. Over the thirty-five years from 1965 through 2003 (with a limited exception at the start of 1998 and one week in August 2003), there has not been a rolling six-month period during which interest rates did not change by at least 50 basis points (100 basis points = 1%) at some point along the yield curve. The 6/50 Rule (6 months/50 basis points) states that during every six-month period, interest rates have moved by more than 50 basis points somewhere along the yield curve over 99 percent of the time since the mid-1960s.

Given that volatility is a fact of life in the realm of interest rates, what does the past record of volatility mean for current interest rates? Figure 4.2 looks at the U.S. Treasury Interest Rate Yield Curve and then draws an imaginary boundary that is 50 basis points on each side of the yield curve. According to The 6/50 Rule, interest rates at some point along the yield curve will move outside the band within the next six months.

Just how extreme have the interest rate moves been? Figure 4.3 reflects nearly 2,000 six-month periods, starting each week since 1968. The chart shows that interest rates have frequently moved 1.5% to 2.5% (150–250 basis points) within six months. Occasionally, they have moved more than 3.5% within six months, and fourteen times they have moved over 7%.

Interest rate volatility can also be expressed in percentage terms, the change in interest rates as a percent of the starting rate. In Figure 4.4, reflecting interest rate changes within the subsequent six months as a percentage of the initial rate, you quickly see that interest rates

Figure 4.2. 50 Basis Point (0.5%) Boundary

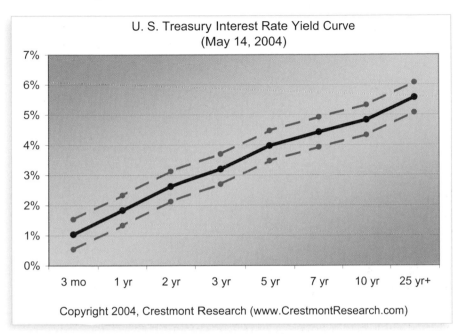

Copyright 2004, Crestmont Research (www.CrestmontResearch.com)

commonly change by as much as 30 percent of their initial rate within half a year. Even during the high interest rate periods in the past, the changes as a percentage of the initial rate are significant. During any six-month period, a 20 percent move has occurred two-thirds of the time—that is, either twenty basis points (0.2%) for short-term rates or 100 basis points (1%) for long-term rates. Since January 2000, in a period of lower interest rates, the moves have averaged nearly 40 percent during six-month periods!

The average investor has tended to ride serenely through the turbulent volatility of interest rates and the bond market. Why? A generally declining trend in interest rates, and thus a generally rising trend in bond prices over the last twenty years, has obscured the volatility of interest rates and bond prices and led to the misperception of stability. Also, media attention focuses far more on stock market action than on the bond market.

The volatility of interest rates matters for at least two reasons: its impact on bond portfolios and its impact on other markets. Within investors' bond portfolios, the market value of bonds changes based

Figure 4.3. Interest Rate Changes within the Subsequent Six Months

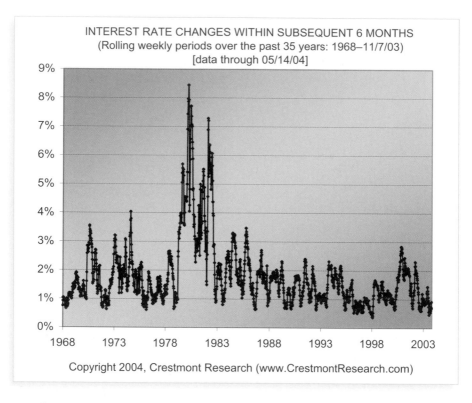

INTEREST RATE CHANGES WITHIN SUBSEQUENT 6 MONTHS
(Rolling weekly periods over the past 35 years: 1968–11/7/03)
[data through 05/14/04]

Copyright 2004, Crestmont Research (www.CrestmontResearch.com)

on changes in interest rates. Just as there is significant volatility in interest rates, there is significant volatility in bond prices. Although buy-and-hold bond investors often ignore the impact of interim volatility, those with interim obligations may find a need for funds when values have cycled downward. Since bond market volatility over the past two decades has largely been to the upside, investors are generally desensitized to the ravages of rising interest rates.

As interest rates and bond prices became more volatile in the decades following the 1960s, traders and investors attracted to volatility moved into the markets. Language, too, began to reflect the increased volatility, leverage, and speculation in the marketplace. Vigilantes, raiders, and poison pills came face to face with strips, tigers, and naked calls. As volatility increased, not only did speculators enter the fixed income arena, but also a more sophisticated breed of

Figure 4.4. Interest Rate Changes in Percentages

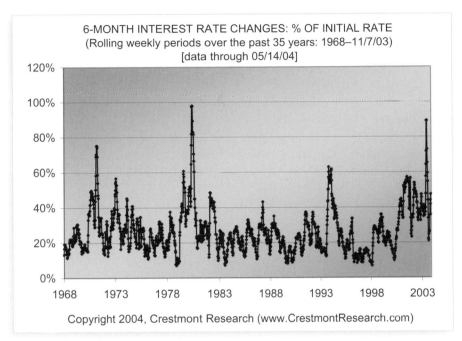

6-MONTH INTEREST RATE CHANGES: % OF INITIAL RATE
(Rolling weekly periods over the past 35 years: 1968–11/7/03)
[data through 05/14/04]

Copyright 2004, Crestmont Research (www.CrestmontResearch.com)

investor arrived. Investors who understood the new tools and strategies of risk management began both to hedge the risks of volatility and to exploit the opportunities unearthed by volatility.

Speculators, volatility, and the people who know how to hedge it are here to stay. Despite the lingering images of the financial markets from decades ago, clearly the land of your grandfather's banker no longer exists.

Summary

Prior to the 1960s, interest rates were relatively disconnected from inflation. As the financial markets evolved, the relationship between inflation and interest rates—an accepted fact of modern finance—developed into a strong and relatively consistent relationship. Despite investors' perception that interest rates in the near term are stable, interest rates have been highly volatile since the 1960s. Modern investment tools and techniques enable investors to harness this volatility to increase portfolio returns.

Key Concepts for This Section: Market History

1. Valuation matters. Over periods of decades, the average rarely happens; above-average returns occur when P/E ratios start low and rise; and below-average returns occur when P/E ratios start high and decline.

2. The financial markets are much more volatile than most investors realize! Volatility matters. Two gremlins can devastate the returns that are actually realized: negative numbers and the dispersion of returns.

SECTION III

SECULAR CYCLES

CHAPTER 5

SECULAR CYCLES

Seasons of the Stock Market: Secular Cycles

Savvy farmers know the seasons and understand the importance of planting and tending to their crops during the most favorable growing periods. In other words, they deposit their seeds in the soil when they have the least risk of loss and the highest probability of securing a successful harvest. The seasons are fundamental to the activities of farmers, and the climate in the financial markets can make the difference between profit and loss for investors.

Likewise, the stock market has seasons—the multiyear periods known as secular bull or secular bear markets. By distinguishing between favorable and unfavorable market seasons, investors can lower their risk and increase their success. Further, skilled investors can employ the appropriate techniques during each market season—the same way a farmer knows to plant vegetables in the spring and winter wheat in late fall.

Bond Market Seasons

Most bond investors know the joy of watching their accounts rise in value as they receive interest payments and as the prices of their bonds increase. The two components of interest payments and bond-price changes are known as the "total return." The two components, however, work independently and can move in different directions. All too many bond investors have experienced the sadness of watching the interest payments be offset by declines in the value of their bonds. When this occurs, total returns can be low or negative. An understanding of these principles as they relate to bonds will also shed light on stock market seasons.

Bond prices increase when interest rates decrease. This occurs because most bonds pay a fixed rate of interest. As market interest rates increase, a bond with the same (now lower than market) rate of interest declines in value. The price falls to the point that the existing interest payments will provide the new market interest rate. For example, if you have a $1,000 bond with an interest payment of $50, the yield is 5%. If market interest rates rise to 6%, the bond value will fall so that the $50 interest payments plus the payment of the principal ($1,000) at maturity will yield 6%. So, when interest rates are rising, bond values fall. The declining bond value offsets the income from the interest payments and lowers the total return to the bond investor.

When interest rates are declining, however, bond values rise. A rising bond value plus the income from the interest payments creates a double-win condition and increases the total return. Rising bond prices are a positive occurrence for investors, but they may also require vigilance, since a bond that moves above par value because of declining interest rates will return to par value at maturity. An investor's decision about whether to sell the bond at a higher value or hold it to maturity should be based upon the investor's underlying strategy and the outlook for the bond market.

Bonds are often called "fixed income" securities. They represent borrowed money that will be repaid at a future date with interest that is paid based upon a predetermined schedule. As a result, the holder or investor in bonds expects to receive income from the investment in the form of interest over the life of the bond and then receive the principal amount at maturity. The interest rate can be a single rate throughout the term of the bond, or a variable rate based on market conditions. Either way, the bondholder's investment return is fixed, based on interest and principal.

The two conditions, rising or falling interest rates, represent the environments for bonds that create secular bear markets (lower total returns) and secular bull markets (higher total returns). Conceptually, it is the same in the stock market: there are periods when the key factors line up for high total returns and periods when the factors offset each other, resulting in lower total returns. The first step is to explore the profile of the secular periods and then explain the most significant factor that serves as the catalyst for secular periods.

Stock Market Seasons

Stock market seasons can extend for years. While a few stock market seasons have completed their cycles in only four years, most average about twelve, and some have run over twenty years. These seasons should not be confused with ice ages, when almost everything becomes idle and virtually nothing grows. Rather, these are periods much like the seasons of the year, with unique climate conditions. For the farmer, spring provides the warmth, the rain, and the rising trend in temperatures that ignite bountiful crops. Winter provides a frigid environment that constrains growth and limits the farmer's total production.

Since 1900, investors have enjoyed four secular bull markets and endured four secular bear markets. Currently, the market is in the early phase of the next secular bear market period. Unfortunately, most current investors tend to think of market history in terms of the secular bull market that ran from 1982–1999, a period during which declines tended to be very short-lived. As a result, many are inclined to think of the market declines from spring of 2000 to fall of 2002 as having been sufficient to take care of bear market business. While those declines served to undo the excesses of the late 1990s, the market has not reached the lower valuations that have historically characterized bear market bottoms. In addition, investors might wish to take a deep breath and understand that secular bear markets can last a long time; some have lasted sixteen and twenty years.

Historically, secular bull markets have run as long as 24 years (1942–1965) and as short as 4 (1933–1936). On average, they have lasted 13.5 years in length. Secular bear markets, for their part, have also run for extended periods of time. They have averaged 11.3 years and have ranged from 4 years (1929–1932) to 20 years (1901–1920).

Secular Market Profile

Just as trends in temperature drive farmers' planting cycles, and trends in interest rates drive the bond market cycles, so do the trends in the expansion or contraction in price/earnings ratios (P/E ratios) drive the long-term seasons of the stock market. The cycles presented in figure 5.1, Secular Market Profile, correspond to peaks and troughs in P/E ratios, often over extended periods of years. For example, the most recent secular bull market began with a P/E of 7 and climaxed with the highest P/E in the last 100+ years, a stratospheric 42. If the last cycle had ended without experiencing a bubble condition, P/E ratios should have peaked in the low 20s, a level that would have been more consistent with the prior secular bull market tops.

By contrast, the 1966–1981 bear market saw the beginning P/E of 21 decline over the years to an ending level of 9. And even though earnings grew significantly during the period, a sleepy investor who chose to emulate Rip Van Winkle would have awakened after sixteen years to find the S&P 500 at a lower level than when he fell asleep. The decrease in P/Es more than offset significant increases in earnings, leaving Rip little to show for a great deal of time.

Not to upset the sweet dreams of current buy-and-hold investors who invest for the long term, but they may wish to contemplate the implications of a market P/E ratio in the low-to-mid 20s, the level during late 2004, on their prospects for future returns. While a rising P/E ratio accentuates the benefits of rising earnings and enhances the total return from stock market investments, a declining P/E ratio offsets the benefits of rising earnings and mutes the total return available in the stock market. Since cycles, by their nature, tend to fluctuate above and below a midrange, the current position of riding historically high on the wave indicates a much higher likelihood from here of a decline than a rise in P/E ratios. In addition, in the past, relatively highly valued markets rarely returned to average without continuing further downward to relatively lower valuation levels. The good news? Eventually, markets recover from excessively low valuations, pass upward through average, and again visit the land of relatively high valuation. For the foreseeable future beginning in the early 2000s, though, it is likely that the stock market has entered a long-term period of P/E contraction or stability.

Bulls Don't Look Like Bears

Look at the secular bull market periods shown in Figure 5.1. You see mostly green. With apologies to Kermit the Frog, it *is* easy being green, at least during secular bull markets. Green represents positive returns. Extended periods of profitability in the market—periods represented by long stretches of green on the chart—occur when P/E ratios are in a rising trend. And since corporate earnings have generally increased over time, the compounding effect of rising P/Es and earnings growth makes it easy to have extended periods of positive returns. As a result, most secular bull markets string together long-running series of winning years. They have few, if any, down years, and the down years that surface tend to be modest declines averaging near 4%.

Most important, bull markets mint money for investors. The 1982–1999 bull market launched the Dow Jones Industrial Average from 875 to 11,497, an increase of over 1,200 percent. It made millionaires of the neighbor next door. The guy across the fence who put $100,000 into the Dow Jones Industrial Average index in 1982 would have found himself a millionaire with over $1,200,000 by 1999, excluding the impact of dividends, taxes, and transaction costs.

Those with open eyes and minds can see when a bull market trend is underway. The most telltale sign of a secular bull market is a general rise in P/E ratios. In the words of Edwin LeFevre in his popular book, *Reminiscences of a Stock Operator:*

> Nobody should be puzzled as to whether a market is a bull or a bear market after it fairly starts. The trend is evident to a man who has an open mind and reasonably clear sight, for it is never wise for a speculator to fit his facts to his theories.

When P/E ratios are already at relatively high levels, however, there is little potential for the market to receive any benefit from further increases in P/E ratios.

Figure 5.1. Secular Bull and Bear Markets Profile

SECULAR BULL & BEAR MARKETS PROFILE

Market Cycle From	Market Cycle To	(#) Total Years	Market	P/E Ratio Beg.	P/E Ratio End	Inflation Beg.	Inflation End	(#) Positive Years	(#) Negative Years	(%) Positive Years	(%) Negative Years	Max Pos. Yrs In Row	Max Neg. Yrs In Row	Avg Gain In Pos. Years	Avg Loss In Neg. Years	Change Begin To End
1901	1920	20	BEAR	23	5	-2%	16%	9	11	45%	55%	2	3	30%	-17%	2%
1921	1928	8	BULL	5	22	-11%	-2%	7	1	88%	13%	5	1	24%	-3%	317%
1929	1932	4	BEAR	28	8	0%	-10%	0	4	0%	100%	0	4	n/a	-32%	-80%
1933	1936	4	BULL	11	19	-5%	1%	4	0	100%	0%	4	0	34%	n/a	200%
1937	1941	5	BEAR	19	12	4%	5%	1	4	20%	80%	1	3	28%	-16%	-38%
1942	1965	24	BULL	9	23	11%	2%	18	6	75%	25%	4	1	16%	-8%	774%
1966	1981	16	BEAR	21	9	3%	10%	9	7	56%	44%	3	2	13%	-15%	-10%
1982	1999	18	BULL	7	42	6%	2%	16	2	89%	11%	9	1	18%	-4%	1214%
2000	????		BEAR	42		3%		1	3	25%	75%	1	3	25%	-10%	-3%
WEIGHTED AVERAGE BEAR (excluding 2000)										42%	58%	2.1	2.7	21%	-18%	-14%
WEIGHTED AVERAGE BULL										83%	17%	5.8	0.9	19%	-5%	810%

Notes: The index and returns reflect the Dow Jones Industrial Average at year-end from Dow Jones & Company. The P/E ratio is based upon the S&P 500 as developed and presented by Robert Shiller (Yale; Irrational Exuberance). Bull & Bear Market classifications are based upon Crestmont's assessment of cycles using peak and trough P/E ratios, inflation trends, and other analysis. The presentation does not include dividends, taxes, inflation adjustments, or transaction costs.

RETURN PATTERN (Red = down year; Green = up year; #% = annual change in the index; starting and ending DJIA index is presented on the ends of the rows)

1901–1920: BEAR	71	-9%	0%	-24%	42%	38%	-2%	-38%	47%	15%	-18%	0%	8%	-10%	-31%	82%	-4%	-22%	11%	30%	-33%					72
P/E Ratio		23	22	18	16	19	19	13	13	15	14	14	14	12	11	12	12	9	6	7	5					
CPI: Inflation		-2%	6%	1%	0%	1%	3%	6%	-4%	8%	4%	-8%	7%	3%	1%	1%	8%	17%	18%	15%	16%					
1921–1928: BULL	72	13%	22%	-3%	26%	30%	0%	29%	48%																	300
P/E Ratio		5	8	8	8	10	12	16	22																	
CPI: Inflation		-11%	-6%	2%	0%	2%	1%	-2%	-2%																	
1929–1932: BEAR	300	-17%	-34%	-53%	-23%																					60
P/E Ratio		28	22	15	8																					
CPI: Inflation		0%	-2%	-9%	-10%																					
1933–1936: BULL	60	67%	4%	39%	25%																					180
P/E Ratio		11	12	13	19																					
CPI: Inflation		-5%	3%	2%	1%																					
1937–1941: BEAR	180	-33%	28%	-3%	-13%	-15%																				111
P/E Ratio		19	14	16	15	12																				
CPI: Inflation		4%	-2%	-1%	1%	5%																				
1942–1965: BULL	111	8%	14%	12%	27%	-8%	2%	-2%	13%	18%	14%	8%	-4%	44%	21%	2%	-13%	34%	16%	-9%	19%	-11%	17%	15%	11%	969
P/E Ratio		9	11	11	13	14	11	11	10	11	12	13	12	14	18	18	16	15	18	17	21	19	20	23	23	
CPI: Inflation		11%	6%	2%	2%	8%	14%	8%	-1%	1%	8%	2%	1%	1%	0%	1%	3%	3%	1%	2%	1%	1%	1%	1%	2%	
1966–1981: BEAR	969	-19%	15%	4%	-15%	5%	6%	15%	-17%	-28%	38%	18%	-17%	-3%	4%	15%	-9%									875
P/E Ratio		21	22	22	19	15	17	18	16	11	10	12	10	9	9	9	9									
CPI: Inflation		3%	3%	4%	5%	6%	4%	3%	6%	11%	9%	6%	7%	8%	11%	13%	10%									
1982–1999: BULL	875	20%	20%	-4%	28%	23%	2%	12%	27%	-4%	20%	4%	14%	2%	33%	26%	23%	16%	25%							11497
P/E Ratio		7	10	9	11	13	16	14	17	17	18	20	21	21	23	26	31	36	42							
CPI: Inflation		6%	3%	4%	4%	2%	4%	4%	5%	5%	4%	3%	3%	3%	3%	3%	2%	2%	2%							
2000–????: BEAR	11497	-6%	-7%	-17%	25%																					
P/E Ratio		42	32	26	24																					
CPI: Inflation		3%	3%	2%	2%																					

Bears Don't Look Like Bulls

In contrast to the consistency of secular bull markets, most secular bear cycles tend to be violent and choppy, with sharp declines followed by abrupt increases. If an amusement park could replicate the ride, it would easily be the most popular with thrill seekers. But for investors, secular bears are similar to haunted houses filled with uncertainty, fright, laughter, and an exit door near the entrance. In many cases, secular bear market investors find major stock market indices virtually unchanged at the end of extended periods of years. Along the way, though, the bear market is often characterized by violent downswings and hair-raising climbs spread over numerous years.

Importantly, though, while many bear markets end up about where they started, some end up far below their starting points. In those cases, one way to end up with a small fortune at the end of the bear market is to start with a large fortune at its beginning. In the 1929–32 bear market, the market began at a level of 300. By 1932, the market had plummeted to 60. In other words $100,000 invested in 1929 shrank to roughly $20,000—before dividends and transaction costs —by 1932.

For those who lost, though, the losses were often devastating. Many came to believe, as Mark Twain said in an earlier era, that the market was a dangerous place. October, he noted, was "one of the peculiarly dangerous months to speculate in stocks. The others," he continued, "are July, January, September, April, November, May, March, June, December, August, and February."

Stock Market Profile Across Secular Periods

By expanding the Significant Swings analysis from chapter 3, figure 5.2 reveals that the distribution of the return profile differs greatly between secular bull and secular bear markets. Even when the data is separated into secular periods, the frequency of years inside the 10% and 16% ranges remains consistent. The revelation is that the extremes reflect a contrasting pattern.

Across the past 103 years, 50% of the years ended within the broader range of −16% to +16%. When the years are again delineated

Figure 5.2. Stock Market Dispersion during Secular Cycles

Dow Jones Industrial Average
DISPERSION OF ANNUAL STOCK MARKET CHANGES
Percent Of Years During Secular Cycles
(8+ Cycles: 1901-2003)

RANGE	103 Yrs AVG	54 Yrs BULL	49 Yrs BEAR
<-10%	21%	4%	42%
-10% to +10%	30%	30%	29%
>+10%	49%	67%	29%

RANGE	103 Yrs AVG	54 Yrs BULL	49 Yrs BEAR
<-16%	16%	0%	33%
-16% to +16%	50%	50%	49%
>+16%	35%	50%	18%

into secular periods, the frequency of years within the broader range remains fairly constant during both secular bull periods and secular bear periods. Note that secular bulls have 50% of the years inside the range and that secular bears have 49% within the range. The volatility of dispersion again remains fairly constant across secular periods.

Note that over the entire 103 years, 30% of the years ended within the range of –10% to +10%, the so-called single-digit years. When the years are delineated into secular periods—the secular bulls with generally rising P/E ratios and the secular bears with generally declining P/Es—the frequency of single-digit years remains fairly constant during both secular bull periods and secular bear periods. Note that secular bulls have 30% single-digit years and that secular bears have 29% single-digit years. The volatility of dispersion remains fairly constant across secular periods.

The most significant dynamic of the analysis relates to the frequencies outside of the range. Across all periods, 35% of the periods reflect changes that are greater than +16%. Further, 16% of the periods present themselves below –16%. In the long run, having twice as many super-positive periods helps to offset the super-negative periods.

When the years are divided among secular bull periods and secular bear periods, the contrast is illuminating. During the periods of generally rising P/E ratios, none of the years were below –16%! All of the years outside of the broader range of –16% to +16% were super-positive years in excess of +16%. During the periods of generally declining P/E ratios, there were almost twice as many years below –16% as there were above +16%. The super-negatives were almost double the super-positives.

Over the secular bull market of the 1980s and 1990s, all of the years with high volatility (as measured by the annual market change) showed upside volatility and super-positive years. As the markets now have entered a secular bear period, the volatility will include both sides of the spectrum. Beware, however, that the incidences of downside volatility are likely to overpower the occurrences of upside volatility. To most investors and market spectators, the markets will feel quite different over the next decade or more when compared to the past two decades. Further, an investor's approach to the markets should be quite different during the current secular bear market.

In secular bull markets for example, half the years show gains greater than +16%, and only 4% of the years show negative returns below –10%. By contrast, in secular bear markets, 33% of the years show losses exceeding –16%, while only 29% of the years show gains in excess of +10%. Clearly, secular bull markets treat most investors very well. Keep in mind, though: secular bear markets damage the portfolios of investors who use the buy-and-hold approach.

Summary

Secular bull markets and secular bear markets are driven by the trend in P/E ratios. Secular bull markets tend to show much volatility to the upside and little volatility to the downside. Secular bear markets exhibit significant swings both up and down, with significantly more downside volatility than upside volatility.

Inflation, Deflation, and Market Seasons

The music starts, and everyone walks in a circle. It is time for monetary musical chairs, in which the participants represent money in the economy, and the chairs represent goods in the economy. If a chair is taken away, someone will be without a seat when the music stops. This represents too much money chasing too few goods—that is, monetary inflation. Add a chair and the opposite occurs—deflation or too little money chasing too many goods.

Inflationary and deflationary trends influence whether long-term stock market seasons are favorable or unfavorable. More specifically, expanding or contracting P/E ratios determine whether a market season is favorable or unfavorable, and inflationary and deflationary trends correspond to and drive the changes in P/E ratios. Periods of rising P/E ratios correspond to periods in which inflation moves toward price stability (low inflation). Periods of falling P/E ratios correspond to periods in which inflation moves away from price stability, either toward greater inflation or greater deflation. The 1966–1982 bear market, for example, corresponds to a move from relatively low levels of inflation to higher levels of inflation, a move away from price stability. On the other hand, the 1982–1999 bull market corresponds to a period of declining inflation in which inflation moved closer to price stability.

Although the United States has not experienced an extended period of deflation in more than six decades, the impact of moving toward or away from price stability applies during times of deflation as well. The 1921–1928 bull market, for example, moved from deep deflation to lesser deflation, a move in the direction of price stability. In contrast, the 1929–1932 bear market corresponded to a move away from price stability, a move from price stability to deflation.

In summary, earnings rise during both secular periods. Secular bull markets benefit from rising valuations (rising P/Es). Secular bear markets result from declining valuations (declining P/Es). Secular bull markets are great periods for equity asset class returns. Secular bear markets are disappointing periods for equity asset class returns. Investors who buy the market when it is accompanied by low P/Es enjoy the potential for significant gains as P/Es expand. On the other hand, investors who buy the market when P/Es are high, eventually face contracting P/Es which are powerful enough to overcome rising earnings per share. Therefore, the lessons of history indicate that investors who buy a highly priced market face a great risk of disappointment.

Dispelling the Myth: It's Not the Economy

Despite the general contention that the economy and the stock market are closely connected, the facts get in the way of confirming conventional wisdom. For example, from 1966 to 1981, the economy grew on average at a rate of 9.6% per year, as shown on figure 5.3. The Dow Jones Industrial Average not only failed to grow, but declined across this period of strong economic growth.

Surely, if the economy were to grow at a slower pace, say an average of 6.2% per year from 1982 through 1999, the market would do even worse. Not so! The DJIA grew an astounding 15.4% a year on average during this period of slower economic growth. The point cannot be overemphasized: the economy and the market can behave independently for very significant periods of time. During secular bull and secular bear markets, P/E contraction or expansion can far outweigh the impact of economic growth.

Looking at the last hundred years, stocks fell by an average of 4.2% per year during bear markets while nominal GDP grew an average of 6.9% during the same bear markets. During bull markets, however, stocks gained an average of 14.6% per year, while nominal GDP grew an average of 6.3% per year. Surprisingly, nominal GDP actually grew faster on average during bear markets than during bull markets! Although economic growth does increase the earnings portion of the price/earnings ratio, the trend in the overall level of the P/E ratio is frequently the largest driver of actual returns. Periods of high nominal growth in GDP result from periods of high inflation—since real GDP generally increases at a relatively consistent pace. Therefore,

Figure 5.3. Stock Market and Economic Growth

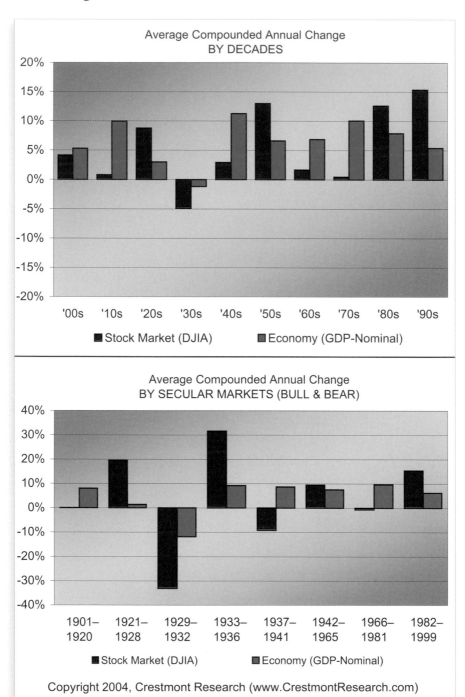

Figure 5.3. (continued)

AVERAGE ANNUAL CHANGE (COMPOUNDED)

DECADE	DJIA Stocks	GDP Nominal
1900s	4.1%	5.3%
1910s	0.8%	10.0%
1920s	8.8%	3.0%
1930s	-4.9%	-1.2%
1940s	2.9%	11.3%
1950s	13.0%	6.6%
1960s	1.7%	6.9%
1970s	0.5%	10.0%
1980s	12.6%	7.9%
1990s	15.4%	5.4%

AVERAGE ANNUAL CHANGE (COMPOUNDED)

SECULAR CYCLE	DJIA Stocks	GDP Nominal
1901–1920 (Bear)	0.1%	8.0%
1921–1928 (Bull)	19.5%	1.4%
1929–1932 (Bear)	-33.1%	-11.8%
1933–1936 (Bull)	31.6%	9.2%
1937–1941 (Bear)	-9.2%	8.6%
1942–1965 (Bull)	9.5%	7.5%
1966–1981 (Bear)	-0.6%	9.6%
1982–1999 (Bull)	15.4%	6.2%
Secular Bear Avg	-4.2%	6.9%
Secular Bull Avg	14.6%	6.3%

the high inflation that creates the above-average periods of nominal GDP growth also causes P/E ratios to decline, thereby resulting in relatively low stock market returns.

The Y-Curve Effect

As reflected in figure 5.4, moves in inflation away from price stability have caused P/E ratios to decline and moves in inflation toward price stability have driven rising P/E ratios. The increase in inflation in the 1940s, for example, corresponded to a decline in P/E ratios. More recently, the move from the high inflation of the early 1980s down toward very low inflation in recent years corresponded to a long rise in P/E ratios from the early 1980s to 2000. Also note that during the first forty years of the twentieth century, the economy experienced deflation from time to time. When the economy moved away from price stability and into deflation, P/E ratios tended to decline.

The "Y-Curve Effect," a scatter plot of P/E ratios and inflation since 1900 on figure 5.4, reveals an intriguing phenomenon. The highest levels of inflation and the most extreme levels of deflation correspond to the lowest P/E ratios. In other words, moves toward extremes of inflation or deflation drive down P/E ratios. The graphical presentation of the relationship between P/E ratios and inflation reveals a pattern that reflects the letter "Y" lying on its left side. Interestingly, the "Y-Curve Effect" indicates that P/Es decline during deflation despite low interest rates. This is consistent with the modern financial theories, including the dividend discount model, which provides that the current value of a stock equals the value today of all future dividends. As a result, the dividends received in the future are expected to provide a fair return on the investment based on the price paid initially. Generally, low inflation and interest rates provide a high-valuation multiple for financial securities. So, as interest rates decline, P/Es generally rise.

Once deflation occurs, however, interest rates stay low. Some might think that this would further inflate values. Yet, in this case, since earnings, and thus dividends, would be expected to decline during deflation, the current value of future dividends declines, and P/E ratios fall accordingly. In the other direction, rising inflation poses a problem for future P/Es. As inflation rises, interest rates rise. As interest rates rise, the required rate of return rises to keep stocks competitive with bonds—which in turn lowers the current value of stocks. As a result, P/Es decline along the upper fork of the Y-Curve. The best environment for high valuations occurs when inflation is low and stable.

Figure 5.4. P/E Ratio and Inflation

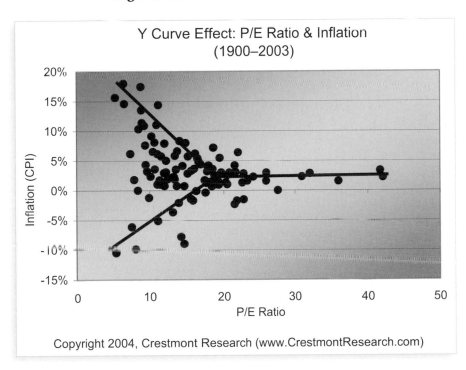

As of late 2004, inflation is relatively low and stable; as a result, P/Es are relatively high. A continuation of the current high P/E is only likely if stable, low inflation rates are sustained. Keep in mind, however, there are very few circumstances that can drive P/Es higher from the current levels. Historically, it took bubbles in the market, or temporary declines in earnings during recessions, for P/Es to be above the low twenties. During bubbles, P/Es rise as prices move to irrational and unsustainable levels. During recessions, earnings temporarily decline, and the calculated P/E ratio can increase due to a decrease in the denominator of the ratio. Even when stock prices decline, the decline in earnings is often greater and still results in a higher ratio. The temporary increases in the P/E due to the decline in earnings during recessions disappear once earnings have been restored to normal levels during the subsequent economic recovery.

The challenge in the current environment — to at least maintain P/Es at current levels in the twenties — is that the United States has never before been able to sustain price stability for an extended period of time. Historically, the relatively brief periods of price stability have been followed either by periods of rising inflation or deflation. Therefore, there is a risk that P/Es may begin to decline toward or below the historical average near sixteen if history is repeated and inflation cannot be held at price stability for an extended period. Some hope, however, that the Fed will be able to maintain inflation near price stability, and that P/Es can be sustained at currently high levels.

Valuation Matters

Valuation is the concept of price in relation to value. To distinguish the difference, consider the following question: which has more value, a car priced at $10,000 or a ring for $1,000? Unless more is known about the items, you know only their prices. If the car is an old jalopy, it may not be worth $1,000, and the price of $10,000 could be highly overvalued. Likewise, if the ring is set with large precious gems, it may be worth much more than its price and would be quite undervalued if priced at $1,000.

For many items, value can be a difficult number to determine. If there are a limited number of buyers and sellers, or if the item is unique, valuation is very subjective. For most goods and services, value is the price that someone is willing to pay.

For financial investments, the price can be more rationally determined. Financial assets are securities that represent future cash flows. A buyer acquires the asset for a return based on future cash receipts. If you know that an investment will only return $90 in the future, it would not be wise to pay $100.

Yet, there is a price that you would be willing to pay for the $90 in the future. Depending on how long you have to wait and the uncertainty of receiving it, there is a price today that provides a fair return on your investment. Therefore, the price affects the ultimate rate of return from the investment.

For example, if a bond has a scheduled interest payment of $500 per year, has a face value of $10,000, and interest rates for similar bonds are 5%, an investor should be willing to pay $10,000 for the bond. By paying $10,000, the investor will receive a yield of 5% until the bond matures and returns the principal value of $10,000. Since the 5% yield is equal to the market yield on similar bonds, the bond is priced in line with the market. If the price of the same bond is more than $10,000, however, then the interest payment will represent a yield lower than 5% and the investor should choose another bond.

In this instance, two factors cause the yield to fall below the market rate of 5%. First, if an investor pays $11,000, for example, the interest payment of $500 is less than 5% of the price paid. Additionally, the investor will receive $10,000 at maturity, the actual face value of the bond, and the decline in investment value from $11,000 at purchase to $10,000 at maturity will represent a reduction in the effective yield from the bond. There are additional aspects to bonds, yields, and bond pricing, but the purpose of these examples is to describe that most bonds are still relatively straightforward to value. Bonds generally have scheduled cash flows from interest payments, and the principal value is returned at a fixed maturity date.

Stocks are more challenging to value, since the future cash flows are derived from earnings and dividends, which are much less certain than a bond's interest payments; still, the fundamental concepts of value are similar. The higher that the price is in relation to future cash flows, the lower the ultimate rate of return. For example, consider a company with earnings per share of $1 that are expected to grow at 5% per year. An investor or analyst can project into the future the expected future earnings and potential dividends. Consider two potential prices for the stock: $10 per share and $20 per share. Keep in mind that the future earnings will be the same under both purchase-price scenarios. The operating performance of the company is not affected by the investor's purchase price for its stock.

Figure 5.5. Impact of Starting P/Es

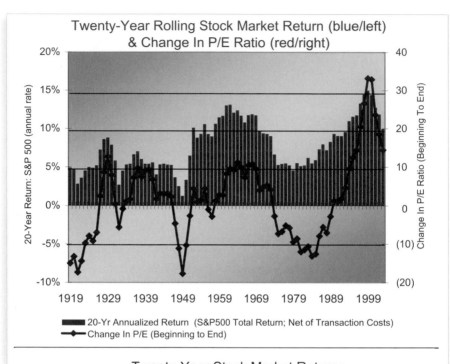

Copyright 2004, Crestmont Research (www.CrestmontResearch.com)

When the purchase price of the stock is $10, the future rate of return will be higher than if the stock price were $20. The investor will have invested less money and will receive the same cash return as under the higher-price scenario. As the amount paid for the stock increases, the calculated rate of return declines. Since future cash flows are not affected by the purchase price the investor paid for the stock, valuation matters.

For bonds, the value is determined based on the interest rate in relation to similar bonds. For stocks, the value is determined based upon the measure of the price in relation to the current earnings—the price/earnings ratio (P/E). If earnings are expected to grow over the long term at a fast rate, then the price today can reflect a higher ratio to earnings than if the expected earnings growth is slow. Similarly, if the expected rate of return is lower, then the price today can be higher than if the expected return is higher. The valuation of stocks is much more complex than bonds. In this chapter, several measures of valuation are explored. In chapter 7, a more detailed understanding of stock market valuation is presented through the framework known as *Financial Physics*.

Importance of Starting P/Es

"Buy bargains," says Sir John Templeton, and chart 5.5 shows why investors do well to heed his advice.

The figure displays a central fact of investment life: valuations matter. Buying an expensive market (a high P/E market) increases the risk of negative to very low returns over a twenty-year period. In fact, buying an expensive market almost precludes the opportunity to have high returns over the two-decade period. On the other hand, buying an inexpensive market (a low P/E market) greatly diminishes the odds of ending up with negative returns, while significantly increasing the potential for very high returns over a twenty-year period.

One might ask if assessing ending P/Es is not just as important as starting P/Es. Ending P/Es are important, but no one can accurately predict what P/Es will be twenty years into the future. A starting P/E, though, is readily known. As a result, investors can make assessments about potential future returns based on the range of likely scenarios and the direction for the level of P/E ratios. When P/E ratios are generally high, many of the scenarios are likely to include lower future P/E ratios. When P/E ratios are generally low, the scenarios may favor rising P/Es. As a result, periods that start with high P/E ratios tend to result in below-average returns due to declining P/Es; likewise, periods that start with low P/E ratios tend to have above-average returns due to rising P/Es.

On the subject of ending P/Es, many faithfully followed long-term investment plans have found their end results torpedoed by declining P/Es in the later years of the plan. Many investors approaching retirement saw half or more of their lifetime savings vanish during the market declines following the spring of 2000. Vigilant attention to the risk inherent in a portfolio is vital at all times, and is particularly important as investors approach retirement or long-term goals. In the current environment of relatively high P/Es, there is a much greater chance of declining or stable P/Es than there is the likelihood of rising P/Es. Chapter 8 explains the reasons why there is a rational limit to market P/Es, a limit that creates a ceiling in the low to mid-twenties, except during bubbles and periods with temporary distortions in earnings.

Summary

Secular cycles represent seasons in the financial markets. These seasons respond to the trends in inflation, the driver of returns for financial assets. Secular bull markets and secular bear markets have distinct characteristics. These secular market profiles are defined by the magnitude of the ultimate gains as well as by the upside and downside volatility each year. The secular cycles are not driven by economic growth; rather, they are driven by the trend in inflation. One of the best indicators of future returns is the starting level of valuation. Initially high valuations lead to below-average returns, while initially low valuations lead to above-average valuations. Chapter 6 reveals the current market cycle and its implications for future returns.

Chapter 6

The Current Cycle

Remember the bull market? Then the historic millennium bubble? Investors bought stock in companies without earnings and made money anyway. Eyeball hits replaced cash flow as the metric for future performance. In California, silicon and software created billionaires, and the new Gatsbys quickly shed the trappings of corporate wealth. They exchanged ties for T-shirts, and shed pinstripes altogether. When the stock market gains seemed unlimited, the options that mattered were stock options, and many people had them: founders, friends, key executives, and many employees. As stock prices soared beyond the stratosphere, option values surged past the moon, creating vast wealth where only a business plan had existed months before.

And not just option holders got rich. Other workers without options benefited as their IRA and 401(k) accounts scaled new heights. Butchers, bakers, and engineers became millionaires. As long as the rising tide carried all boats higher, it seemed that any investment strategy worked.

While many investment strategies produced profits during the market bubble, the end came abruptly—as it generally does with financial investments that are based on irrational assumptions. The bull market peaked in 2000 with the NASDAQ cresting at 5,048.62, the Dow posting 11,722.98, and the S&P 500 reaching 1,527.46. The subsequent three years each reflected declines in the market. As the market deflated, few stocks, portfolios, or investors were spared.

The decline in the NASDAQ was the most dramatic with that stock market index eventually falling 80 percent from its peak. Put in practical terms, a NASDAQ millionaire became a fifth of a millionaire; 401(k) retirement accounts shrank to be less than 101(k)'s, and portfolio values plummeted.

Following the decline, and beginning in April 2002, the S&P 500 rallied over 30 percent. The NASDAQ did even better with a gain of over 90 percent. While a 90 percent rally off of the bottom is impressive, a 90 percent rally does little to overcome an 80 percent decline, and in late 2004 the NASDAQ remained at less than one-half of its peak value. Put in dollar terms, a $1,000,000 portfolio that loses 80 percent shrinks to $200,000. A subsequent 90 percent gain, adding $180,000 to the account, only brings the portfolio back to $380,000. A portfolio that has experienced a decline of 80 percent requires a 400 percent gain to return the portfolio to its initial value.

Current Market Cycle

Stand back from the clamor of stock market chatter, and you can hear several distinct tunes. Market cheerleaders sing the praises of what they claim is a new bull market. More skeptical observers suggest that the 2003 rally may have been merely one of the periodic rallies that occur intermittently during the course of long-term secular bear markets. Still others pose the possibility that the 2000–2002 declines served only to correct the extreme valuations that accompanied the bubble. From the perspective of the latter group, a long-term secular bear market may just now be unfolding.

Bear Tracks

At present, there are four significant signs that we are in the early stages of a secular bear market:

1) High P/Es;
2) Low dividend yields;
3) Low inflation;
4) Low interest rates.

High P/E's

If the P/E at the peak of the bubble were the pinnacle on Everest, the current P/E is at least the top of the Matterhorn. The P/E on the S&P 500 index during late 2004 is in the mid-twenties. It is nearly the highest P/E of the last century, excluding the bubble years of the late 1990s and a brief portion of 1929. Also, it is almost 50 percent higher than the average P/E over the last century. More ominous, perhaps, the current P/E is slightly higher than the P/E that existed at the beginning of two of the longest secular bear markets in U.S. history (the 1901–1920 and the 1966–1981 bear markets).

Some argue, however, that if forward-looking earnings were inserted in the P/E ratio, the market would then be valued much more closely to its long-term average valuation. Forward-looking earnings reflect the earnings expected over the subsequent year rather than those that are "in the bank." The inconsistency for this particular argument is that historical measures such as those used in Figure 6.1 are based upon trailing earnings, not forward earnings. If the

Figure 6.1. S&P 500 P/E Ratio Since 1900

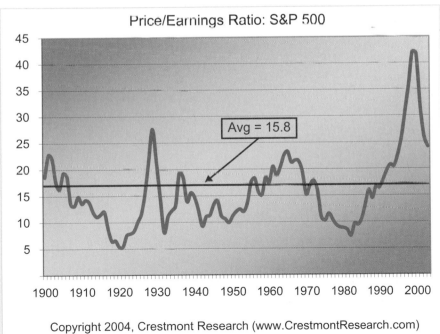

Copyright 2004, Crestmont Research (www.CrestmontResearch.com)

historical chart were constructed using forward earnings, the average P/E historically would be less than 15, and current "forward-based" P/Es would still be high compared to their historical counterparts.

Therefore, the first data point—P/Es that are well above average—indicates a relatively low probability of further increases in P/Es and clearly indicates a high probability of stable or declining P/E ratios. As a result, the current P/E ratio portends a secular bear market for stocks.

Low Dividend Yields

As reflected in figure 6.2, dividend yields are near their lowest levels of the last century. Currently, they return little more than a penny or two on each dollar invested. While low dividend levels by themselves do not precipitate bear markets, they correspond to and often reflect high valuation levels for stocks. As a result, most bear markets have begun with dividends at low levels. Bull markets, by contrast, tend to start with a base of high dividends.

Figure 6.2. S&P 500 Dividend Yield Since 1900

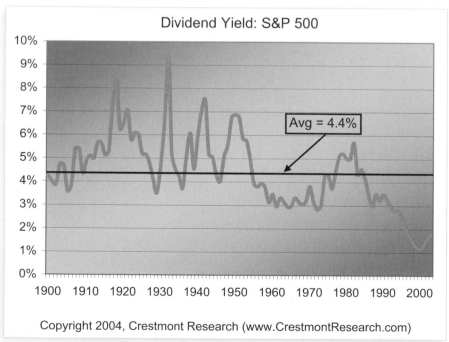

Dividends can be an indication of valuation because of the relationship of dividends to earnings. Dividends have been paid from earnings at a fairly consistent rate historically. Therefore, as the ratio of price to earnings increases, so does the ratio of price to dividends. Since the dividend yield represents the ratio of dividends to price—the inverse of the price to dividends ratio—as the price/earnings ratio increases, the dividend yield declines. So a rising valuation mathematically decreases the dividend yield. Using this relationship in reverse, a low dividend yield is often an indication of high valuations in the stock market.

Therefore, the second data point—dividend yields that are well below average—indicates that valuations are relatively high, and potentially signals a secular bear market for stocks.

Low Inflation Starting to Rise

Low inflation is good for the financial markets, but low inflation historically has not been sustained. As inflation has trended higher or fallen into deflation, secular bull market cycles have ended and secular bear markets have emerged. It is significant to note that the United States has never maintained price stability for extended periods of time, and therefore low inflation has tended to be the crossroads for the next trend to either higher inflation or to deflation.

If price stability were maintained going forward, P/E ratios might remain at current levels in the low to mid-twenties. A move to higher inflation or to deflation, however, will bring P/Es down. A declining trend in P/Es creates a secular bear market. Currently, according to several measures, the level of inflation as measured by the consumer price index (CPI) remains reasonably near price stability and below the historical average of 3.3%.

Inflation presents major problems for investors, as Charles D. Ellis notes in his book, *Winning the Loser's Game* —

All investors share one formidable and all too easily underestimated adversary: inflation. This adversary is particularly dangerous for individual investors.... For individual investors, inflation has usually been the major problem—not the attention-getting daily or cyclical changes in securities prices that most investors fret about. The

corrosive power of inflation is truly daunting: At 5 percent inflation, the purchasing power of your money is cut in half in less than
15 years—and cut in half again in the next 15 years. At 7 percent,
your purchasing power drops to 25 percent of its present level in
just 21 years—the elapsed time between "early" retirement at 61
and age 82, an increasingly normal life expectancy. This is clearly
serious business, particularly when the individual is retired and has
no way to add capital to offset the dreadful erosion of purchasing
power caused by inflation.

Figure 6.3. S&P 500 Inflation: CPI Since 1900

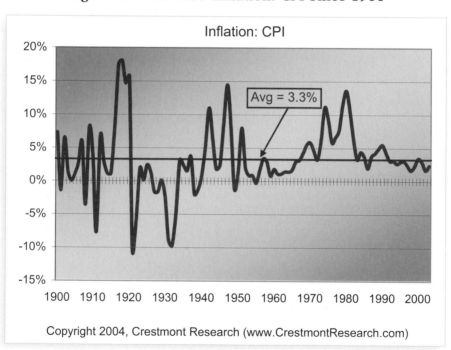

Copyright 2004, Crestmont Research (www.CrestmontResearch.com)

While inflation may take several forms, the erosion of purchasing
power often stems from the ability of a government to print money
or expand credit. One writer lamented the ability of government to
ruin the value of perfectly good paper simply by adding ink. In the
somewhat shorter term, a move either to higher inflation or to deflation tends to be accompanied by declining P/E ratios, the telltale
element of secular bear markets.

Therefore, the third data point—inflation that is well below average and at levels of price stability—is positioned at a crossroads point where increases or decreases would be adverse to stock market valuations. The risk of moves away from price stability indicates the potential for a secular bear market for stocks.

Relatively Low Interest Rates

The descent from a roller coaster's highest point can be exhilarating. But it is the quick turn back up from the bottom that produces the crushing G-forces. Likewise, with interest rates, a long period of declining rates produces exhilaration in the economy and in the markets. But a sharp move higher off the bottom can produce economic G-forces that crush stock and bond valuations.

Currently, interest rates are at relatively low levels in relation to the past 40 years. The risk of declining bond prices from a rise in interest rates has become significant. Jim Grant of Grant's Interest Rate Observer says that the usual reference to U.S. Treasury securities as providing *risk-free interest* has been turned on its head and represents more risk than return. Now, he says, "Treasury securities come closer to offering *interest-free risk.*"

As with low inflation, low interest rates are beneficial to the stock investor. Low interest rates actually are a strong ally of high stock prices. The problem arises if the trend in inflation and interest rates reverses and they begin to rise. At that point, P/Es, stock prices, and bond prices often begin to fall.

As of 2004, long-term interest rates are relatively low, but not historically low. The probabilities are close to evenly divided on the issue of whether long-term interest rates will rise or fall over the next few years. Many market experts are calling for a rise in interest rates. A rise would be consistent with a rise in inflation. There is also the possibility for the Fed to maintain inflation near price stability. If they were to be successful in containing inflation, long-term interest rates could decline modestly further.

Therefore, the fourth data point—interest rates that are relatively low in relation to the past forty years—reflects conditions of relatively high valuation for financial assets. Rising interest rates would confirm a secular bear market for stocks; however, further declines for interest rates would support currently high P/Es, but cannot drive P/Es substantially higher to create another secular bull market.

The Best of All Possible Worlds

In Voltaire's *Candide,* Dr. Pangloss stands as a believer that the flawed world he faces represents "the best of all possible worlds." With all respect to the doctor, imagine for a moment the best of all possible worlds for investing in the stock market. Stocks would sell at bargain prices. They would pay huge dividends. Inflation would be moving toward price stability, thereby spurring higher P/E ratios, and interest rates would be solidly moving lower—also prompting P/E expansion.

In fact, none of the four favorable conditions exists today. Instead, their opposites—high valuations, low dividends, and potentially rising inflation and interest rates—rule the day. Despite the claims of Dr. Pangloss' talking-head descendants that all is well, current conditions

Figure 6.4. Interest Rates: 20-year Treasury Bond Since 1900

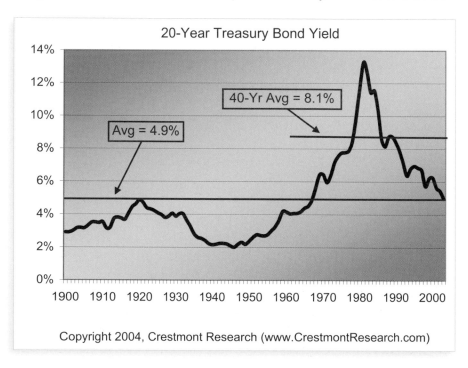

Copyright 2004, Crestmont Research (www.CrestmontResearch.com)

reflect those usually found early in secular bear markets. Rather than the ungrounded optimism of Dr. Pangloss, the current times call for the clear-eyed realism of Voltaire, who, in addition to being a leading writer of his day, proved himself a most successful speculator in corn, bacon, and other investments. He even participated in an investment syndicate and used a statistically based strategy to win the national lottery while eliminating virtually all of the customary risk; his pool bought essentially all of the lottery tickets after a number of lotteries without winners had increased the potential winnings to unprecedented levels.

Dividends do more than provide pleasure to their recipients; they help investors assess the expensiveness or cheapness of the market. While P/Es remain the dominant measure of market valuation for many investors, the market's dividend yield (dividend per share divided by stock price) also provides a useful guide to the market's level of valuation. In fact, it can provide a particularly hardy measure of market valuation.

Many major companies pay dividends, cash payments representing a portion of their profits, to their shareholders on a quarterly, semiannual, or annual basis. Because investors become attached to the regular dividend payments, and because an omitted or decreased dividend payment will cause many investors to sell the stock, companies are careful to keep dividends consistent with the trend in long-term earnings.

Dividend Yield and P/E Ratio: Correlated Partners

Figure 6.5 presents the relationship between dividend yield and P/E ratio from 1900 to 2003. Clearly very low dividend yields correlate with very expensive markets (high P/Es), and very high dividend yields correspond to markets selling at bargain prices (low P/Es). The relationship continues convincingly between the extremes as well; dividend yields tend to increase as markets decline in value, and decrease as markets rise and become more expensive.

Although this could seem coincidental, the relationship is fundamentally and mathematically based. The dividend yield is the percentage return on a stock from the dividend payments during a year. The ratio for dividend yield results from dividing the dividend by the price of the stock or index of stocks, thus D/P. The price/earnings ratio is represented by the relationship P/E. When the P/E ratio is inverted, it reflects a measure known as the earnings yield, the level of earnings in relation to the price or E/P. Since dividends are paid from earnings at a rate that has historically averaged 50 percent, the D/P ratio averages one half of the E/P ratio. A change in the earnings yield of a stock has a similar effect on the dividend yield; they move in the same direction. Yet, when earnings yield is expressed as a P/E ratio, as the ratio of price to earnings (P/E) increases, the ratio of dividends to price (D/P) moves in the opposite direction. As a result, when P/Es rise, dividend yields necessarily decrease; as P/Es decline, dividend yields increase.

Figure 6.5. Dividend Yield and P/Es

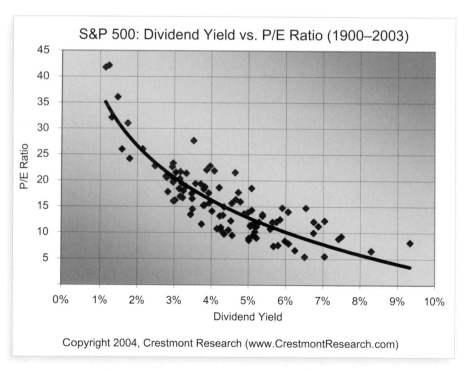

Companies determine their dividends based on the amount of operating profits and the internal capital needs at the company. The price of a stock is determined by the market, and reflects a decision each investor makes when buying the stock. The dividend yield, therefore, is determined by the level of dividends as well as the market price of the stock. For example, if the annual dividends on a company's stock are $2 per share, a price of $40 per share provides a 5% dividend yield. Yet if the price is $67 per share, the dividend yield is 3%. Keep in mind that the level of dividends that a company pays on its stock is completely unaffected by the purchase price paid by an investor—dividends are determined based upon profits and internal capital needs. Therefore, in periods of above-average valuation (high P/Es), investors can expect below-average dividend yields. Likewise, in periods of below-average valuation, investors can expect above-average dividend yields. As a warning to those wanting higher dividend yields in the current environment, it is unrealistic to expect average or better dividend yields in periods of above-average valuation.

The Dividend Insight

Dividend yields can be a complementary measure of the stock market's valuation. While investors most often use the P/E ratio as the measure of market valuation, P/Es can be distorted during recessions that temporarily reduce earnings. Also, dividends are generally more stable than earnings and are unaffected by the temporary adjustments or one-time accounting charges to earnings that affect P/E ratios. As a result, overall dividend yields can be used as a measure of the level of valuation in the market. Currently, the dividend yield measure confirms the P/E ratio's signal of relatively high valuation. In recent years and through 2004, dividend yields portray a market with high valuations, high risk, and a low probability of satisfactory returns for some years to come.

As highly recognized financial writer Richard Russell has commented:

> Earnings can run all over the place, they can be manipulated, they can be figured in various ways, and no two analysts tend to agree about whether the S&P should be looked at from the standpoint of trailing earnings, forward earning, core earnings, you name it.

Dividends are different. There's no argument about dividends. You know what they are, there's no adjusting, misstating, monkeying around with dividends. Charles H. Dow used the dividend yield on the Dow as his gauge when deciding whether stocks were overvalued or undervalued.

Today's Dividend Yield

What is the dividend yield on the S&P 500 today? It is below 2%, one of the lowest levels in history—not a good sign for those hoping that valuations have declined to historically attractive levels. In the background, you can almost hear the assertion of market cheerleaders: "Sure, dividends are low, but expect dividend yields to return to the historical norm of 3.5% or higher." And it may do so eventually, if earnings and dividends rise over time without much change in the market's price, or if there were to be a decline in stock market's price. To return to the historical average dividend yield immediately, the market would have to fall by over 30 percent.

Astute investors, like great hitters in baseball, keep their eyes on the ball. An investor who focuses on his wish for a higher dividend yield is like a hitter who dreams of a perfect pitch when he should be directing his full attention to the pitch at hand. Both risk striking out. The key to success for both the hitter and the investor is to see current reality clearly.

Looking Ahead

Speculation about the future abounds. Rarely, though, is it grounded in a clear understanding of the interrelationships between economic growth, earnings growth, inflation, interest rates, and stock valuations (P/E ratios). The next three figures, each titled Valuation Matters, offer a detailed look at potential returns between now and 2010 as well as a clear view of the foundations of the exceptional returns earned during the 1982–1999 bull market in both stock and bonds. The figures dissect the source of returns for stocks and bonds using the concept of a return bar. The return bar breaks out the individual components of total return. For stocks, returns are built from earnings growth, dividends, and the expansion or contraction of P/E multiples in the market. Bond returns have two components: the yield from interest payments, and gains or losses in value from the trend in interest rates.

Figure 6.6, Valuation Matters: 1982 to 1999, dissects the sources of returns for stocks and bonds during the last secular bull market. During the secular bull in the past two decades, earnings growth contributed 5.9% to stock returns. Dividend yields averaged 3.1%, to drive total returns near 9%. The greatest contributor to total returns, however, was the expansion of market P/E ratios from less than 10 to well above 20. The increase in valuation added 8% to returns. As a result, total returns compounded at 17% per year over those eighteen years.

Bonds yielded 12% over the same period. Since interest rates started the period at well over 10%, the average interest payment yield provided 8.3% of the return. As interest rates declined, bond values increased and added a little more than 3.6%. In total, the combination thrilled bond investors with a 12% total return. Clearly, for investors in financial assets, the last secular bull market was incredibly rewarding. Through this analysis, you can see the individual components that provided the gains. This template also provides the framework to assess future returns for both stocks and bonds.

Figure 6.7, Valuation Matters: Low Inflation, poses an optimistic scenario and assumes maintaining both price stability and very high stock market valuations. Based on these assumptions, stocks would produce a total return of 6.2% per year before transaction costs. Since this scenario assumes low, stable inflation near 1.5%, the total real return would be 4.7% per year on average between 2005 and 2010. Bonds, for their part, would return 5% per year before inflation and 3.5% per year after inflation over the same period.

For stocks, if inflation remains constant and averages 1.5%, the economy would experience below-average nominal growth of approximately 4.5%. As a result, earnings growth would be approximately 4% and would contribute 4% to stock returns. At current levels of valuation, the dividend yield is likely to be near 2.2%. In total, stock returns before transaction costs, inflation, and taxes would be a modest 6.2%.

For long-term bonds, the coupon interest rate in late 2004 is near 5%. If inflation remains the same, interest rates should remain the

Figure 6.6. Valuation Matters: 1982–1999

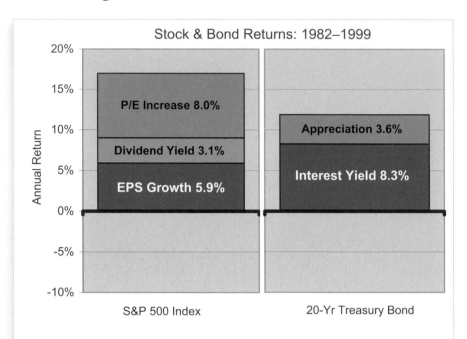

Figure 6.7. Valuation Matters: Low Inflation

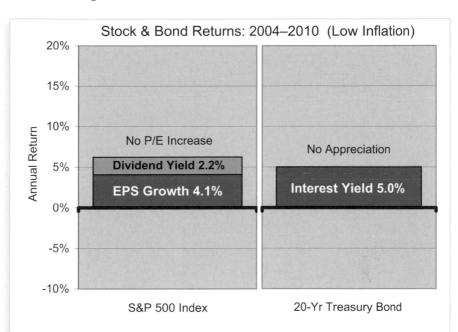

same or decline somewhat. As a result, there would be little change in the principal value of bonds. Thus the total return will equal the coupon yield of 5%.

Figure 6.8, Valuation Matters: Average Inflation, is built upon the assumption that inflation rises modestly to average 3% over the period — close to the historical average of slightly more than 3%. In this scenario, a modest rise in inflation would partner with a modest rise in interest rates as well as a decline in P/E ratios. For inflation to average 3%, it would need to gradually rise from near 1.5% currently to 4.5% in 2010. Based on the general relationship between P/E ratios and inflation, inflation of 4.5% (slightly above the historical average) drives the P/E ratio to approximately 13.5 (slightly below the historical average). The combination of rising inflation and interest rates, as well as a decline in P/E ratios, would likely produce total returns before transaction costs reflecting a loss of –0.2% from 2005 through 2010. Based upon inflation averaging 3%, the total real returns would be a loss of approximately –3.2% per year on average for stocks. Bonds would return 0.4% per year before inflation and a loss of –2.6% per year after inflation over the same period.

For stocks, if inflation averages 3%, it will end the period at 4.5%. The economy would experience average nominal growth of near 6% and earnings growth will contribute approximately 5.4% to stock returns. As valuation levels decline, the dividend yield will increase and average 2.9%. Rising inflation will depress P/E valuations. The above-average inflation of 4.5% will drive P/E ratios to a below-average level near 13.5. The effect is a valuation loss of –8.5%. In total, stock returns before transaction costs, inflation, and taxes would be a disappointing loss of –.2%.

For bonds, the coupon interest rate will rise over time and average 6%. As interest rates rise, existing bond values will decline and usurp 3.8% of the value. As a result, the principal decline offsets part of the coupon. Thus the total return for bonds from 2005 through 2010 will be a disappointing 2.2%.

Potential Investment Solutions

A clear-eyed view of the present and a realistic view of possible future scenarios are central to an investor's ability to structure profitable

Figure 6.8. Valuation Matters: Average Inflation

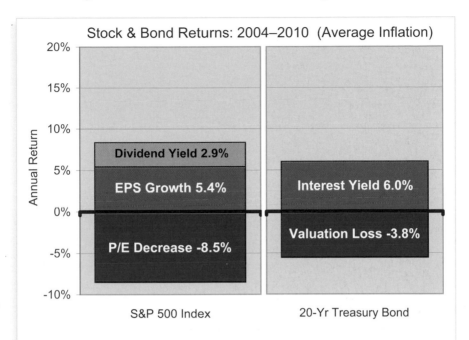

investment solutions. The early stages of secular bear markets pose substantial risks as well as significant opportunities. Several upcoming chapters explore viable approaches for sound investing in the current market climate.

The next two chapters present a framework for identifying the drivers of returns in the stock market and the causes of secular stock market cycles. The section begins with details about the *Financial Physics* model and concludes with an application of its principles to forecast scenarios for stock market returns through the end of the decade. First, below is a recap of the key principles and concepts from section III.

Key Concepts for This Section: Secular Cycles

1. The stock market experiences extended periods of secular bull markets and secular bear markets based on the trend in P/E ratios, which is driven by the trend in inflation.

2. The Y-Curve Effect reflects the strong relationship between P/E ratios and inflation or deflation.

3. The current financial conditions indicate relatively low or negative returns from stocks and bonds.

SECTION IV

FINANCIAL PHYSICS

CHAPTER 7

FINANCIAL PHYSICS

$\mathbf{W}$hile the laws of physics provide predictability for the future speed and direction of a spacecraft hurtling through space, what rules exist to govern the future movements of the market? Are there underlying principles on which rational intermediate-term forecasts can be made? For those seeking to understand the potential returns available in the stock market in five, ten, or twenty years, Crestmont's *Financial Physics* model provides a foundation that enables an investor to determine his or her own perspective on the stock market's future, develop rational forecasts, and discern the difference between information and misinformation from market pundits.

Predicting the Future of the Stock Market

The stock market is a collection of the stocks of individual companies. The principles that are used to value individual stocks are the same as those used to value the overall stock market. These principles relate to valuing financial assets based on their expected cash flows. The more cash flow, the higher the value. Several factors affect the value of the cash flows. These include the timing of the cash flows (near-term cash flows are worth more than cash flows received further into the future), the rate at which the cash flows increase over time (a faster growth rate is worth more), and the certainty of the cash flows (consistency increases the value). For the stock market, the cash flows are represented by earnings and dividends.

As investors weigh all the factors that affect values, the market collectively determines its overall level of valuation. In the stock market, the level of valuation is measured with a ratio known as the price/earnings ratio (P/E). The P/E reflects the number of years of current earnings that investors are willing to pay for stocks today. Thus the market price can be determined by multiplying earnings (or earnings per share, EPS) by the price/earnings ratio (P/E).

In other words, the price level of the stock market or an individual stock can be explained by two variables, EPS and P/E. For a discussion of the overall stock market, a representative index can be used. The S&P 500 Index is a recognized and respected index that is often used as a proxy for the overall stock market. For this discussion, EPS represents the aggregate profits earned by the companies in the S&P 500 Index, thus reflecting the earnings of a broad range of companies. The second variable, the P/E, represents the ratio of the market price of the S&P 500 to its earnings. Multiplying EPS and P/E creates the price of the market.

$$\text{MARKET PRICE} = \text{EARNINGS PER SHARE} \times \frac{\text{PRICE}}{\text{EARNINGS}}$$

For example, if the aggregate earnings for the S&P 500 are $50 per share and the P/E ratio is 20, then the market price of the stock index would be 1,000.

$$\text{MARKET PRICE} = \text{EARNINGS PER SHARE} \times \frac{\text{PRICE}}{\text{EARNINGS}}$$

$$1{,}000 = \$50 \times 20$$

While the current P/E can represent a useful guide to investors to assess whether the market is currently cheap or expensive, investors focus on the future. They yearn to know the price of the stock market at some date well into the future. Although you know the price you pay today, it is the price in the future that will determine whether the investment was a good choice or a bad one.

To develop a reasonable assessment of the stock market in the future, you need a reasonable estimate of future EPS and a reasonable estimate of the future P/E. The approach of multiplying EPS and P/E provides the expected future market price when the estimates for those components can be reasonably determined.

So, is it possible to reasonably forecast both EPS and the P/E into the intermediate future of five to twenty years from now? Yes. The *Financial Physics* model provides a framework for making rational estimates about future EPS, future P/E ratios, and the future level of the stock market. To you as an investor, the practical benefit of the model is the insight about potential returns in the market over the next decade or so. As you develop your estimate of future returns, be sure to relate your assumptions to historical values to assess whether they are reasonable. As of late 2004, rational assumptions would reflect an environment that is unfavorable for stock market investments; the details are explained later in this chapter.

The following section of this chapter builds the *Financial Physics* model and shows its role as a big-picture or macro model for the stock market. The subsequent section of the chapter will illustrate how the *Financial Physics* model can be used as a tool for valuing the market and predicting future price levels for it. Since unpacking a lot of economics and financial concepts—especially at the same time—can be challenging, the discussion will walk you step by step through an interactive tour of *Financial Physics*.

As you will see by the end of the tour, the *Financial Physics* model identifies that inflation is the common element in the longer-term relationship between the economy and the stock market. Although on the surface the economy and the stock market appear to have an inconsistent relationship, the missing link lies in the effect of inflation on valuations. The *Financial Physics* model explains the fundamental effect of inflation on the economy and the stock market. This practical explanation, and your understanding of the concepts, will arm you with insights that will enable you to capitalize on solid investment advice and avoid mistakes that are driven by hopeful, but incorrect, statements.

Building the *Financial Physics* Model

By now, you are probably wondering, "What exactly is *Financial Physics*"?

Financial Physics represents the interconnected relationships among key elements in the economy and the financial markets that determine the stock market's overall direction. It reflects the link between growth in the economy, growth in earnings, and overall stock market valuation as reflected by the P/E ratio. *Financial Physics* explains why and how inflation and deflation drive total economic growth, corporate earnings, and rising or falling P/E ratios. The trend in the P/E ratio determines whether stock market returns are greater than or less than earnings growth.

So, what exactly does that mean? Before going into all of the details, it may be helpful to have a quick summary of the model, its components, and the way to interpret its elements. After a short description, the discussion will delve into the specifics. The *Financial Physics* model is graphically presented in figure 7.1.

Note the components in the *Financial Physics* model. First, there are three ingredients from the economy: real gross domestic product (Real GDP), inflation, and nominal gross domestic product (Nominal GDP). Next, two elements are added from finance: the price/earnings ratio (P/E) and earnings per share (EPS), which combine to produce the price level of the stock market. You will recognize that the finance components are the same elements discussed at the beginning of this chapter.

Figure 7.1. *Financial Physics* Model

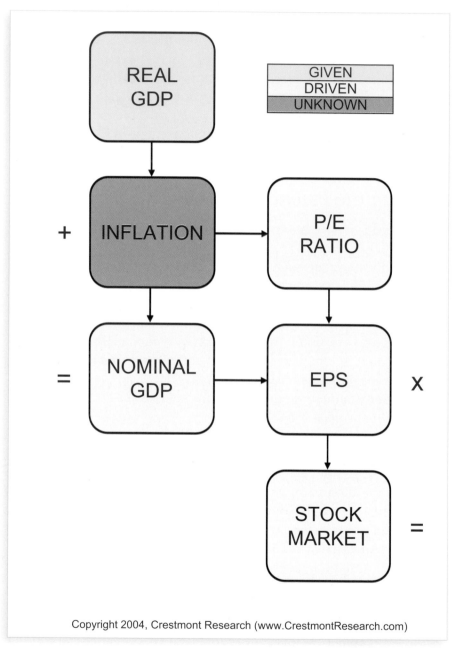

Although you can see the factors in the model, you may be wondering how they relate to each other. The first ingredient, Real GDP, is designated in the model as a *Given* because growth in the economy (before factoring in Inflation) has been remarkably consistent over the past century, especially the past thirty-five years. It has been very close to 3% per year on average for each of the last three decades and for the century overall.

Therefore, the first major point is that real growth in the economy has averaged about 3% per year.

The next ingredient, Inflation, is the key to the model. The reasons for its importance will become apparent shortly. For now, please recognize that inflation influences the value of many of the other components in the model, yet the future direction of inflation is *Unknown*. It drives Nominal GDP, which can be used to predict or estimate earnings in the future. Even more important, the trend in inflation drives P/E ratios higher or lower and thus dramatically impacts the valuation level of the stock market. The future trend for this unknown variable will drive the ultimate direction and level of returns from the stock market.

Therefore, the second major point is that the future trends in inflation, an *Unknown* variable, drive several of the other ingredients in the model. With the basic concepts in place, it is time to take a closer look at the model and its components.

Key Elements of the *Financial Physics* Model

To help you understand the details, here are some definitions from the economics side of the model:

1) Real gross domestic product, known as Real GDP, is essentially the amount of goods and services in the economy before inflation. Real GDP increases when companies in the economy sell more units.

2) Inflation refers to price increases due to an increase in the amount of money in the economy in relation to the amount of goods and services in it. The loss of purchasing power due to the excess money is known as monetary inflation.

3) Nominal gross domestic product, known as Nominal GDP, is Real

GDP plus Inflation. So Nominal GDP includes not only the unit growth of Real GDP, but also the effect of inflation on prices. Essentially, Nominal GDP represents the total sales of all companies in the economy.

The three economics ingredients are familiar to economists, but may not be known to all investors. Likewise, investors know the financial components, so here are a few definitions to reinforce the understanding of the economists on the tour.

Definitions of the financial ingredients in the model:

1) Earnings per share (EPS) represents the net profits for a company, divided by the number of shares of the company's stock held by stockholders. The *Financial Physics* model relates to the overall stock market using the S&P 500 Index as a proxy for the market. Thus EPS in the model is the combined profits per share of all companies in the S&P 500 Index.

2) The price/earnings ratio (P/E) is the ratio of the current price to current EPS. In effect, P/E represents the total number of years it would take for current earnings to pay the value of the S&P 500 Index.

Both of these concepts were previously discussed, and represent the traditional concepts of stock market valuation. It is worth noting that all the key factors are readily available to investors, and the value of the *Financial Physics* model is that it shows how established relationships between the key elements can be used to provide a rational perspective about the stock market's future.

The next stage in the tour is to explore the historical details of economic growth. You will find that economic growth has been remarkably consistent over the past century. The details will reinforce one of the principles of *Financial Physics*: real economic growth can be assumed to be relatively stable near 3% over time.

Consistent Growth in Real GDP

Figure 7.2 provides a closer look at the historical growth in Real GDP. Real GDP represents the absolute level of the economy before inflation. It represents the combined revenues of all companies, based on the number of units sold and excluding the impact of any price changes due to inflation or deflation.

For example, consider an economy with only one product: pencils. If the number of pencils (units) sold remains the same from year to year, Real GDP will remain the same. If the number of pencils (units) sold increases by 3%, the Real GDP would increase by 3%.

Real GDP growth is the number most often reported in the press after the government releases its quarterly estimates. The key concept to note is that real GDP relates to the growth in units produced throughout the economy.

As figure 7.2 reflects, consistent growth has been the hallmark of Real GDP in the U.S. over the past century. The population grew fairly steadily over the years, and the people and machines in the economy became more productive at a relatively consistent rate. Obviously, there were growth spurts and recessions, but, over the decades, real economic growth has been relatively consistent around the average growth rate.

In fact, during the past hundred years, annual Real GDP growth has averaged 3.5%. Most decades during that time, it has averaged between 3% and 4.5%. Strikingly, during the last three decades — decades that included a severe bear market, a major bull market, and the greatest bubble in U.S. market history — Real GDP growth averaged 3.3%, 3%, and 3% for the 1970s, 1980s, and 1990s respectively.

Although it may be surprising that real growth has been so consistent over the last three decades, you may be wondering what has happened since the start of the current century in 2000.

In the first four years of the new millennium, Real GDP growth has been below 3%. To bring the decade average back to the historical average, the next six years would need to average more than 3%. So it is not surprising that real growth was more than 3% during 2003 and 2004.

Based on more than a century of consistent history, the first building block to *Financial Physics* is that Real GDP growth is remarkably consistent and has averaged roughly 3% annually.

The second building block, adding inflation to Real GDP, will provide a component that helps identify the relationship between earnings per share and economic growth.

Figure 7.2. Economic Growth: Constant over Time

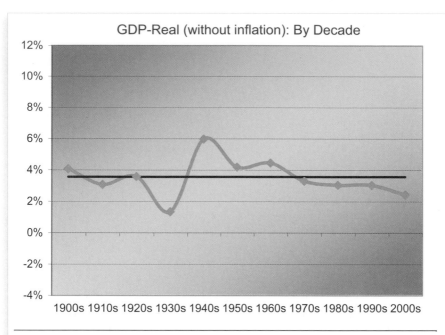

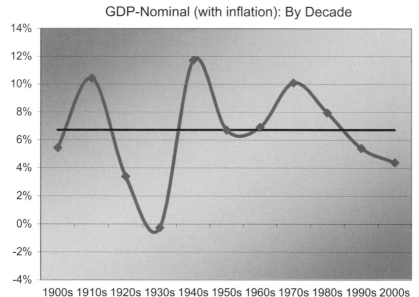

Figure 7.2. (continued)

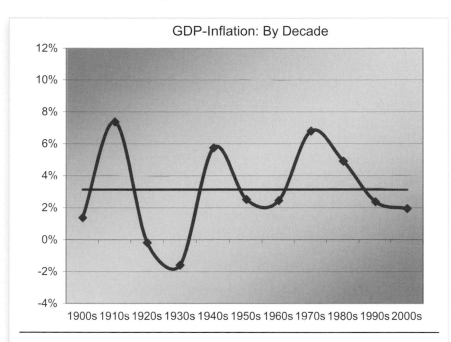

	Annual Simple Average		
BY DECADE	GDP NOMINAL	GDP REAL	GDP INFLATION
1900s	5.4%	4.1%	1.4%
1910s	10.4%	3.0%	7.4%
1920s	3.4%	3.6%	-0.2%
1930s	-0.3%	1.3%	-1.6%
1940s	11.7%	6.0%	5.7%
1950s	6.7%	4.2%	2.5%
1960s	6.9%	4.4%	2.5%
1970s	10.1%	3.3%	6.8%
1980s	7.9%	3.0%	4.9%
1990s	5.4%	3.0%	2.4%
2000–2003	4.4%	2.4%	2.0%
1900–2003	6.7%	3.5%	3.1%

Copyright 2004, Crestmont Research (www.CrestmontResearch.com)

Nominal GDP Leads to Sales,
Which Leads to Earnings

As mentioned previously, Nominal GDP again is simply Real GDP plus inflation. For example, if Real GDP growth is 3% and inflation is 2%, Nominal GDP growth would be 5%. Using the pencil-based economy in the prior example, if the number of pencils sold increases by 3% and the price of pencils increases by 2%, Nominal GDP growth would be 5%.

If the average Real GDP growth has been near 3%, what is the normal level for Nominal GDP growth?

Nominal GDP has varied more than Real GDP because inflation has cycled within a fairly wide range. On average over the last century, however, annual Nominal GDP growth has averaged 6.7%, reflecting average Real GDP growth of 3.5% plus average inflation in GDP of 3.2%.

With that in mind, how does Nominal GDP relate to companies?

In practical terms, Nominal GDP may be seen as the combined reported revenues or sales of all companies. So, when discussing overall growth in the economy, there are two components that enable companies to sell more goods and services. These are the number of goods sold and the effect on prices from monetary inflation. Together, they represent the combined sales of companies in the economy. In the U.S., the combined sales of all companies have grown at an average of 6.7% over the past century.

With the second building block in place, that overall growth in the economy is the result of real economic growth and inflation, the tour is ready to move to the third building block. The third building block is the connection between economic growth and earnings.

A key relationship in the *Financial Physics* model is that earnings emanate from sales, and tend to grow at roughly the same rate as sales. For the S&P 500 Index, dominated by larger companies, the growth rate in earnings is slightly slower than the overall economy. Keep in mind that the economy also has a number of startup companies and fast-growing small businesses that increase the average. The relationship between sales and earnings is much like the relationship between a stalwart nanny and a puppy tethered together for a brisk walk. Occasionally, the puppy may run ahead, but at the end of the day it goes where the nanny goes, usually lagging slightly.

With the link between economic growth and earnings growth established, the next detail is to further explore the relationship and establish its strength. After another step or two, the relationship can be explained with numbers and can then be used to project future earnings.

As managers, owners, and investors know from experience, earnings are much more volatile than sales. Recessions can significantly reduce earnings, although the impact is temporary. Following recessions or other soft periods for earnings, there generally is a period of fast earnings growth to get earnings back in line with sales.

Over the past century, as reflected in figure 7.3, earnings for the S&P 500 companies have grown on average by 6.1% per year. That is slightly lower than the sales growth of the whole economy, since the overall growth in the economy includes new startup companies and small businesses that are often faster growing. A key point is to recognize that the relationship between sales growth and earnings growth is fundamental—earnings come from sales.

One of the most common financial misunderstandings relates to earnings growth and economic growth. Earnings over the past century have not grown faster than sales. Despite the facts, some market enthusiasts try to argue that earnings can grow faster than sales for extended periods of time. Unfortunately, this cannot be true.

If earnings were to grow faster than sales for very long, earnings would ultimately overtake sales. Clearly earnings cannot exceed sales, and so over the long term, sales growth constrains earnings growth. In addition, overall earnings do not grow much slower than sales. If they did, earnings would ultimately become insignificant. Economic forces maintain earnings in a natural relationship to sales.

This discussion confirms the third building block of *Financial Physics*: earnings growth is fundamentally related to economic growth. The details show that Nominal GDP growth (Real GDP plus inflation) has averaged 6.7% annually over the last century. As a result, earnings growth, which is driven by sales growth, has increased an average of 6.1% annually over the past century.

Figure 7.3. Earnings Per Share Related to Economic Growth

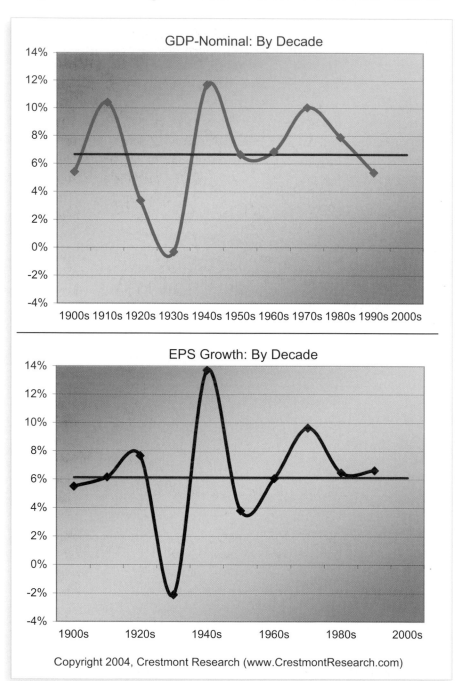

Figure 7.3. (continued)

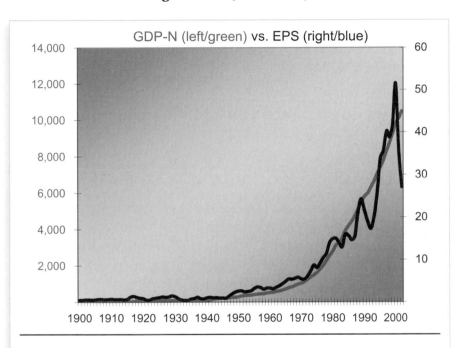

BY DECADE	Annual Simple Average	
	GDP NOMINAL	EPS GROWTH
1900s	5.4%	5.5%
1910s	10.4%	6.2%
1920s	3.4%	7.7%
1930s	-0.3%	-2.1%
1940s	11.7%	13.7%
1950s	6.7%	3.8%
1960s	6.9%	6.1%
1970s	10.1%	9.7%
1980s	7.9%	6.5%
1990s	5.4%	6.7%
2000–2003	4.4%	0.3%
1900–2003	6.7%	6.1%

Predicting Earnings per Share

Figure 7.4 provides the graphical relationship between the growth in Nominal GDP and the growth in S&P 500 earnings. Here is how it predicts future EPS:

1) Since Real GDP growth has been relatively consistent, it is reasonable to assume future growth of 3% over intermediate periods of five to twenty years or more.

2) Add average inflation of 3.2% to predict average future Nominal GDP growth of 6.2%.

3) Since the relationship between Nominal GDP growth and EPS growth is strong and based on principles of economics, an estimate of future Nominal GDP can be used to determine expected earnings per share. Well-established statistical tools can be employed to use the value of Nominal GDP to predict earnings per share.

4) The estimated future EPS, predicted using an estimate of future Nominal GDP, presents a centerline around which earnings per share can be expected to cycle over time.

The process just described determines estimates for EPS for each year in the future. This EPS series essentially represents the expected level and growth in earnings in the future. Although temporary influences affect earnings during shorter-term periods of time, the EPS centerline provides a fundamentally-determined path that is useful for intermediate-term projections of earnings.

Although the *Financial Physics* model may seem reasonable, you certainly can ask whether it has been tested. One way to verify its validity is to use the same approach as described above, starting at a point years ago in order to assess the model's accuracy over actual points in history.

Testing the Model for EPS Estimation

Using only data that was available in 1975, the model was used to predict earnings per share through 2007. Since the methodology is fundamentally based, rather than statistically based, this approach should reasonably assess the model's validity and accuracy. The year 1975 was chosen since it was three-quarters of the way through the last century. That provided a good base of seventy-five years of economic data and also was long enough ago, more than twenty-five years, to see how the model performed over time.

First, using this approach, Nominal GDP is extrapolated using standard statistical techniques. This provides a projection for Nominal GDP, a base measure of economic growth, into the future through 2007. Then EPS is predicted, based on its long-term relationship with Nominal GDP, for each year through 2007.

Figure 7.5 clearly reflects that the results of the analysis provide a baseline that EPS has followed for twenty-eight years. This confirming historical analysis predicts a baseline EPS value for 2007 that is virtually the same as the analysis using data through 2003!

Please keep in mind that this methodology of predicting EPS trends is fundamentally based and historically proven. This analysis strongly confirms the third building block in the *Financial Physics* model—earnings are predictable based on their fundamental relationship to the economy.

If you are convinced so far of the ability to estimate the trend in EPS, the fourth building block of *Financial Physics* will introduce the concept of valuation in relation to price. On the finance side of the model, EPS is multiplied by the P/E ratio to determine the price level of the market. So, what determines the P/E ratio? This is the essential question that ties the principles of economics to the principles of finance within the *Financial Physics* model.

Inflation Drives the Price/Earnings Ratio

The fourth building block is the most significant element of *Financial Physics* and stock market valuation: Inflation is the primary driver of the P/E ratio.

You may have heard that interest rates are the primary driver of P/E ratios. If so, you have lots of company. To visualize the relationship between interest rates and P/E ratios, a graph has been developed to compare the P/E ratio to interest rates, using a version of the P/E known as the earnings yield. The earnings yield is the inverse

Figure 7.4. Earnings per Share Is Highly Predictable over Time

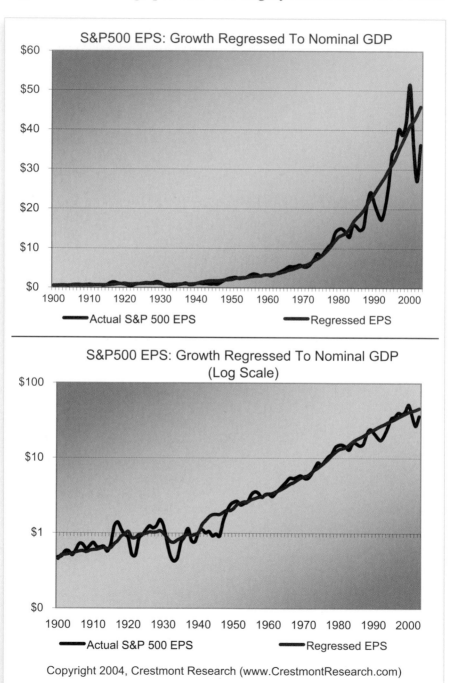

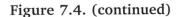

Figure 7.4. (continued)

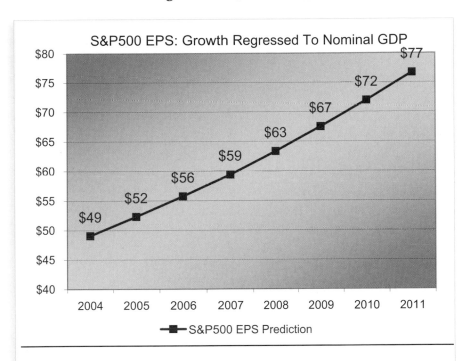

	2004	2005	2006	2007	2008
S&P 500 EPS	**$49.05**	**$52.28**	**$55.72**	**$59.38**	**$63.30**

Figure 7.5. EPS Predicted from 1975

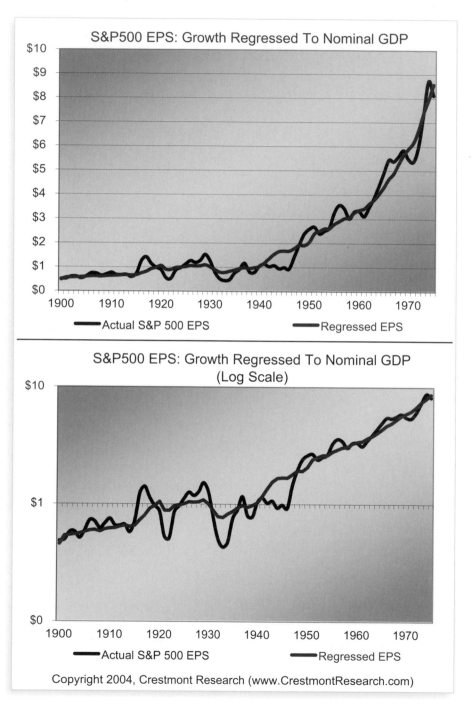

Figure 7.5. (continued)

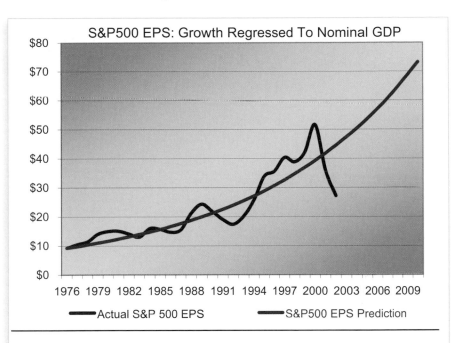

S&P500 EPS: Growth Regressed To Nominal GDP

	2004	**2005**	**2006**	**2007**	**2008**
S&P 500 EPS (1975 predicted)	$50.23	$53.46	$56.91	$60.58	$64.49
Note: FULL SERIES (2003 predicted)	$49.05	$52.28	$55.72	$59.38	$63.30

Note: EPS prediction based upon GDP data from 1901-1975

of the P/E; it is presented as E/P rather than P/E, which provides a more consistent comparison, since interest rates represent the yield on bonds and the earnings yield represents the yield on stocks. In figure 7.6, you will see that interest rates and P/E ratios had an inconsistent relationship during the first two-thirds of the past century. This corresponds to a similar dynamic that was described in chapter 4, relating to the inconsistency between interest rates and inflation during the early part of the century. P/Es did track inflation, which cycled throughout the past century. It was interest rates that were disconnected with economic reality until the 1960s.

Another relationship that is often accepted today, that P/E ratios rise when interest rates fall, does not work during periods of deflation. During deflation, when interest rates can fall only to 0%, P/E ratios tend to fall rather than rise.

At this point on the tour, it may be helpful to revisit the relationship between interest rates and inflation that was discussed in chapter 4.

Figure 7.6. P/E Ratios and Interest Rates: 1900–2003

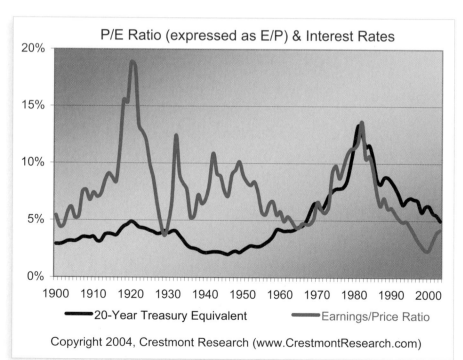

Copyright 2004, Crestmont Research (www.CrestmontResearch.com)

The relationship was inconsistent for the first two-thirds of the past century. As a result of several factors, it has become more consistent during the past forty years, as the financial markets have become more sophisticated.

So, if *Financial Physics* identifies inflation as the driver of rising or falling P/Es, what explains the fundamental reason that inflation has such a pivotal effect?

Crestmont has named the impact of inflation on P/Es as the "Y-Curve Effect." As you will see in figure 7.7, P/E ratios tend to rise when inflation moves toward price stability, periods of stable, low inflation. When inflation moves away from price stability, either from low inflation toward higher inflation or from low inflation to deflation, P/E ratios tend to decline.

When inflation rises, the return that investors want from stocks increases because they wish to be compensated for the rise in inflation. As a result, stock prices decline to a lower level where they can

Figure 7.7. P/E Ratios and Inflation: 1900–2003

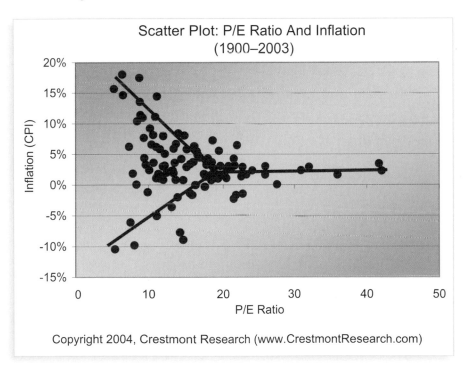

Copyright 2004, Crestmont Research (www.CrestmontResearch.com)

provide higher future returns. When inflation falls into deflation, the result is a decline in future earnings. If earnings are expected to decline in the future, the current price will decline as well. You can see that from a level of very low inflation, a trend in either direction is not good for stock prices.

A somewhat similar relationship exists for those who relish drinking a hot cup of black coffee in the morning. If the coffee is within a narrow temperature range, the experience is positive for the drinker. But if the coffee becomes much hotter or cooler, the experience turns decidedly negative. Right now, the inflation temperature is almost perfect.

As the tour of *Financial Physics* comes to an end, the implication that inflation is near the perfect level right now means that a move toward higher inflation or a move into deflation would likely result in declining P/E ratios. This is quite different than the experience of investors during the 1980s and 1990s when inflation started at high levels and stock prices were low. As inflation declined over those two decades, the stock market rose and returns were high. Now that valuations are at high levels, the conditions cannot provide the results to which investors had become accustomed.

In conclusion, here are the key points from the tour of *Financial Physics*:

Key Points on *Financial Physics*

- Economic growth (GDP-Real), excluding inflation, is relatively consistent over long periods of time.

- Earnings per share (EPS) grows relatively consistently with nominal economic growth (GDP-Nominal).

- EPS can be predicted using estimates of future Nominal GDP.

- Based on the prediction of EPS into the future, an investor needs only a perspective on inflation to determine P/Es and, therefore, the return environment available in the stock market over the next five, ten, or twenty years.

Crestmont's *Financial Physics* model is also a tool for valuing the market and predicting its future price level. The model combines basic principles of economics and basic principles of finance. Econo-mists will quickly identify with its economic ingredients; investors will quickly identify with its financial ingredients. The model's key value is the identification of the relationships between economics and finance.

Financial Physics: Valuation and Prediction

Financial Physics provides a rational framework for using the inter-relationships between economics and finance to estimate future EPS and future P/E ratios, and thus future levels in the stock market. The result for investors is a perspective on expected future returns from the market. With that perspective, investors are better positioned to develop an investment strategy for financial success. The follow-ing part of the chapter will build on the previous tour of *Financial Physics* by providing additional details and reiterating key elements of the model.

Cannonballs and the Stock Market

Tired of hitting their own soldiers in the back with cannonballs, ear-ly military leaders sought to predict the trajectory of cannonballs in flight. As they grasped the basic principles of physics, they eventually succeeded in forecasting a cannonball's path with greater precision. As a result, the effectiveness of the artillery increased dramatically, and the leaders enjoyed the heartfelt thanks of their frontline troops.

Can the future of the stock market be predicted with similar pre-cision? In the short run, swings of emotion ranging from unhinged pessimism to irrational exuberance dominate market swings and un-dermine the predictability of the stock market. In the intermediate term, though, the interrelationships between economic growth, EPS, inflation, rising or falling P/E ratios, and stock market valuations make rational predictions possible.

Estimating Future Earnings

By estimating future growth in the economy, an estimate of future earnings can be developed. The U.S. economy has grown at 6.7% per year on average over the past century. This 6.7% growth consists of real growth averaging 3.5% per year, plus inflation, which has averaged 3.2% per year. As the economy has grown, company earnings have grown at a similar, yet slightly lower, rate. As reflected in figure 7.8, this relationship is based on fundamental principles of economics — growth in the economy reflects growth in sales, and growth in sales tends to be reflected in growth in earnings.

Because of the relatively consistent growth in the economy across periods of ten years or more, and because of the close relationship between growth in the economy and growth in earnings, the long-term trend in EPS can be extended into the future to produce a rational estimate of future EPS. As reflected in figure 7.9, this string of estimated future EPS provides a trendline stretching into the future, a trendline around which actual EPS would be expected to fluctuate.

Estimating Future P/Es

The other element essential to estimating the future market level is the future P/E ratio. As seen in figure 7.10, trends in inflation drive the direction of P/E ratios. Specifically, the moves away from price stability (very low inflation) — either toward higher inflation or toward deflation — drive P/E ratios lower. The moves toward price stability drive P/E ratios higher. Historical data provides a basis for estimating future P/E ratios based on an assumption about the level of inflation.

The *Financial Physics* model not only provides a means of estimating future P/E levels, but also allows the investor to see the impact of higher or lower inflation and interest rates on projected future market levels. *Financial Physics* enables the investor to incorporate his or her own assumptions about inflation and interest rates into the forecasting process. Its flexibility enhances both its usefulness and its power as a tool for analysis.

Estimating Future Market Levels: An Example

As of this writing in late 2004, the S&P 500 rests near 1,150. Suppose you would like to know a reasonable estimate for the S&P 500 index in 2008. To determine the future index, you would need estimates for the two component variables: future EPS and the future P/E ratio. For the estimate of future EPS, you can use the values provided by figure 7.9. That estimate of future EPS is based upon the

Figure 7.8. Earnings per Share Related to Economic Growth

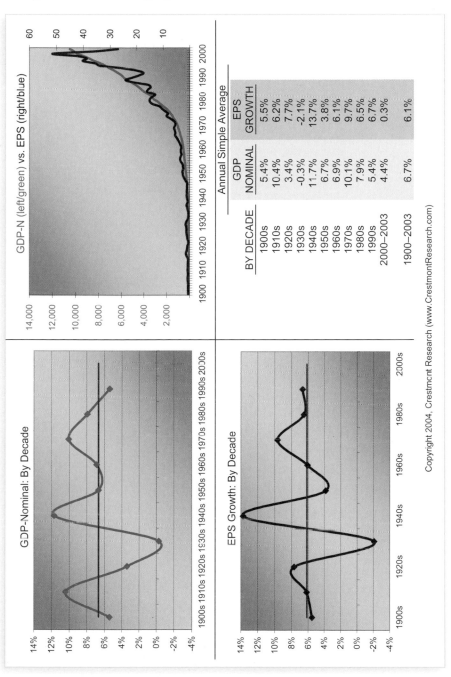

BY DECADE	GDP NOMINAL	EPS GROWTH
1900s	5.4%	5.5%
1910s	10.4%	6.2%
1920s	3.4%	7.7%
1930s	-0.3%	-2.1%
1940s	11.7%	13.7%
1950s	6.7%	3.8%
1960s	6.9%	6.1%
1970s	10.1%	9.7%
1980s	7.9%	6.5%
1990s	5.4%	6.7%
2000–2003	4.4%	0.3%
1900–2003	6.7%	6.1%

Annual Simple Average

GDP-N (left/green) vs. EPS (right/blue)

GDP-Nominal: By Decade

EPS Growth: By Decade

Copyright 2004, Crestmont Research (www.CrestmontResearch.com)

Figure 7.9. EPS Predictable Over Time

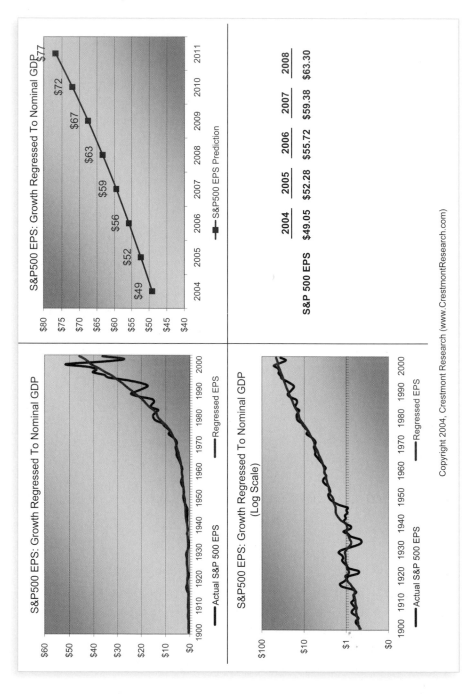

long-term historical real growth in the economy of 3.5% plus inflation of 3.2%. Added together, the resulting nominal growth of 6.7%
is similar to historical growth rates. Therefore, based on the projected future growth in the economy, EPS extrapolated into the future
should be about $63.30 in 2008.

Next, based on the Y-Curve Effect, the P/E that corresponds to the
inflation-level assumption of 3.2% is 16.9. This number can be ap-
proximated using the inflation and P/E data on figure 7.10. Now,
with both a reasonable estimate for EPS in 2008 and a reasonable
estimate for the P/E ratio in 2008, you can make a reasonable estimate for the S&P 500 stock index in 2008.

The estimated level of 1,069.77 for the S&P 500 in 2008 consti-
tutes a gravity point around which the actual value would be expected to fluctuate higher and lower. Economic growth was included in
the calculation, as was earnings growth. How can the estimated future level of the market be below its initial level of 1,150? Why are
positive ingredients over several years producing a negative expected return?

Increasing Earnings and Declining Market

The estimated level of 1,069.77 for the S&P 500 in 2008 is about 7
percent below its value in late 2004, even though earnings are expected to grow over the next 4 years. Here the *Financial Physics* model shows one facet of its usefulness. Many investors might assume
that the growth in EPS over the next several years would very likely result in a higher market. A contraction in P/E ratios, however,

could offset the impact of EPS growth. Expectations based on only one factor, such as EPS, often soar like hot-air balloons. The *Financial Physics* model helps tether future expectations to the reality of the actual interrelationships between the economy, EPS, inflation, and rising or falling P/E ratios.

Results from Applying *Financial Physics* Model

Note the insights provided by applying the *Financial Physics* model. In the illustration above, the estimated ending value for the S&P 500 is below the initial level of the market, even though the assumptions were benign. Relatively modest inflation was assumed, as well as an ending P/E ratio that was only slightly above average. Yet, even though earnings were assumed to grow significantly over the years, the estimated ending value for the S&P 500 reflects a decline from its level near the end of 2004.

Supposing that the assumptions provided an ending P/E of 13, reflecting inflation of 5% per year, then the estimated ending value for the market after four years of EPS growth would reflect a loss of over 20 percent. And assuming a P/E of 13 would not be making a radical assumption. Bear market bottoms in the past tended to occur far below that.

And lower P/Es are possible going forward because of the Y-Curve Effect in figure 7.10. Recent inflation by most measures is close to perfect; it is very close to price stability. Either a move toward higher inflation or a move down into deflation will likely cause P/E ratios to decline from current levels. The best scenario would be for inflation to remain at low levels of price stability, but the results would still reflect returns well below the historical average. The next chapter will present further details about a reasonable expectation for stock market returns during a period of price stability.

For an historical perspective, consider the current P/E of 23 against the historical average of near 16. Keep in mind that that the historical decline in P/Es has rarely stopped at the long-term average. Rather, markets have tended to move to extremes, and the average bear market has ended with P/Es close to 10. As an extreme example, the estimated EPS in 2008 of $63 per share and a P/E of 10 would yield an S&P 500 Index value of 630, a level that is 60 percent of

Figure 7.10. Relationship of P/E Ratios and Inflation

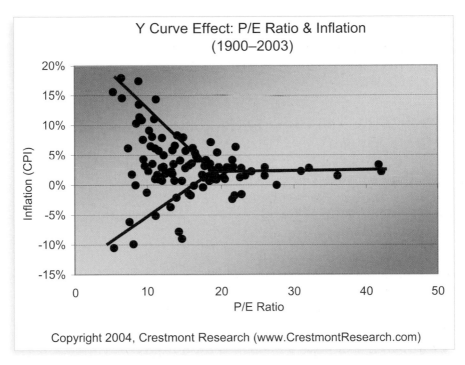

Copyright 2004, Crestmont Research (www.CrestmontResearch.com)

the value in late 2004. Even if the P/E were to settle at the historical average near 16, the S&P 500 Index would still reflect a decline of 12 percent to 1,008. Upcoming chapters outline tools and strategies for dealing with the potentially challenging markets.

Although the stock market has come down from the bubble valuations of 2000, it may yet be in the position of a mountain climber who has descended 10,000 feet from the 27,000-foot summit of Everest. Despite the significant descent, the climber should not anticipate that sea level is near. In fact, the air is still thin, and the vast majority of the world lies below the current position.

History as a Guide

Eight secular periods driven by the inflation and P/E cycle have occurred over the past century. They have ranged from four years to over twenty years in length and have produced four secular bull markets and four secular bear markets lasting an average of twelve and a half years each. Gains during secular bull markets have sometimes been spectacular, while bear markets have produced results ranging from unsatisfactory to devastating for investors who maintained a buy-and-hold strategy. Effective and profitable investment strategies are considerably different for secular bull markets and secular bear markets. A look at those strategies and when they should be applied is the subject of the last four chapters. Importantly, investors who apply the right strategies at the right time can profit in both secular bull and secular bear markets.

The next chapter explores the implications of *Financial Physics* in the current environment and relates its concepts to the components of stock market returns. The information from *Financial Physics* can be used with traditional financial models to predict future stock market returns and rationally assess the market climate that investors currently confront.

CHAPTER 8

IMPLICATIONS FROM
FINANCIAL PHYSICS

As Louis and Clark journeyed west in search of a north-west passage, they and their scouts would climb prominent lookout points to survey the terrain ahead and put into perspective the progress they had already made. This chapter serves a similar purpose. It starts by synthesizing key ideas from the first seven chapters and then charts the course for the remainder of the book. Two key sections conclude the chapter: "Dissecting Returns" and the "Valuation Cascade." Dissecting Returns illustrates the likely course of stock market returns over the rest of the decade. The Valuation Cascade presents a compelling case for a natural upper limit to sustainable price/earnings ratios (P/Es), and thus a natural limit to sustainable stock market valuation.

The Voyage So Far

Volatile Markets

During the descent from 30,000 feet toward the Aspen airport in the midst of the Rocky Mountains, the volatility of the landscape becomes striking. Jagged peaks alternate with steep canyons. Similarly, as you look more closely at both the stock and the bond markets, you will see far greater volatility than most investors realize.

Over the past hundred years, the annual change in stocks—half of the time—is more than 16 percent, either up or down. Bonds, for their part, are volatile as well. Over the past thirty-five years, over every six-month period, interest rates at some point on the yield curve have changed more than 0.5% (50 basis points) 99 percent of the time, and more than 1% (100 basis points) 80 percent of the time.

Both the stock and bond markets enjoyed secular or long-term bull markets from 1982 to 1999. And since the bigger moves in the market that occur during secular bull markets are almost always to the upside, many investors—like seasonal tourists who experience only the good days—lose sight of the harsh downside of volatility in the markets.

When P/E ratios trend upward, the periods of relatively high changes are almost always on the upside. On the other hand, when P/Es trend down from historically high levels, the periods of relatively large changes are more often on the downside. A buy-and-hold approach works during periods of secular bull markets, but in periods of secular bear markets, more effective and robust strategies are needed if investors are to profit and achieve their investment objectives.

Economic Growth and Stock Market Returns

The lack of correlation between economic growth and stock market returns for extended periods of time surprises most investors. Real growth in the economy and in earnings per share (EPS) averaged virtually the same rate from the mid-1960s to the early 1980s as from the early 1980s through 1999. While real economic growth was remarkably consistent over the two secular cycles, stock market returns differed dramatically.

Despite substantial growth in both the economy and earnings from 1965–1981, the market ended at the same level at which it had begun sixteen years earlier. By contrast, 1982–1999, a period of lower nominal economic and EPS growth, saw the market soar more than tenfold to produce one of the greatest bull markets in history. An investment of $100,000 in the S&P 500 in 1982 was worth well over $1 million by the end of 1999.

Financial Physics Explains Market Performance

Financial Physics is the combination of well-respected principles of economics and recognized principles of finance.

The economy, as measured by real gross domestic product (Real GDP), has grown at a fairly constant rate, averaging just above 3% per year over the past century, and almost exactly 3% during each of the past three decades. Real GDP plus inflation reflects nominal economic growth and corresponds to the sales of U.S. companies. Earnings of public companies grow at a rate just below nominal gross domestic product (Nominal GDP), because the economy includes both the public companies and higher-growth entrepreneurial companies.

If the P/E ratio remained constant, the market's moves would be driven only by the growth in EPS—which is driven by the growth in Nominal GDP. The major driver to stock market returns above or below economic growth is the trend in P/E ratios, and the trend in P/Es is driven by the trend in inflation. If inflation is headed away from price stability (low inflation near 1%), P/Es fall; if inflation is headed toward 1%, P/Es rise. The compounding effect of rising earnings and rising P/Es creates periods in the stock market known as secular bull markets; the mitigating effect of declining P/Es on rising earnings creates periods in the stock market known as secular bear markets.

Today the stock market is in the early stages of what historically has presented itself as a secular bear market. The conditions include low inflation, high P/E ratios, low dividend yields, and relatively low long-term interest rates. Additionally, the conditions are opposite of those that precede secular bull markets.

What's Next

Row, Not Sail

Secular bear markets often exhibit high volatility. They combine breathtaking declines with sharp rallies and require more active investment strategies than do secular bull markets. Crestmont's calls these "Row, Not Sail" strategies because they require actions rather than simply buying and holding. These actions include more pro-active investment management, more frequent rebalancing, option writing, and the use of higher-yielding securities, hedge funds, and other dynamic process strategies. Chapter 10 is dedicated to discussing the concepts related to "Row, Not Sail."

Current Outlook

Valuations, as measured by P/E ratios, are at historically high levels. With inflation near price stability, it is extremely unlikely that the market can sustain an extended period of P/E ratio increases from the current levels. Without P/Es increasing, returns from the stock market are limited to EPS growth and dividends. Rising P/Es would be necessary to drive another secular bull market. Since investors cannot expect another secular bull market from here, the other two alternatives are a secular bear market or a bear in hibernation. If inflation trends higher, or if deflation occurs, a traditional secular bear market can be expected. If inflation is held at price stability for an extended period, the secular bear will remain dormant, and total returns should be consistent with earnings growth plus dividends—therefore approximately 6% annually. After transaction costs of approximately 2%, total net returns from the stock market will be approximately 4% annually.

The reason to refer to the market's condition as a bear in hibernation, rather than a sleeping bull, is that bull markets do not start from high-valuation levels—bears do! If inflation continues to cycle as it historically has, the current secular bear will continue to roam the markets. If the current environment is sustained for an extended period of time, the next cycle—whenever it happens—will reflect declining P/Es, not rising P/Es.

Going forward, investors should be prepared for the perception of a sluggish economy if inflation is maintained in the range of price stability. Real growth in the economy is likely to chug along and average 3%, the same pace as the last few decades. If inflation stays close to price stability and adds 1%–2% in nominal terms to GDP, then the overall nominal growth in the economy will be 4%–5%. An economy that averages 4%–5% on a nominal basis will feel sluggish in relation to an economy that has historically averaged 6.5%–7%. Yet the real gains in the economy, wealth, and standard of living would be similar to historical levels.

Absolute Return Reality

In the next chapter, progressive approaches to investing are explored. There are distinct differences between the traditional relative return approach and the progressive absolute return approach. Although some absolute return investments are risky and speculative, most operate as businesses that seek consistent profitability. Profit consistency does not happen automatically; it is not the proverbial free lunch. The absolute return approach requires tremendous skill and commitment to generate profits relatively consistently regardless of market direction. By contrast, most traditional money managers seek returns over the long term based on the risk of the capital markets, structuring their portfolios to concentrate on market risk and eliminate the risks associated with individual companies. As a result, the patterns of returns from traditional money managers tie closely to the performance of the market. The relative return approach requires tremendous patience to realize gains over time and to endure the secular cycles of the markets. Chapter 9 explores the differences between the relative return approach to investing and the absolute return approach.

Current market conditions are positioned for higher risks and lower rewards than average. It is a good time for investors to develop stronger business plans for investing — plans that both consider the expected market environment and incorporate the strategies for wealth development and wealth preservation that do not depend on strong stock market gains. Chapters 11 and 12 provide specific techniques for investing in secular bear markets and discuss the ongoing evolution in the field of investment management.

Valuation Cascade:
Natural Upper Limit for P/Es

In early 2000, the stock market soared far above the irrational exuberance levels Alan Greenspan had identified in 1996. Giddy with success and momentum, the market rose on the wings of imagination, hope, and greed. In many cases, the market relied on earnings that were the product of aggressive accounting and sometimes fraud. In doing so, it mirrored the flight of Icarus in Greek mythology.

Burning with the desire to fly, Icarus made wings for himself from feathers held together by wax. Intoxicated with his early successes and heedless of the warnings of sober advisors, he flew closer and closer to the sun. At the height of his temporary success, reality reasserted itself, the heat from the sun melted the wax on his wings, and he plunged to his demise.

So too did the investors of early 2000 find flights of valuation fancy to be temporary and unsustainable. The NASDAQ, which had soared highest, plummeted over 80 percent in the course of seventeen months. And even after a sizable percentage bounce off the bottom in 2003, it remained at almost one-third of its peak price in late 2004. Clearly, the market can fly temporarily to extraordinary heights of valuation, but it has never been able to maintain levels of extreme overvaluation for long periods of time. This section reveals why there is a natural limit to sustainable market valuations and P/Es. Before delving into the details, a few points of background will be useful for the discussion.

Overview of Rational Investing and Valuations

Irrational speculators sometimes buy stocks or bonds at any price on the basis of the greater fool theory: they are willing to pay unreasonably high prices for securities because they feel that a greater fool will come along and willingly buy their securities at an even higher price and reward them with a profit. Eventually, though, there comes a point when there is no greater fool, and rational sellers begin to drive prices down toward a fair value.

Rational investors tie the price they are willing to pay for a stock or bond to its intrinsic value. The intrinsic value is based on the expected cash flows and profits that they can reasonably expect to derive from the underlying company or the financial security itself. Investors understand that the price they pay should relate to the cash return that they expect to ultimately receive. The return generally comes in two components: the cash they receive while holding

the investment—interest or dividends—plus the amount they receive from eventually selling the bond or stock. Regarding the future
sales proceeds, rational investors expect that the buyer in the future
will also look to the future profits and cash flows and thus will likely be making a rational decision. As a result, rational investors rely
on rational pricing in the financial markets. Irrational investors rely
on hope—and hope is not a strategy.

Return from Bonds

The return from a bond that is held to maturity and that does not default is readily known. An investor who pays $1,000 for a bond that
will be worth $1,000 at maturity and that pays 7% interest will re-
ceive $70 per year in interest over the life of the bond and then re-
ceive his $1,000 principal value back when the bond matures. If the
investor desires or requires a 7% return on his investments, he can
buy the bond at a price of $1,000 and be satisfied.

Imagine that the $1,000 bond, which yields 7%, is the only invest-
ment opportunity available. If the investor desires or requires a higher
rate of return, say 8%, he cannot achieve his goal by paying $1,000
for the bond. The investment simply will not return more than 7%.
The investor who requires the higher rate of return must exercise patience and discipline and wait to buy the bond at a discount in order
to be able to achieve the return.

The known cash flow from the bond, as well as the investor's required rate of return, define very precisely the price that a rational
investor will pay for the bond. This relationship between an investment's cash flow, the investor's required rate of return, and the price
of the investment is the fundamental relationship of finance. It governs the behavior of rational investors and prompts the reversion of
overvalued or undervalued bonds to more reasonable prices.

Return from Stocks

The return from stocks is far less predictable than that from bonds.
While dividend payments tend to be reasonably stable and generally increase over time, they vary based on the growth in earnings and
corporate needs. Also, stocks represent corporations that structurally
have an infinite life. Thus they have no defined maturity date at which

the investor can be assured of receiving a return of his investment. Rather, the investor can only realize his profit or loss by selling the stock at the then current price, a price that will reflect the then current dominant market emotion—exuberance, despair, or boredom.

While the difficulties mentioned previously make valuing stocks a challenge, reasonable valuations can nevertheless be estimated. Both the dividends and future growth in earnings can rationally be estimated and the investor can determine his required rate of return. With those elements in place, the investor can determine the price that he can pay for the stock in order to achieve his expected rate of return. In the following discussion, the focus is on the overall stock market rather than individual companies. Nonetheless, the concepts apply similarly to individual stocks.

Future Cash Flows and the Desired Rate of Return

The long-term average growth rate of the economy before inflation has been a fairly consistent 3% per year, as shown in the discussion of *Financial Physics* in chapter 7. Once inflation is added, the result is the nominal growth rate of the economy. Since corporate earnings growth has closely tracked the economy, though at a slightly slower rate, a reliable proxy for earnings growth can be developed by estimating economic growth. Given the solid consistency of real economic growth, the unknown variable remains inflation, as highlighted by *Financial Physics*. So, with an estimate of future inflation, future cash flows can be predicted.

A fundamental premise of investing is that riskier investments should offer the potential for higher returns than safer investments. In other words, rational investors would not choose to buy riskier investments unless they offered the potential for higher returns than safer investments. Stocks are riskier than bonds, so if you have an estimate of future bond yields, you can expect that the desired rate of return on stocks will be higher than that on bonds. This excess of the desired rate of return for stock above bond yields is known as the equity risk premium.

There is a cascade of steps between short-term cash returns and the desired return from the stock market. Each step down the cascade is based on additional elements of risk, and therefore will usually be priced to offer higher returns than the higher steps in the cascade. While the expected return relationships between less risky and more risky investments can fluctuate, they will not get too far out of line, or market participants will capitalize on the mispricing and cause the pricing relationships to be appropriately restored.

To use the cascade, start with the safest investment and work your way through riskier bonds, ultimately determining an estimate for the desired rate of return for stocks. Since U.S. Treasury bills are a safe haven for short-term cash and are considered "risk-free," they demand only protection against the loss of value due to monetary inflation and thus offer very low rates of return. Longer-term Treasury bonds offer a higher rate of return — or risk premium — because they carry time risk, the risk that inflation and interest rates may rise over the life of the bond and make its fixed interest rate less valuable than it appeared in the beginning. Corporate bonds tend to offer higher returns than U.S. Treasury bonds because they carry more risk; they are backed only by a corporation, rather than being backed by the full faith and credit of the United States government.

Stockholders get paid only after corporations pay their bondholders and only if there is money left over. Thus stocks carry more risk than bonds, and the desired or required rate of return for stocks should be higher than the interest rate on long-term corporate bonds. Since the desired rate of return moves incrementally higher from the safest bonds to the riskiest stocks, this approach develops an interlocking cascade between future cash flows of securities of different risk levels and the desired returns of investors using the now familiar friend, or foe, inflation.

Academic Simplification

While some may wonder if the term "academic simplification" qualifies as an oxymoron, in this case it states a fact. Finance scholars have taken the complicated process of calculating the value of stocks and synthesized that process into a helpful equation known as the dividend discount model. Essentially, the equation takes today's dividends, increases them at a specified growth rate, and then provides the price today that a rational investor could pay for the stock in order to realize the desired rate of return.

For example, assume earnings (EPS) of $2 per share, and the average dividend payout ratio of 50 percent results in dividends of $1 per share. If inflation is approximately 1%–2% per year, then earnings would be expected to grow at approximately 4% based on the *Financial Physics* principles, and investors should expect a return from stocks of about 6.5% before transaction costs and taxes. This is verified through two approaches. First, the expected total return from stocks of 6.5% is based upon earnings growth of 4% plus a dividend yield near 2.5%. Secondly, the relationships in the Valuation Cascade suggest that 6.5% would be the appropriate return level based on the relationship of stock returns and various interest rates.

Using these assumptions, the well-respected dividend discount model presented in figure 8.1 determines that the appropriate price would be $40 for a stock with dividends of $1, desired return of 6.5%, and expected growth of 4%. When the dividends of $1 are divided by the difference between 6.5% and 4% (i.e., 2.5%), the result is $40. Based upon EPS of $2, the P/E is 20. Keep in mind that a price of more than $40 will result in lower future returns. Likewise, a lower price would provide higher returns. The purchase price affects returns because it affects the amount of money invested; it does not affect the amount of future cash flows that provide the return.

There are three variables for the dividend discount model that provide the current fair value market price. The fair value price is the value today that will provide the expected return from an investment,

Figure 8.1. Dividend Discount Model

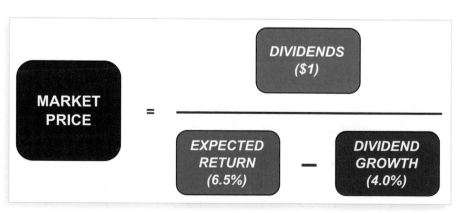

based on its expected future dividends in perpetuity. The first variable is dividends, the amount per share that is distributed to stockholders. The second is the expected return; the percentage return that is appropriate for the investment, based on the rate of inflation and a premium for the risk of the security. The third variable is the expected growth rate of the dividend over time, a percentage often closely tied to the growth in earnings. In addition to using the dividend discount model to value individual stocks, the model can be used to value the overall stock market.

Too often, traditional investment advice focuses on one element of the picture, often earnings growth, while ignoring the interrelated ingredients of the overall picture. A realistic forecast of stock market returns can be developed with the interconnected assumptions provided by the *Financial Physics* model, combined with the methodology of the Valuation Cascade, and ultimately brought together by the rational analysis of the dividend discount model.

Valuation Cascade

The Valuation Cascade provides a methodology for understanding the relationship of stock market valuations to inflation. It demonstrates through the relationships in the financial markets that there is a natural limit, a rational pinnacle, to P/E ratios in the overall stock market. The process starts with inflation and flows down a number of steps to present a corresponding P/E ratio. The Valuation Cascade explains the relationship between inflation and P/Es that was empirically identified in chapter 7 and highlights the reason for the peak in P/Es that corresponds to inflation near price stability. Further, the cascade quantifies the natural limit to P/E ratios beyond which investors would no longer find stocks attractive using a rational approach to value and returns.

The first component is inflation and its relationship to risk-free interest rates. Since U.S. Treasury bills have a maturity of less than one year and are guaranteed by the United States government, they are considered to be short-term, risk-free investments. As a result, without intervention, the market tends to price their yield just above the rate of monetary inflation in order to compensate the investor for the loss of value from inflation. Treasury bills have little other risk associated with them and therefore do not deserve or receive additional return.

You do not need to be a conspiracy theorist to believe that short-term interest rates are controlled by the Federal Reserve. When the Fed intends to stimulate the economy, they lower short-term interest rates below the equilibrium level, generally the level of inflation. Likewise, at other times, the rate is raised to reduce the demand for credit and fight inflation. Nonetheless, when not artificially set by the Fed, the short-term interest rate on Treasury bills (also known as T-Bills) tends to float near the inflation rate. During much of the past forty years, the Fed has been acting to reduce the rate of inflation. As a result, the interest rate on T-Bills has averaged more than the rate of inflation. Although some analyses may reflect a spread of 0.5% or slightly more, the natural rate for T-Bills when the Fed is maintaining a more neutral position should be much closer to the rate of monetary inflation. For the Valuation Cascade, a spread of 0.1% is included.

U.S. Treasury bonds (T-Bonds) have time risk, since they require the investor to commit to a fixed rate of interest for a long time. To compensate the investor for the risk, T-Bonds normally have a premium yield to T-Bills; that is, they normally offer a higher return than T-Bills. As reflected in figure 8.2, that premium has generally been about 100 basis points (1%) above short-term rates. On some rare occasions, though, T-Bonds may temporarily offer lower yields than T-Bills, if the Fed has artificially raised short-term rates.

Companies also borrow money from the financial markets in the form of bonds. Since companies have credit risk that is greater than the U.S. government, corporate bonds have a positive spread above Treasury bonds; in other words, they offer a higher yield than do T-Bonds. That spread tends to vary depending on market conditions, though it is generally higher in more uncertain, higher-inflation, periods. The increase in spreads included in figure 8.3 is intended to be representative of the effect on spreads across various scenarios, and does not necessarily reflect precise historical spreads. For the Valuation Cascade, a realized spread of 0.50% is included at low inflation levels, and a slightly higher spread is included in scenarios of deflation or higher inflation.

Figure 8.2. Spread between 20-year T-Bonds & 1-year T-Bills

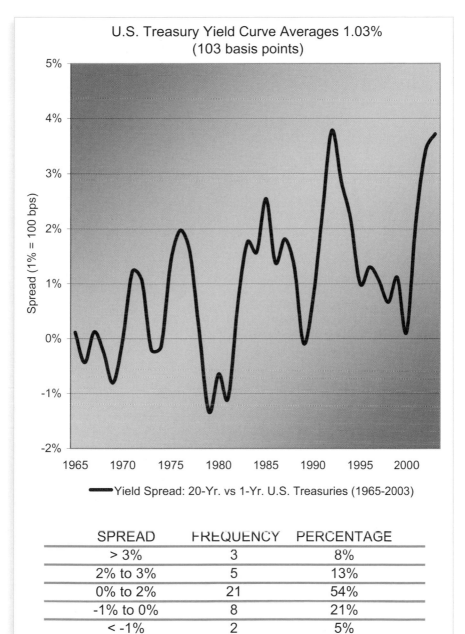

U.S. Treasury Yield Curve Averages 1.03%
(103 basis points)

Yield Spread: 20-Yr. vs 1-Yr. U.S. Treasuries (1965-2003)

SPREAD	FREQUENCY	PERCENTAGE
> 3%	3	8%
2% to 3%	5	13%
0% to 2%	21	54%
-1% to 0%	8	21%
< -1%	2	5%

Stocks represent claims on corporate earnings and assets after all other creditors, including the bondholders, have been satisfied. As a result, the required rate of return on stocks is higher than the return on bonds, resulting in a spread for stocks that is above the return on bonds. That spread also varies for reasons similar to the spread on corporate bonds. As a result, figure 8.3 presents different variables for each scenario. The included spreads reflect the equity premium representative of historical returns, excluding the effects of changes in the level of P/Es. The variability in the corporate bond spread and the stock market return spread reflects the impact of greater risk during periods of deflation and higher inflation.

For example, the historical average inflation rate has been approximately 3.2%, earnings growth has averaged 5.9%, and dividends have averaged near 3.5%. The closest scenario to the historical average is Scenario D in figure 8.3. There you can see that the valuation cascade and equity premium provide an expected return for stocks of 8.35%—consistent with historical earnings growth plus dividends. Although some analyses do reflect higher returns from stocks over certain long-term periods, be aware that they include enhanced gains due to increases in the P/E ratio, which cannot occur perpetually. Gains or losses from changes in the P/E ratio should be a separate assumption for stock returns. In periods of low P/Es, gains from increasing P/Es may be appropriate; in periods of high P/Es, further increases in the P/E ratio are not consistent with financial principles or history. The Valuation Cascade provides insights into the natural limit to P/E ratios and the impact of inflation on P/Es.

A Practical Example

This example uses Scenario B, the low-inflation, price-stability scenario, to illustrate the value of the Valuation Cascade table in figure 8.3. Start with inflation of 1%. This suggests a normalized Treasury bill rate of close to 1%, maybe 0.1% higher due to transaction costs and minimal returns due to uncertainties.

Since long-term Treasury bonds have time risk beyond Treasury bills, there is an appropriate premium. Based on modern history, this adds approximately 1% (the historical risk premium of T-Bonds over T-Bills) to produce a T-Bond yield of 2.1%. Since corporate bonds are

Figure 8.3. Valuation Cascade: Impact of Inflation on P/E Ratios

Scenario	A	B	C	D	E
Inflation Assumption	-3.00%	1.00%	2.00%	3.00%	5.00%
Treasury Bills	0.10%	1.10%	2.10%	3.10%	5.10%
Treasury Bonds					
Spread	1.00%	1.00%	1.00%	1.00%	1.00%
Yield	1.10%	2.10%	3.10%	4.10%	6.10%
Corporate Bonds					
Spread	0.75%	0.50%	0.63%	0.75%	1.00%
Yield	1.85%	2.60%	3.73%	4.85%	7.10%
Stock Market Returns					
Spread	3.50%	3.00%	3.25%	3.50%	4.00%
Gross Return	5.35%	5.60%	6.98%	8.35%	11.10%
Economic Growth					
Real GDP	3.00%	3.00%	3.00%	3.00%	3.00%
Nominal GDP	0.00%	4.00%	5.00%	6.00%	8.00%
EPS Growth	0.00%	3.60%	4.50%	5.40%	7.20%
Stock Market Valuation					
Example EPS	$50	$50	$50	$50	$50
Dividend Payout Ratio	50%	50%	50%	50%	50%
Dividends Per Share	$25	$25	$25	$25	$25
Required Return	5.4%	5.6%	7.0%	8.4%	11.1%
Expected Growth Rate	0.0%	3.6%	4.5%	5.4%	7.2%
DDM Value: Price $Div/(Return - Growth)	$467	$1,250	$1,010	$847	$641
P/E Ratio	9	25	20	17	13

riskier than Treasury bonds, it is reasonable to expect typical corporate bonds to pay about 0.5% more than Treasury bonds. So, corporate bonds, under this scenario, would average 2.6% yields.

Finally, since stocks are riskier than corporate bonds, they should offer a higher return than corporate bonds. A reasonable estimate is that stocks should offer at least 3% more return than corporate bonds in order to compensate investors for the extra risk in owning stocks. So, if Treasury bills yield 1.1% returns, stocks should offer a return of about 5.6% in order to be reasonably—or fairly—valued. If stocks under this scenario were priced to return only 4%, they would be overvalued and would offer less return than an investor should require. On the other hand, if stocks under these conditions were priced to offer 10%, they would be selling at bargain prices and would offer high potential returns.

Continuing down the table, an estimate of inflation of 1% will provide nominal growth in the economy of approximately 4% (since real growth has averaged 3%) and overall earnings and dividend growth of about 3.6% (slightly lower than economic growth). Using the dividend discount model equation from figure 8.1 and the information in figure 8.3, the dividend growth rate of 3.6% is subtracted from the required rated of return from equities of 5.6% to give a difference of 2%. Assuming that earnings are $50 per share and dividends are $25 per share, the dividend of $25 is then divided by the 2% difference to provide an approximate value for the stock of $1,250—representing a P/E ratio of 25, close to the P/E ratio of the market as of late 2004.

Further, as presented in chapters 5 and 6, the P/E has historically peaked in the low to mid-20s. The Valuation Cascade explains that there is a natural peak to P/E ratios. The irrational bubble of the late 1990s propelled P/Es to unsustainable heights; the period of the early 2000s has only deflated the bubble to levels of rational valuation. In other words, current levels of valuation remain high in relation to historical levels of P/Es.

Before proceeding, it may be helpful to confirm and support the previous analysis with a second approach to assessing returns. As discussed earlier, the concept of total return is based on adding the dividend yield and the expected growth in earnings to determine the total expected return from stocks. The other element of gains and losses, those due to increases or decreases in the P/E ratio, are not core gains. Instead, they are revaluation changes due to changing market conditions. When assessing fair value in a current market environment, total return consists of the core components of dividend yield and earnings growth.

The example of Scenario B can be confirmed in terms of total return. For an estimate of dividend yield, the relationship between P/Es and dividend yield discussed in chapter 5 and earlier in this chapter suggests a dividend yield near 2%, based on the P/E for Scenario B of 25. For an estimate of earnings growth, the relationship of earnings growth to economic growth discussed in chapter 8 suggests a growth rate of 3.6%, based on inflation of 1% and the resulting nominal economic growth of 4%. The result of adding the dividend yield of 2% and earnings growth of 3.6% is a total return of approximately 5.6%. This confirms the level of return presented in Scenario B of the Valuation Cascade in figure 8.3.

The cascade then repeats the process for several additional inflation and deflation scenarios with illuminating results. The two variables, earnings growth and desired returns, are linked by inflation—a dynamic described by *Financial Physics*. As inflation rises, the increase in earnings is not enough to offset the impact of higher return requirements, and the result is declining P/Es. In periods of deflation, the required return does not go below 0%. Yet the growth in earnings soon becomes negative, and return requirements increase due to the uncertainties of deflation. As a result, P/Es decline under deflation as well.

Fair Value and Average Returns

The concept of fair value is sometimes confused with the concept of average returns. If a financial asset is priced at fair value, it does not necessarily mean that an investor can expect it to provide average returns. A more detailed explanation of fair value and average returns will highlight the differences and arm you with further information to help identify some of the illogical reasoning that some pundits present.

Fair value for an investment is the price that provides an appropriate level of future returns based upon the risk of the investment and the anticipated market environment. For example, when inflation is relatively low and is expected to remain low, a U.S. Treasury bond priced to yield a return of 4% could be close to its fair value. The current price provides an appropriate level of future returns based on the risk of the investment and the anticipated market environment. It is important to note, however, that the annual return of 4% at fair value is well below the average return that has happened in the past. Over the last hundred years, for example, Treasury bond yields have averaged 4.9%. Fair value, then, is a condition at a point in time; average returns are the result of a series of points in time.

Fair value for an investment is not a permanent value. Rather the fair value for an investment changes when the investment environment changes. Just as a hiker adjusts layers of clothing depending on the temperature and climate, so the future returns demanded by rational investors change as the investment environment shifts. And when the future returns demanded by investors change, the fair value of an investment changes. If, for example, inflation were to rise to higher levels, investors would demand higher returns from bonds to offset the impact of higher inflation. The Treasury bond yielding 4% would no longer provide a return sufficient to compensate for the risk of the investment and also cover higher inflation. As a result the market would lower the price of the bond to a level where its fixed series of interest payments would then return a higher yield of perhaps 5% or 6% to a new purchaser of the bond. The bond would then be fairly valued in its new environment; its then current price would produce an appropriate level of future returns based on the risk of the investment.

The concept of fair value has two cousins: undervalued and overvalued. If the interest rate on Treasury bonds in the market is 4% and someone offers to sell you a similar Treasury bond at a price that yields 5%, that bond is undervalued. It is priced to offer a higher than expected return. On the other hand, if someone offers to sell you a similar bond priced to yield only 3%, that bond is overvalued, because its current price will deliver a return lower than the expected and widely available 4% return. Clearly, the concept of fair value can be applied similarly to stocks and other investments as well.

In addition to understanding fair value, investors should keep clearly in mind that bond prices fall when interest rates rise. Some market pundits use illogical reasoning that sometimes confuses investors. As a result, some investors believe that bond prices rise when interest rates increase. The illogical reasoning is that rising interest rates provide higher interest payments which, in turn, should make bonds more valuable and cause their prices to rise. In fact, the opposite occurs. Why? Because the future cash flows for an existing bond do not change as interest rates rise, they remain fixed. As a result, the prices of existing bonds actually fall to provide the higher returns demanded by higher interest rates in the market.

Similarly, with stocks, as inflation and interest rates rise, prices generally decline to enable stocks to have a future return that is appropriately higher for the new market conditions. Although earnings may increase somewhat due to higher inflation, the impact of higher earnings is not enough to offset the price declines prompted by the demand for higher future returns.

In the current environment, when you hear that the market is fairly valued, beware the pundit who implies that it is positioned for average returns in the future. Additionally, a statement that the market is overvalued because P/E ratios are above average likewise reflects a misunderstanding of the concepts of fair value and average returns. Keep in mind that historical average returns in the stock market represent the aggregation of below-average returns and above-average returns. The average has rarely occurred! Fair value in the current environment will provide below-average returns, since valuations are now above average. Sometime in the future, when valuations are again below average, fair value will provide above-average returns.

Summary of Valuation Cascade

Not only do P/Es peak at price stability (near 1% inflation), there is a natural limit to the level of P/E ratios. *Yes, there is a natural limit to the level of sustainable P/E ratios!*

Icarus could not fly to the sun, and P/Es cannot be sustained on a broad basis much above the low to mid-20s because of limits on the real growth rate of the economy and the market's requirement that equities be priced to return more than bonds. It took a bubble in the late 1990s to break through this natural barrier temporarily. It is not a coincidence, though, that many of the secular-cycle tops over the last hundred years peaked with P/Es in the 20s. Interestingly, the relationships shown through the Valuation Cascade also tend to explain why P/E ratios have often bottomed out just below 10 during periods of low market valuations.

Dissecting Returns:
Forecasting Stock Market Returns

Would you like to know future stock market returns? Sell your *Farmer's Almanac* and forget looking at the stars or throwing darts. Logic can guide you to the land of reasonable expectations. But first, a warning: the historical average returns often cited by market cheerleaders are not a reasonable expectation based on the relatively high levels of P/Es in the stock market. Returns depend on where you start and where you finish, and as of late 2004, the stock market was starting from historically high P/Es. Further increases in the P/E ratio are highly unlikely from the current level.

The total return from stocks consists of two components: dividends plus the change in the price. Therefore, to forecast stock market returns going forward, reasonable estimates for future dividend yields and future price changes are needed. The first component, dividend yield, is closely related to the level of P/Es. The second component, future gains or losses, can be developed through the *Financial Physics* model. Before starting the process of forecasting future returns, a short summary of relevant concepts may be helpful.

Dividend Yields

Dividend yields are closely related to P/E ratios. As P/Es and stock prices rise, the dividend yield falls. This occurs because dividends are paid from earnings. The portion of earnings paid out as dividends is known as the dividend payout ratio. Although the ratio has cycled over time, it has averaged close to 50 percent for the companies in the S&P 500 index over the past five decades.

The P/E ratio is calculated using two components: price and earnings per share (EPS). The dividend yield, the dividend divided by the stock price, is calculated using two components: price and dividends per share. Since P/E and dividend yield share the component of price in common, and, since dividends relate directly to EPS, the relationship between P/E and dividend yield is direct. This is the reason for the strong relationship reflected in figure 8.4. In addition, this explains fundamentally why levels of high valuation provide low dividend yields.

There will be more details about dividend yields shortly. At this point, for the first component of total returns, it is important to note that dividend yields are directly related to the level of valuation in the stock market.

Next follows a short summary of the fundamental axioms of *Financial Physics*, which provides the information needed to forecast future changes in the stock market. With the background about

Figure 8.4. S&P 500: Dividend Yield vs. P/E

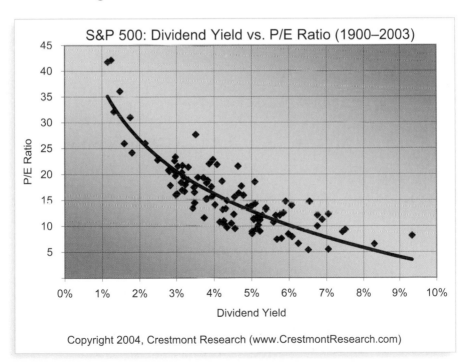

dividend yields and market valuation, the essential components will be in place to predict future stock market returns.

Axioms of *Financial Physics*

The relationships of the *Financial Physics* model, presented in figure 8.5, tie together economic growth, earnings, inflation, and the level of market valuations. The following summary of the key axioms from chapter 7 provides further building blocks toward a realistic stock market forecast.

1) GDP-Real: Real growth in the economy has averaged close to 3% per year for most of the past century, especially the past three decades.

Thus GDP-R = 3%.

2) GDP-Nominal: Nominal growth in the economy reflects real economic growth plus inflation.

Thus GDP-N = GDP-R + Inflation.

3) EPS Growth: Earnings per share of the larger public companies in the S&P 500 Index has been slightly lower historically than overall GDP-N growth.

Thus, in the future,
GDP-N growth = 6.2%; EPS growth = 5.6%; Inflation = 3.2%.

4) P/E Ratio: This measure of stock market valuation is affected inversely by the directional trend and level of inflation or deflation.

Thus if EPS growth rises due to inflation,
P/E ratios will decline to average or below-average levels.

5) Realistic Expectations: Inflation currently is relatively low and stable; there are many factors that could potentially contain inflation at near price stability.

Thus if GDP-R grows at average historical levels of about
3% and inflation holds at near 1.5%, then Nominal GDP
will grow at 4.5%; thus EPS growth will average 4%.

Figure 8.5. *Financial Physics* Model

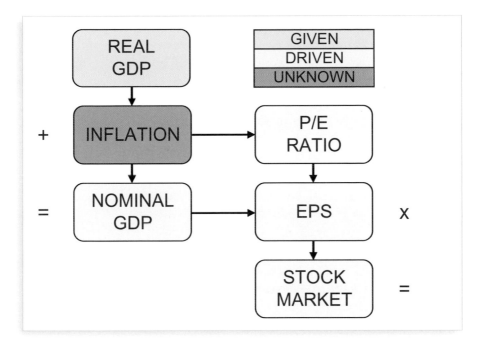

Predicting Stock Market Returns

Astronomers predict the timing of an eclipse or the path of a planet's orbit with great precision because the laws of momentum, gravity, and inertia provide strong grounds for making astronomical predictions. Although the precise future of the stock market is far less predictable, thoughtful investors can make reasonable stock market forecasts over intermediate time frames of five to twenty years. While recognizing that crowd psychology drives market prices in the short term, savvy investors can make rational intermediate-term forecasts—estimates tethered to financial reality.

As reflected in figure 8.6, there are two components to total return in the stock market: (A) the dividend yield, plus (B) gains from changes in the prices of stocks in the market. These are the same considerations for total return in your investment portfolio. The increase or decrease in the value of your account will be the result of dividends that you receive and the price appreciation or decline of stocks or mutual funds in your portfolio. A description of each component is provided below.

To develop a more detailed perspective of the second component, market price change, there are two additional components to consider. The change in the market's price — or in the price of any individual stock — relates to the change in earnings multiplied by the change in the P/E ratio. For example, if earnings did not grow and the P/E ratio remained the same, the price would not change. If earnings start and end at $2 per share and are valued with a P/E ratio of 15, the result will be a price of $30 at the start of the period as well as at the end.

In addition, if the P/E ratio remains the same and earnings grow by 10 percent, the price will increase by 10 percent. Earnings that start at $2 per share and grow by 10 percent will be $2.20 per share at the end of the period. When multiplied by a P/E ratio of 15, the price will be $33 — 10 percent more than the starting price.

Lastly, if earnings are unchanged, the only source of gains (or losses) would be the change in the P/E ratio. Earnings that start and end at $2 per share when P/E ratios increase by 20 percent from 15 to

Figure 8.6. Components of Total Return

(A) Dividends: Dividends are readily known since they show up as cash in your account. As reflected in figure 8.4, the dividend yield is affected by the level of valuation (P/E). Dividends are paid from earnings and have generally ranged from 35 percent to 60 percent of earnings, and have averaged about 50 percent. When stocks are priced high relative to earnings, the dividend yield will be lower than when stocks are more reasonably priced.

(B) Market Price Change: Market Price Change = (Y) Earnings Change + (Z) P/E Ratio Change

18 will provide an ending price of $36—20 percent more than the starting price.

Therefore, as reflected in figure 8.7, the two components of changes in the market price are (Y) the change in earnings and (Z) the change in the P/E ratio. A description of each component is provided below.

Figure 8.7. Market Price Change Components

(Y) Earnings (of the public companies) have grown at a rate slightly below economic growth (GDP-Nominal); this variable is based on the dollar increase or decrease in the market's earnings per share.

(Z) P/E Ratios (level of valuation) are driven by inflation; this variable is based on the actual number change in the P/E ratio.

The Historical Perspective

Six years remain in this decade, 2005 through 2010. The methodology of dissecting the total return into its components can be used to provide an historical perspective of what has driven returns. There have been ninety-nine rolling six-year periods since 1900. The first was 1900–1905, the second 1901–1906, and the most recent was 1998–2003. This provides a significant number of scenarios across which to consider the potential returns over the remainder of this decade.

Figure 8.8 provides a bar reflecting the annualized total return for each six-year period since 1900. The annualized total returns have covered a broad range from a loss of –7% to a gain of 25%.

Figure 8.9 presents the components of the annualized total return—EPS growth, dividend yield, and the effect of changes in the P/E ratio—for every six-year scenario since 1900. The figure

Figure 8.8. Six-Year Annualized Returns Since 1900

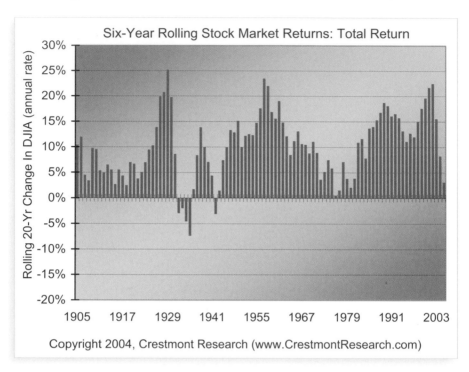

Copyright 2004, Crestmont Research (www.CrestmontResearch.com)

reveals relatively consistent earnings growth, especially after the depression of the 1930s. Within each bar, the contribution of EPS to total return is reflected in blue. Further, figure 8.9 reflects the contribution of dividends to total returns, which have tended to be greater in periods of low P/Es and lesser when P/Es were at higher valuations. The contribution of dividend yield to total return is reflected in brown. The relationship between dividends and P/Es was discussed in detail in chapter 5.

The third component, the impact of changes in the P/E ratio, clearly has had the greatest impact on determining the magnitude of the annualized total return. When the P/E ratio has increased over the six-year period, the increase in valuation levels adds to total return—as reflected in green on the top of EPS and dividends. When the P/E ratio has decreased over the six-year period, the decrease in valuation levels reduces the total return—as reflected in red below EPS and dividend component of total return.

Figure 8.9. Six-Year Annualized Return Components

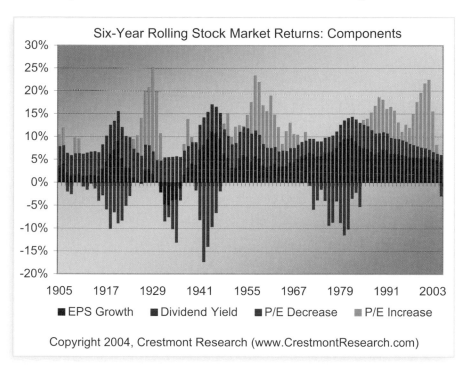

Six-Year Rolling Stock Market Returns: Components

■ EPS Growth   ■ Dividend Yield   ■ P/E Decrease   ■ P/E Increase

Copyright 2004, Crestmont Research (www.CrestmontResearch.com)

The change in the P/E ratio has a significant impact on total return. Over the remainder of this decade, a decline in P/E ratios would reduce total returns below the level provided by EPS and dividends. If there is no change in the P/E ratio, the level of return will be limited to EPS growth and dividends. From the currently high level of P/E ratios, it cannot be expected that P/Es will provide a green-bar addition to total returns.

The Forecast

What returns can reasonably be expected over the next six years? A chart presenting the likely scenarios appears in figure 8.10. It is based on the relationships expressed in the *Financial Physics* model and the formula for total return. Scenarios that are unlikely or impossible are reflected by dashes. For example, it would not be consistent to expect high P/E ratios with high inflation or high nominal growth in the economy with low inflation. Both of these examples would be inconsistent with basic principles of economics and finance as well as historical experience.

For total return, the two components are price changes and dividend yields. The chart presents the two key drivers of price change on the top and side axis, P/E ratio on the left and EPS growth on the top. The second component, dividend yield, is placed to the left of the P/E ratio. Based upon the direct relationship between P/E ratios and dividend yields, as presented in figure 8.4, an estimated dividend yield can be determined for each level of P/E ratio.

Finally, for reference, the implied inflation rate is listed to the right of the chart. As presented in the Y-Curve Effect analysis from chapter 7, the P/E ratio is directly related to the level of inflation. Similar to the method used for the estimated dividend yield, an estimate of inflation can be associated with each level of P/E ratio. The inflation estimate is used primarily to determine the likely scenarios for EPS growth. As provided by the *Financial Physics* model, EPS growth is heavily influenced by the level of inflation included in nominal economic growth.

The chart of expected stock market returns over the rest of the decade is presented in figure 8.10. Keep in mind that the numbers are approximations and may be affected slightly by a variety of factors; they are intended to represent reasonable estimates of the relationships and results that can be expected over the remainder of this decade. An example may help to illustrate the methodology of the chart. Assume that you believe inflation will remain stable through 2010 at near price stability of 1.5%. That would provide for P/E ratios to be sustained in the low 20s—for this example, assume 23 at the start and the end of the period. If the P/E ratio is 23, the expected dividend yield over time will be close to 2.2%. Further, the inflation rate has implications for EPS growth. Assuming that annual real growth in the economy continues on its historical trend of 3%, Nominal GDP would grow at 4.5% and EPS would increase close to 4% annually. Therefore, the intersection of the 23 P/E and 4% EPS growth provides a 6.2% annual return—2.2% from dividends and 4% from the price increase based on projected EPS growth and a 23 P/E in 2010. As noted in the chart, the 6.2% annual return is before transaction costs, which can total 2% or more annually.

Figure 8.10. Future Stock Market Return Scenarios

Avg Dividend Yield	2010 P/E Ratio	AVERAGE EPS GROWTH					2010 Inflation
		4.0%	5.0%	6.5%	8.5%	10.0%	
2.0%	27	8.9%	-	-	-	-	1%-2%
2.1%	25	7.6%	-	-	-	-	1%-2%
2.2%	23	6.2%	-	-	-	-	1%-2%
2.3%	20	4.0%	-	-	-	-	1%-2%
2.6%	17	1.5%	2.6%	-	-	-	2%-3%
2.8%	15	-	1.0%	-	-	-	3%-4%
3.0%	13	-	-	0.6%	-	-	4%-5%
3.6%	10	-	-	-	-0.6%	-	7%-8%
4.7%	7	-	-	-	-4.3%	-3.1%	11%-12%

The table header above reads: **Gross Pre-Tax Returns From The Stock Market (annual compounded return 2005–2010)**

Note: Starting P/E, based upon S&P data and Crestmont's analysis, is 23; base S&P 500 Index is 1,125; trailing 2004 'historically consistent' EPS is $49; inflation and EPS trend ratably from 2004 to 2010. Returns are before transaction costs, which can be 2% or more annually.

Copyright 2004, Crestmont Research (www.CrestmontResearch.com)

Limited Returns and Market Vulnerability

The level of the stock market, earnings, P/E ratios, and inflation during much of 2004 reflected a reasonably fair value. The implications, however, are that future returns are vulnerable to a trend in inflation away from price stability. Even if inflation were to stay at price stability, the returns would likely be limited to earnings growth of near 4% plus dividends of approximately 2.2%, a dividend level appropriate for P/Es in the low 20s. A trend toward higher inflation or deflation would result in lower P/Es and potentially negative returns.

The implications for individuals are somewhat similar, yet different than the implications for institutions with longer investment horizons. The term "institutions" generally refers to endowments, foundations, pension plans, and other perpetual organizations that professionally manage investments to partially or completely fund their obligations. For individuals, should future returns not meet their objective for retirement, there are the painful choices of working longer, living on less, or providing less to their descendants. For institutions with fixed obligations and budget expectations, the alternative of working longer is not available. Their only choice is to reduce outlays, often in the form of benefits to their constituents.

Living off the Farm

For institutions, the investment portfolio is often a primary or significant source of funding for their obligations. Universities, for example, rely on their endowments to fund a portion of their operations and to provide scholarships to students. These endowments rely on donations and investment returns to provide the source of funds for these obligations. Extended periods of low market returns or losses can be quite challenging: not only can these periods suppress donations, but also the investment income may not be sufficient to meet the annual budgeted needs. During these years, the endowment is required to use a portion of the principal to meet its obligations.

Many institutional investors have sufficient capital to deal with extended periods of tapping into the principal value of their portfolios, yet the long-term effects can be quite detrimental and can create a spiraling decline. A relevant analogy is the family farm. If the blueberry crop does not produce well one year, the farmer can either cut back on cobbler or can sell off a few acres to keep the sweets on the table. If, however, he sells a few acres, there will be less land to plant the next year—almost assuring that future crops will not achieve their bountiful past. And unless the crop is well above average, it will be difficult to reacquire the original land. If there are a few tough years in a row, the loss of land can begin to spiral. The farm soon reaches the point where its crops can no longer be expected to sustain the farmer, and the main harvest becomes an annual real estate transaction. Likewise for institutions, extended periods of poor market conditions can lead to extended periods of depleting principal. As each year passes, the base dwindles, ultimately requiring that benefits or initiatives be scaled back much more severely than ever considered.

For individuals who have long horizons and supplement their lifestyles with investment income, the unexpected use of principal can quickly compound into a crisis. Hope is not a strategy, and good assumptions are crucial to planning.

Impact of Assumptions on Planning

The most important numbers in the assumptions used by individual and institutional investors are the projected future returns and the projected future costs. When projecting future returns, it is important to remember that the average historical returns represent a composite of periods that have had returns above the average and periods when it was below. The economic and financial conditions that drive above-average returns are distinct from the conditions that drive below-average returns. Periods of above-average return have been driven by the overall increases in the valuation of financial assets that occur as inflation trends toward the price stability of low inflation. Periods of below-average returns occur when inflation departs from price stability toward deflation or higher inflation. Based on the current low level of inflation and the relatively high level of valuation in stocks and other financial assets, investors should be cautious about including return assumptions related to average or above-average returns.

For costs, the most significant uncontrollable variable is inflation. To maintain a financial plan that is consistent in its assumptions, expectations regarding future inflation should be consistent across the elements of costs as well as returns. A financial plan's ability to meet the investor's objectives is as dependent on the expected returns from the portfolio as it is on accurately estimating future obligations.

Over the past two decades, inflation and interest rates declined, and financial assets appropriately adjusted in value and rose significantly. As a result, individuals appeared to be ahead of plan for retirement, and institutions became over-funded in relation to their expected liabilities. From here, many investors want to keep all of the benefits of having been in a period of "above average'" and assume the "average" going forward.

At this juncture, however, average performance is probably the most unlikely of all assumptions. From current levels of valuation, future returns are priced to be below average. Based on the financial relationships of the market and the economy, further valuation gains are unlikely without another temporary bubble period. And finally, any movement back toward average market conditions will adversely affect investor returns.

A rise in interest rates will reduce the total returns in bonds, and a decline in P/E ratios toward the historical average will produce below-average stock market returns. And since this would generally occur due to rising inflation and interest rates, future costs could be higher than expected. This does not represent an unusually dramatic scenario, only one that restores the above-average gains of the past two decades to the average.

What should investors do to address the challenges of the current financial market environment? The following two chapters explore different approaches to investment philosophy, and highlight the changes needed to deal with the new conditions now in place following the end of the most recent secular bull market. Whether the current environment is a secular bear market or a bear in hibernation, the tools and techniques that worked well during the 1980s and 1990s are not the most effective ones for the rest of this decade or longer.

Key Concepts for This Section:
Financial Physics

1. Crestmont's *Financial Physics* model aligns the interconnected relationships between the economy and the financial markets that determine the stock market's overall direction.

2. P/E ratios for the market have a sustainable peak or limit in the range of 20–25 when inflation is near price stability—very close to where P/Es were in 2004.

SECTION V

INVESTMENT PHILOSOPHY

CHAPTER 9

INVESTMENT PHILOSOPHY

Billionaire Ross Perot earned money as a child by selling Christmas cards. He was smart, and by late January, he had learned one of his first powerful business insights. Though he had made good money selling Christmas cards, he knew he wanted a business that could operate in all seasons. He did not want his income to be at the mercy of favorable and unfavorable seasons.

Similarly, investors who seek consistent returns gravitate to an absolute return investment philosophy—the investment philosophy that has consistent profitability as its key objective. As a result, absolute return strategies become particularly valuable during secular bear markets. Before exploring the details of the absolute return approach, it may be helpful to describe the basic concepts of the traditional relative return philosophy.

Relative Return Investing

Even though the goal of consistent profitability may sound inherently reasonable and appealing, most investment advisors, money managers, and investors do not at present use an absolute return approach to investing. Instead, they apply a relative return philosophy, a philosophy primarily based on the Modern Portfolio Theory, Efficient Market Hypothesis, and Capital Asset Pricing Model ideas of Harry Markowitz, Eugene Fama, and William Sharpe.

What do relative return investors and managers do? They invest in different asset classes, such as stocks or bonds, by buying a wide range of stocks, bonds, or mutual funds. They thereby diversify across the asset class, with the objective that their investments will perform in line with a benchmark index such as the S&P 500 Index or the Lehman Bond Aggregate. While they may shift the individual components of the portfolio, they maintain a diversified exposure to the stock or bond markets as a whole.

For stock market investing, they expect to profit by participating in the long-term growth of the economy. Relative return investors intentionally accept stock market risk and volatility in the shorter term, because they expect to profit in the long term. They believe that long-term growth in the economy will result in higher earnings for corporations, and that higher earnings will eventually translate into higher stock prices. The reality is, though, that "eventually" sometimes proves to be far longer than many investors anticipate.

Note that while investors may hope for consistent returns from the stock market, consistent returns are not what the relative return stock portfolio is designed to achieve. The relative return portfolio will, by definition, largely mirror the movements of the market and thus be subject to the gains and losses resulting from favorable and unfavorable market seasons. Diversification across other asset classes will tend to reduce the volatility of the overall portfolio, since most other asset classes are less volatile than stocks, and some asset classes are not highly correlated. It does not, however, address one of the inherent weaknesses of relative return investing—the tendency of the portfolio to both rise and fall in tandem with the overall market.

Contrasting Absolute Return and Relative Return

You have probably heard the story about the race between the tortoise and the hare. Once again, that fable provides insights, this time related to investment philosophy. The tortoise's slow and steady pace exemplifies the approach known in the financial community as absolute return investing. The hare's sprints and rests epitomize the approach known as relative return investing.

The absolute return approach and the relative return approach have differences, strengths, and weaknesses. Each approach can be appropriate in certain market conditions. Since relative return investing has been used over the past few decades as the traditional approach, it will be familiar to most readers. Given the current market conditions and outlook, the absolute return approach should be particularly interesting to investors.

Absolute return investing is a philosophy as well as an approach. It incorporates the objective of investment gains regardless of broad price changes in an asset class or market benchmark. Absolute return investing relies on active skill for returns, rather than on a more passive participation in general market trends. As a result, investing becomes business-like, seeking profits from the activities of the investment manager rather than gains from general market moves, dividends, or interest payments. Further, absolute return investing defines risk as the potential for a loss, and the threshold for success in absolute return investing is profitability. It does not consider either the direction of the markets or the performance in relation to a benchmark; a loss is a loss.

Relative return investing is grounded in a tradition of relatively recent practice and much scholarly research. Its objective is to realize investment gains from the performance of an asset class or benchmark. An asset class is a group of assets whose value tends to change similarly. Stocks are an example of an asset class. An increase in the overall value of the stock market has a similar effect on most individual stocks. As a result, a diversified portfolio of stocks will be highly correlated to the stock market—the price of the portfolio will move in close relation to its market. Similarly, bonds, as an asset class, when grouped into a portfolio, tend to move similarly to the overall bond market. Therefore, the relative return style of investing provides the investor with the returns of the market—as the market provides the returns. It requires a long-term view and patience as the investor endures losses and volatile swings on the way to long-term success.

Relative return investing does require skill, but the skill is that of effectively participating in the asset class and realizing the benchmark return. Since investing for relative returns is highly dependent on the performance of the asset class, the definition of risk relates to the variance from a benchmark, known statistically as "tracking error." If you are down 10% when the market is down 12%, there has been 2% of positive tracking error. If instead your portfolio were down 13%, then the tracking error would be 1%. This explains why relative return practitioners cheer when they are "beating the market"; they seek to have a cumulative series of positive tracking errors to ultimately outperform the market. In practice, very few relative return managers beat their benchmarks consistently over time. As a result, many sophisticated investors have changed their strategy to one that is known as "indexing." The "indexing" approach uses passive funds that closely track the market index to replace the use of active money managers that seek to beat the market while maintaining a close relationship with the index. Whether you use active managers or passive indexes, the relative return style of investing is highly dependent on the direction of the market.

On January 1 of each year, as you reflect on the expectations for your investment portfolio, consider whether it is invested to make a profit regardless of the direction of the stock market, interest rates, and other markets. Suppose you ask your advisor, "Should I *expect* to make money on my investments this year?" If the response includes a comment about the direction of the markets, then you are pursuing a relative return approach; if it reflects an objective of positive returns each year, then you are pursuing an absolute return approach.

Skill-Based Returns vs. Benchmark Returns

Absolute return investing tends to derive its profits from activities that use the skills of the money manager, the skills that are helpful in extracting profits from the market consistently, while reducing the chances of a loss. This includes expertise in identifying both overvalued and undervalued investments, managing risk, and assessing trends in the markets. It often requires the abilities of a private investigator or investigative reporter who does research to uncover trends and essential facts before they are apparent to others. Just as some investigative journalists get the inside scoop better than others, and some basketball players shoot better than others, some investment managers invest better than others. Further, absolute return investing involves controlling risk through expertise in hedging or through the selection of securities. As a result, the emphasis is on the return-to-risk relationship in addition to total return.

A great many relative return managers possess high intelligence and highly refined skills, but those skills are directed toward performing in line with, or slightly ahead of, a benchmark. The benchmark for returns is generally based on asset classes such as stocks or bonds. In addition, asset classes are subdivided into segments; for example, large cap and growth for stocks, and high yield and government for bonds.

To illustrate one way that an absolute return stock market manager might invest differently than a relative return manager, consider the thirty stocks in the index known as the Dow Jones Industrial Average. A relative return manager, who wishes to benefit from the long-term growth of companies in the Dow Jones index, would buy all thirty stocks in the exact proportion that they are represented in the average itself. As a result, the investment portfolio should realize a return comparable to the index.

An absolute return manager, whose goal is consistent profits, might look at the same stocks, employ the firm's research capacity to determine the fifteen stocks that are most overvalued and the fifteen that are most undervalued, and then buy the fifteen most undervalued and sell short the fifteen most overvalued. Selling short is the way to profit from declines in price by selling first at the current price and buying the stock later at a lower price to close out the position. Just as declining prices cause losses in stocks that are purchased, rising prices cause losses for short positions. If this portfolio were constructed randomly, you could expect that gains from one half would offset the losses on the other as the market moved up or down, since most of the stocks would be generally tracking the market. Since the selection was random, there would be under-performers and over-performers on both sides of the portfolio. When the stock market goes up, the purchased longs would increase in value on average in line with the drop in value by the shorts. If however the absolute return manager is successful in generally purchasing the fifteen stocks that over-perform and selling short the stocks that under-perform, the manager will profit from stock-selection skill.

As scholarly and empirical research has demonstrated, most of a stock's price movements are driven by the general trend in the market; the remainder is based on the company's operating performance and other market factors. By holding offsetting purchased and short positions in the example described above, the portfolio becomes somewhat neutralized to the impact of general market movements and generates its returns based on the skills of the investment manager. Those skills can be reflected by correctly choosing undervalued stocks that will appreciate in relation to the overvalued stocks, or by selecting both purchased stocks and short stocks that will generate profits regardless of market conditions. In the relative return approach, the gains or losses occur from trends in the stock market. In the absolute return example, the market trends were neutralized and the gains and losses depend on the manager's skills.

Opportunity Differences

The benchmark indexes used to measure the performance of relative return managers generally limit their choices of strategies and investments. A large-cap, relative return manager is generally required to own large-cap stocks, stocks of larger companies that have a high market value. He is usually not free to include smaller capitalization stocks or to employ strategies other than simply owning the stocks.

By contrast, the absolute return manager generally is not limited by the securities associated with a relative return benchmark. Additionally, he can use a wider range of securities, assets, and strategies. As Alexander M. Ineichen notes in his popular book, *Absolute Returns* —

> The absolute [return] manager invests in the full range of investment opportunities whereas the relative return manager does not. An absolute return manager, for example, can hedge unwanted risk, can change risk profile by levering and de-levering according to changes in opportunity set, can exploit inefficiencies on the short side, or can explore valuation differences among equal or similar financial instruments. For a skilled asset manager, a greater pool of investment opportunities leads to greater performance. There

are also differences in terms of the magnitude of the investment opportunities in addition to differences in the opportunity set. If a relative return manager has a large cap U.S. equity market index as investment benchmark, he or she is forced to exploit inefficiencies in one of the most efficient financial markets in the world. The magnitude of mispricing is unlikely to be large and the cost of finding the inefficiency prohibitively high.

Measures of Success

In the world of relative return investing, mutual fund and institutional money managers rarely lose their investors if they perform in line with the market averages. A manager who loses 20% when the market loses 20% will maintain his investor base. A manager who loses 15% when the market loses 20% will keep his existing investors and will attract additional ones. But a manager who makes 15% when the market gains 20% likely will experience withdrawals by unsatisfied investors. And the manager who makes 15% when the market loses 20% probably runs a hedge fund, which is discussed in greater detail in chapter 12.

Success and compensation in the relative return segment of the industry are generally based on the amount of assets under management. Managers are rewarded for managing larger and larger pools of assets, even though increased size in a traditional portfolio does not necessarily enhance the possibility that the fund will outperform the market averages. In some instances, it can reduce the potential for the fund to exceed its benchmarks.

Different standards tend to be applied in the absolute return segment of the industry. Success is determined by measures of profitability and consistency. Many funds will close once they reach a size where further growth would inhibit performance. In general, most managers receive relatively modest base compensation, and the greatest rewards are provided by performance incentives that are paid only if the managers generate profits for their investors. They risk being fired or going out of business, however, if they lose money. Their compensation guidelines have more in common with the compensation guidelines of highly skilled corporate executives than with the compensation packages of relative return managers.

The compensation package is structured to have a significant portion of the compensation result from performance: annual bonuses and stock options for corporate executives and profit sharing for the absolute return manager.

Risk Can Be a Friend or a Foe

Outside a stock brokerage office in Brattleboro, Vermont, a poster shows a graph of the stock market's rise over the past hundred years. In bold print, the poster's title reads, **WHERE'S THE RISK?** The implication, of course, is that if investors own a portfolio of stocks and wait long enough, they will make money. The relative return approach attempts to use time to define away or mitigate the risk of loss in the market. The mantra is repeated day after day, year after year, to both individual and institutional investors: "Stay the course. Stay fully invested. Invest for the long term. Think long term."

Relative Return Risks

Average returns and long-term probabilities of loss do not tell the whole story. The probability of loss while owning the market over a long enough period of time may indeed be minimal, but the probability of a loss for periods of years, even decades, can vary dramatically depending on the market's level of valuation. The probability of loss may be very high when valuations are high, very low when valuations are low, and modest when valuations are average.

While a subsequent secular bull market can overcome the losses in secular bear markets, some investors may conclude that they cannot afford to be, or are unwilling to be, patient for such long periods of time. Also, long-term thinking does nothing to offset actual market declines, portfolio declines, and net worth declines in shorter time frames of five, ten, or even fifteen years—time frames that are relevant to almost all investors. As a recent example, investors who invested in the S&P 500 index at 1,500 in the year 2000 still have losses in their portfolios five years later.

Portfolio declines affect investors and their relative return managers differently. While a portfolio that tracks the benchmark index perfectly may reflect hard work on the manager's part and may be a cause for celebration among his relative return peers, the investor whose portfolio perfectly tracks a 35% market decline is not on track to accomplish his investment objectives.

There are also opportunity costs to consider in the investment decision process. While market pundits are quick to say that stock returns are positive over longer periods, sometimes they do not consider that investors have other alternatives. Although there may be a sense of security in knowing that stock returns are almost always positive over fifteen-year periods, receiving little or no return on your investment after fifteen years will be quite disappointing. Not only would inflation have diluted the purchasing power of the capital, but also you could have very likely more than doubled your money in bonds over that same period. Thus stocks and all other investments should be reviewed in relation to the other opportunities, not just against breaking even.

Relative return investing relies on the price movement of asset classes—movement that may not occur on a steady basis. The approach is best suited for markets that are trending upward; it should not be considered a timeless strategy. Yet, the relative return approach is viewed by many to have relatively low risk, since it provides good returns in the long run. The relative return advocates use a long-term perspective to mute the risk profile of the approach and to encourage investors to be patient and tolerant of interim shortfalls in performance.

Absolute Return View of Risk

In contrast to the relative return view of risk, the absolute return view is that risk is about the probability of loss and about the amount of money that could be lost. Imbedded in the idea of risk are the concepts of uncertainty and loss. If a loss is certain, it is not a risk, it is a problem. Therefore, risk is a concept of potential loss and the probability or likelihood of sustaining a loss.

There are different measures of risk and different dynamics of risk, but risk itself relates to the uncertainty of a loss, and the dynamic between the uncertainty and the size of a loss determines the risk profile. As a result, most measures of risk relate to the consistency of the periodic returns and the magnitude of the losses. Returns are not judged in relation to a market benchmark; rather returns are measured as absolute gains or losses in the account balance. The absolute return investor would look at the hundred-year matrix of stock market returns and see that the losses incurred over shorter periods of time represent clear evidence of substantial risk in the market—risk of loss and unsatisfactory performance.

Systematic vs. Non-systematic Risk

Modern Portfolio Theory, taught to legions of finance students over the past five decades, includes the concepts of systematic risk and non-systematic risk. Simply stated, systematic risk is the risk associated with the general market (the system); non-systematic risk is the risk associated with individual companies. In effect, these two terms isolate the two factors that affect returns from investing in stocks. The first is the general risk of the market and levels of valuation. The second relates to the series of risks associated with individual companies, including business risks, management risks, competitive risks, etc.

Harry Markowitz changed modern investment practices by saying that investors are not compensated for individual company risks since those factors can be mitigated through diversification. In effect, a portfolio that is fully diversified will sufficiently reduce the impact of risk from individual companies. Markowitz believed that if a risk could be mitigated by diversification, then efficient markets would not provide a return for that risk. Therefore, if markets are efficient, investment returns from stocks are provided only by taking overall market risks.

The concept of efficient markets is embodied in a theory known as the Efficient Market Hypothesis (EMH), introduced in 1970 by Eugene Fama. It states that stock prices always reflect all known information. As a result, stock prices are always perfectly priced, and no investor can have an edge on finding undervalued or overvalued securities. More recent versions of the theory allow for some short-term inefficiencies or market malfunctions, but a version of the efficient market hypothesis is a key assumption for many of the other financial theories that are the basis for relative return investing.

Relative return investors attempt to reduce non-systematic risk—the risk of uniquely poor performance by individual companies—by diversifying across a wide range of stocks or bonds. The impact on the portfolio of any one failing company thus becomes very small. In effect, relative return investors seek to accept systematic risk—the risks associated with stocks or bonds as an asset class. Their belief is that returns occur over the long term, by staying invested throughout the cycles in the market. Yet, there is little recognition of the significance of the stock market or bond market valuation cycles. As a result, few adjustments are made in applying the approach across different market environments. The future returns for investors are constantly based on the long-term average risk and return of the market. Therefore, relative return investing is considered risk-based investing—returns are the compensation for taking the risks of the market.

Absolute return investors, on the other hand, generally seek to eliminate market risk and accept non-systematic or individual stock risk. They seek to avoid the volatility of the market, and focus on skill-based, consistent means of generating profits. Therefore, absolute return investing does not seek returns from the risk level of the investment; rather it seeks returns specifically based on the skills of the investment manager.

For half a century, relative return investment professionals have worked to diversify portfolios to eliminate non-systematic risks and seek gains from systematic (market) risks. At the same time, absolute return investors have worked to hedge away the systematic (market) risks, and seek gains from their skills in selecting mis-valued companies and from taking non-systematic risks. These investors include Alfred W. Jones, who started the first hedge fund about the same time that Dr. Markowitz published his paper on Modern Portfolio Theory.

Dominant vs. Secondary Risk

The concepts of systematic (market) risk and non-systematic (individual securities) risk relate to the nature of the risks inherent in a particular portfolio or strategy. Although in theory the goal of relative return investing is to isolate market risk and the goal of many styles of absolute return investing is to isolate securities risks, the reality of investing leaves most portfolios with components of each type of risk. As a result, one of the risks tends to be dominant and the other tends to be secondary. Traditional portfolios have market risk as dominant, whereas absolute return portfolios tend to have securities risk as dominant.

The approaches toward risk management in traditional and alternative portfolios tend to be different. One of the main tools of risk management is diversification, which is the concept of holding multiple securities in a portfolio, or spreading out risks in the portfolio across multiple positions. A greater number of securities or positions is known as diversification, and a lesser number is known as concentration.

Diversification can play different roles. For traditional, relative return portfolios, diversification is used to reduce the secondary risk (securities) and to concentrate on the dominant risk (market). Further, the goal generally is to include more market risk—since assumption of risk is the source of return. Thus, diversification *increases* the dominant risk.

For absolute return portfolios, the technique of portfolio construction and the implementation of investment strategy are used to reduce that approach's secondary risk, market risk. Diversification is used to spread out the impact of any single investment decision. Since absolute return investing relies on the skills of the manager to select profitable investments, the dominant risk is securities risk. Thus diversification for absolute return portfolios *decreases* the dominant risk.

The significance of understanding dominant and secondary risk across the two investment approaches highlights the fundamental differences in the two approaches. This distinction between dominant and secondary risk provides a framework to evaluate the nature and risks of various investment alternatives. As a result, an investor can more accurately identify to what extent the approach is primarily relative return based or absolute return based, regardless of its stated investment style.

Portfolio Mismanagement

If the first rule of portfolio management is diversification, why do most investors unwittingly concentrate their risks?

Many investors believe that a portfolio constructed with numerous stocks and bonds is diversified. That approach has its roots in the principles of Modern Portfolio Theory (MPT). But when MPT is misapplied, it does not provide the road map to secure investing and leaves investors vulnerable to substantial risk.

A key principle of MPT developed by Harry Markowitz in the early 1950s is simple to understand yet striking in its implications: diversification can eliminate the risks that do not provide returns, while retaining the risks that do provide returns. Later, William F. Sharpe further developed these principles into the Capital Asset Pricing Model (CAPM). From Jonathan Burton's interview with Dr. Sharpe:

> Every investment carries two distinct risks, the CAPM explains. One is the risk of being in the market, which Sharpe called systematic risk. This risk, later dubbed "beta," cannot be diversified away. The other—unsystematic risk—is specific to a company's fortunes. Since this uncertainty can be mitigated through appropriate diversification, Sharpe figured that a portfolio's expected return hinges solely on its beta—its relationship to the overall market. The CAPM helps measure portfolio risk and the return an investor can expect for taking that risk.

In combination, MPT and CAPM have been the basis for structuring investment portfolios for the past several decades. Based on an investor's risk profile, allocations are made across the investment alternatives. Decades ago, there were stocks and bonds, and occasionally an alternative investment. As a result, portfolios were developed from a very limited palette. Yet, the groundbreaking MPT and CAPM principles helped investors and advisors to structure diversified portfolios of stocks and bonds rather than concentrated portfolios.

As simple as that sounds, inasmuch as those concepts are second nature in investing today, Dr. Sharpe determined that market risk is the only risk investors are paid to include in their portfolios. Since the risks associated with individual companies can be diversified away, the systematic market risk is the source of returns. Most investors have heard this principle said another way: "eighty to ninety percent of the returns come from being in the market, and a fraction comes from stock selection." Actually, if an investor is diversified sufficiently to completely achieve the theory, then CAPM indicates that the percentage of the returns that is due to the market should be the entire one hundred percent. As a result, effective diversification under MPT and CAPM should provide investors with investment returns that are consistent with the market returns.

These principles can be related first to stocks and then to bonds. A diversified portfolio of stocks tends to provide the returns of the general stock market. Once individual company risk is diversified, the pure stock market risk remains. Thus, the portfolio moves with the stock market. Stock market returns are driven by earnings growth and valuation changes (as measured by the price/earnings ratio, known as P/E). If P/Es increase, stock market returns are generally high, since the P/E ratio multiplies the effect of rising earnings. If P/E ratios decrease, stock market returns will be low or negative, since declining P/Es generally offset the benefit of rising earnings.

For example, consider a stock that sells for $15 and has earnings per share of $1. The P/E ratio is 15 — $15 divided by $1. If the earnings increase by 5% to $1.05 and the P/E ratio remains the same, the stock price will rise to $15.75, since the stock price equals the earnings per share multiplied by the P/E ratio. If, however, the P/E rises to 20 in addition to the increase in earnings to $1.05, the stock price will be $21.00, a gain of 40% over the initial price of $15.00. As a result, approximately one-eighth (5%) of the gain comes from the 5% growth in earnings, and the balance comes from the increase in the P/E ratio. On the other hand, had the P/E ratio declined to 10 while earnings increased to $1.05, the stock price would be $10.50. Even though earnings grew by 5%, the investor has a loss of 30% on the investment. As you can see, the impact of changes in the P/E ratio can have a dramatic impact on the stock price and an investor's returns.

Similar principles apply to bonds. Once the individual company risks are diversified, the portfolio moves in concert with the bond market, which is largely driven by trends in interest rates. As many investors have experienced, when interest rates decline, bond values increase. Likewise, rising interest rates cause bond values to decline. Thus, if interest rates are falling, the yield from the bond portfolio is supplemented with increases in the value of the bonds; or, if rates are rising, the decline in bond prices offsets some of the portfolio yield, resulting in lower total returns.

Therefore, an investment portfolio that is structured with allocations of 60 percent in a diversified stock portfolio, 30 percent in a diversified bond portfolio, and 10 percent in other investments is concentrated 90 percent across two risks: stock market risk and bond market risk. And over longer periods of time, those two markets tend to move in the same direction.

This does not indicate that the principles of MPT and CPM are not solid; the issue is that the application of the principles has not evolved as the financial markets have become more complex. Dr. Markowitz's publication of MPT in 1952 discussed the concept of "performances of available securities." In 1952, stocks and bonds were the predominant investment alternatives. A portfolio allocated across the two asset classes was about as diversified as you could be.

Many investors today do not realize that mutual funds were uncommon before the 1980s; there were fewer than 300 in the 1960s, and more than 10,000 today. In addition, the investment choices and available securities have exploded over the past two decades. The menu of securities now readily available includes asset backed, foreign, real estate, options, commodities, investment trusts, hedge funds, inflation-protected bonds, etc.

Most investors remember only the market risks and conditions of the past two decades, when the annual trends were strongly in favor of stock and bond investors. Interim dips were always buying opportunities. But, for those with battle scars from the 1970s and before, stock and bond market risks have not always been so forgiving. The driver of stocks, the P/E ratio, is again at historical highs. The driver of bonds, interest rates, is near recent historical lows. Given where both of the traditional asset classes are positioned, the odds appear to favor Mr. Risk over Mr. Return for stocks and bonds.

Over the past several decades, the financial community has also realized that Eugene Fama's Efficient Market Hypothesis, an important assumption for MPT and CAPM, may not be as strict as originally theorized. Financial markets are an efficiency process, rather than an efficient condition. In other words, markets attempt to find the right prices over time, but do not reflect all of the information all of the time. Many alternative investments today, hedge funds, for example, operate to identify and profit from mispricings and inefficiencies, and thereby contribute to the efficiency of the markets.

Returning to Dr. Markowitz, diversification in a portfolio applies to risks, not securities. Other than not being familiar with the investment alternatives, what other logical reason would explain why investors concentrate their portfolios into two major risks when so many options are available?

Risk Misconceptions

Rational investors generally price riskier investments to offer higher ultimate returns than less risky investments. This bedrock concept of finance governs much investment thinking and is a key reason that lower-quality bonds yield more than higher-quality bonds. But the risk/reward relationship is not always as direct as many might assume. Did Jack Welch at GE or Warren Buffett take on higher levels of risk to achieve their higher-than-average levels of return? Most would say no. Welch and Buffett achieved higher returns by exercising higher levels of skill than their counterparts. One might even argue that a portion of their success lies in their ability to reduce risk by identifying particularly high-quality companies to add to their investment and corporate portfolios. Similarly, some investment strategies that use an absolute return approach have been able to generate higher returns over market cycles, while providing demonstrably less risk than the overall market.

Another risk/reward misconception: higher risk, some believe, automatically means the potential for higher rewards. Some investments, though, carry higher risk precisely because they provide a relatively lower opportunity for reward or profit. Risk is not a knob on investments that one turns to get higher returns. Risk is what rational investors assess and price into the expected return of an investment. The reason that lower-quality bonds have higher yields than higher-quality bonds is that investors demand more yield for the riskier bond—the price of the lower-quality bond is set by rational investors who would not pay a price that does not compensate for the risk. That is the function of the market—to set the price and terms of assets or investments based on their expected financial payback after a level of risk and losses is realized.

Source of Returns: Risk vs. Activity

Most investments in financial securities seek returns by taking risk. Other types of investments provide returns from the activity under-lying the investment. For example, bonds with higher risk generally provide higher returns. This is consistent with Dr. Markowitz's Mod-ern Portfolio Theory (MPT). In contrast, investments in farming, for example, provide returns from the activity of growing crops, not from taking the risk of farming. As previously discussed, GE and Berkshire Hathaway were activity- and skill-based investments, rather than risk-based investments.

One goal of risk-based investing is to eliminate the risks that do not provide returns. This concept is central to CAPM and is the basis for diversification in traditional stock portfolios. The goal in activ-ity-based investing is to apply the greatest level of skill to increase returns and reduce risk. The best example is arbitrage investing: si-multaneously buying and selling an asset at a profit with no risk.

Investors should seek to understand the source of returns from in-vestments. For risk-based investments, returns should be commensu-rate with the risk. For activity-based investments, they should seek the best skills. For investments that include both, an investor should seek to identify and assess both elements within the investment.

Expected Returns and Probable Returns

The phrase "expected returns" is used in the financial community as a reference to the rate of return that an investor should require from a certain investment, given its risk profile. In 1952, when Harry Mar-kowitz published the principles of Modern Portfolio Theory in *The Journal of Finance,* he referred to expected returns in his "expected returns—variance of returns" rule. In that context, expected returns "include an allowance for risk."

Therefore, expected returns, other than yields from risk-free Trea-sury bills, include a risk premium—a gross yield before any loss-es. In the example of the higher- and the lower-quality bonds, the lower-quality bond is priced to yield higher interest payments due its greater risks. Consider the example of a higher-quality bond, a U.S. Treasury Bond yielding 5%, and a lower-quality bond issued by a risky company. Due to the greater risk of loss, investors will require that the corporate bond have a higher yield, say 10%. Since there is generally no risk of loss on the Treasury bond, the expected return of 5% will be 5%. But, the expected return of 10% on the corporate bond may be realized at 10% or it may be less if there is a credit loss.

In a portfolio diversified across numerous corporate bonds that yield 10%, it should be expected that the realized portfolio return will be less than 10%. There is a high probability that at least a few losses will occur given the higher risk profile of the bonds. As a result, there will be a difference between "pre-risk expected yield" and "post-risk probable yield." Investors are often seduced into higher-yielding investments without considering the likely post-risk return. This is a crucial concept when considering the risk premium of asset classes, including stocks.

Every security is priced to an expected return based on its risk profile; yet, the probable return for investments with risk is not the expected return.

Market Efficiency: Condition vs. Process

An old story, told in many versions, illustrates the concept of market efficiency. A young student and a scholar on efficient markets are walking across campus. The student notices the scholar's glance toward a dollar bill lying on the sidewalk. As the scholar looks away and walks by the dollar, the curious student asks why he did not pick it up. The scholar continues with a lesson on efficient markets: "The bill must have been an illusion, unworthy of the effort to pick it up. If there ever was a dollar bill on the sidewalk, someone else would have already found it."

Despite conventional wisdom, markets are not efficient… as a condition; markets are an efficiency process.

Traditional theories regarding market efficiency, including Eugene Fama's Efficient Market Hypothesis, hold that markets anytime and always reflect all known information. As a result, at least according to the theory, an investor (without illegal inside information) cannot earn excess profits. This concept is deeply ingrained in modern financial theories and investment practices. So while hoards of investors walk past dollar bills in the market, savvy participants contribute to market efficiency by being the ones who pocket the assumed impossible.

The means by which markets assimilate information is the efficiency process. The dollar bill that fell on the sidewalk is analogous to the new piece of information that becomes available to some in the markets. The first investors to realize and understand the information are the ones that are first able to profit from it. Therein lies one of the benefits of skill-based investing: finding the new information that will affect the value of a security. As a result, markets are an efficiency process. As knowledgeable investors assimilate new information, they act on their new information by purchasing and selling securities. That process, buying to introduce new positive information into prices and selling to introduce new negative information into prices, is the efficiency mechanism of markets. As a result, the investors with the early information are able to benefit from the subsequent movements in price as the information becomes generally known.

For example, assume that the available research reports estimate that revenues and profits for a company are expected to grow by 5 percent. An astute investor walking though the stores of the company notices 10 percent more customers than usual. In addition, a quick look at the loading dock spots 10 percent more delivery trucks bringing inventory to the store. Without inside information, only insightful observations, the investor buys the stock. The price moves up slightly. As other investors recognize the same insights, the price moves up further. By the time the quarterly report is released, much of the price move has occurred and the skillful investors realize a profit for their efforts. Thus, the markets are an efficiency process seeking to include new information in prices as market participants buy and sell securities based on their insights.

The approach toward market efficiency distinguishes relative return investing and absolute return investing. Relative return investors seek to survive the waves of the market by realizing the long-term average return. Gains occur in rising markets and losses in declining markets. Since the long-term trend for stocks has been up, relative return stock market investors have always been proven right over a long enough period of time. Absolute return investors seek gains in all market conditions. They seek to ride the waves and avoid the breaks of the markets, and they seek gains from skill. The results are as distinctly different as their respective approaches.

Return Profiles

Some of the differences between the relative return approach and the absolute return approach can be visually illustrated by comparing the returns of each approach to stock market returns. One of the most significant differences between the two approaches relates to their respective performances during positive and negative market conditions. Thus, to profile the performance of each approach, their respective returns can be contrasted during positive-return days and negative-return days in the stock market. For stock market returns, the S&P 500 Index is used as a representative benchmark.

The analysis starts by developing the data for each day over the years 2002 and 2003. To aggregate the positive-return days (up days) and the negative-return days (down days), the series of daily returns are sorted from the worst down day to the best up day. When the series is plotted on a graph, it presents an upward-sloping blue line from the lower left of extreme negative returns to the upper right of extreme positive returns. When the blue line crosses the 0% return line, there is a delineation of the down days on the left and the up days on the right.

By plotting the returns of a relative return investment against the line in red, the profile of that investment in down days and up days can be visualized. Likewise, on a separate graph, when the returns for an absolute return investment are plotted against the line in red, the profile for that investment can be viewed. For the relative return investment, a popular mutual fund will be used; for the absolute return investment, a somewhat typical equity long/short-style hedge fund will be used.

Figure 9.1 reflects the graph for the relative return mutual fund for 2002 and 2003. As you can see, the return pattern closely tracks the market returns. The slight variances represent a measure known as "tracking error," a risk measure for relative return investments. The key observation is that the relative return mutual fund very closely tracks the return pattern of the stock market. During the down days

Figure 9.1. Relative Return Profile

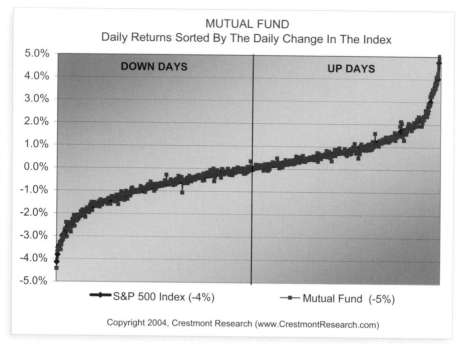

MUTUAL FUND
Daily Returns Sorted By The Daily Change In The Index

DOWN DAYS   UP DAYS

S&P 500 Index (-4%)   Mutual Fund (-5%)

Copyright 2004, Crestmont Research (www.CrestmontResearch.com)

on the left of the graph, the mutual fund is down; during up days, it is up.

Figure 9.2 reflects the graph for the absolute return hedge fund for 2002 and 2003. As you can see, the return pattern distinctly diverges from the market returns. The pattern during down days is substantially similar to the pattern during up days in the market. The hedge fund has significantly neutralized its relationship to the market and has focused on generating returns from the superior skills of stock selection. The key observation is that the performance of the absolute return hedge fund is unrelated to the returns of the market.

The return patterns or style profile for relative return investments are the opposite of the returns from absolute return investments. They reflect the difference between the respective approaches to return generation and risk management. Neither profile should be considered superior; each represents a different style of investment and has different roles in an investment portfolio.

Figure 9.2. Absolute Return Profile

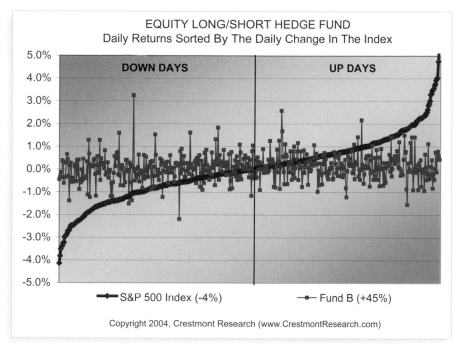

EQUITY LONG/SHORT HEDGE FUND
Daily Returns Sorted By The Daily Change In The Index

A Little History: The Devil's in the Assumptions

The relative return philosophy is based largely on three theories: Harry Markowitz's Modern Portfolio Theory (MPT), Eugene Fama's Efficient Market Hypothesis (EMH), and William Sharpe's Capital Asset Pricing Model (CAPM). Stated simply, MPT "explores how risk averse investors construct portfolios in order to optimize expected returns for a given level of market risk." EMH provides that securities prices reflect all known information and inhibit investors from finding mispriced securities. CAPM provides a framework for constructing portfolios with an optimal reward and risk relationship.

MPT, EMH, and CAPM profoundly influence the thinking of many of the largest institutional investors in the world, and rightly so. They provide valuable insights into issues of risk, market efficiency, investment theory, and portfolio construction. MPT and CAPM, the two that most directly affect investment management and portfolio construction, rely on key assumptions, some of which involve the notions of rational investors and efficient markets. The models also rely on the user to determine appropriate assumptions for future returns to be used as inputs. As Dr. Markowitz stated up-front in his 1952 article on MPT titled "Portfolio Theory" in *The Journal of Finance:*

> The process of selecting a portfolio may be divided into two stages. The first stage starts with observation and experience and ends with beliefs about the future performances of available securities. The second stage starts with the relevant beliefs about future performances and ends with the choice of the portfolio. This paper is concerned with the second stage.

Note his emphasis that MPT is completely reliant on the user to identify the available securities and to develop beliefs about their future performances. If market conditions have an asset class valued at relatively high levels, and thus the asset class is expected to perform below average for a period of time, MPT requires that its assumptions include below-average returns for that asset class. If average returns are assumed, the results from MPT will be wrong.

A fundamental idea of much traditional investment thinking is that markets are efficient. Leading practitioners of absolute return investing, however, make their livings by finding and capitalizing on market inefficiencies. While recognizing a tendency toward efficiency, they think of market efficiency as a process rather than as a consistently existing condition. Recent reports and studies are acknowledging the role that hedge funds and other absolute return investments play in *increasing or improving* market efficiency.

Another assumption—that of the rational investor—raises the eyebrows of many who deal with investors on a daily basis. Many experts would argue that much of the market's volatility reflects the swings of crowd psychology, rather than the rational analysis of all available information. An emerging field of study in finance is behavioral finance, the study of how and why investors make decisions. This crossover between finance and psychology is providing insights into the effect of emotion and irrational behavior on the financial markets.

The appropriateness of when to use a very long-term time horizon is a recurring theme in this book. Additionally, the book highlights the tendency of investors to make inappropriate assumptions for future returns for their time horizons. Estimating future returns is always a challenge, but far too many investors rely on average returns based on history rather than on assessing the likely future returns based on current valuations.

Finally, assumptions about the lack of correlation between the price movements of different asset classes seem to be challenged by the realities of market action. As earlier chapters have noted, secular bear markets for stocks coincide with secular bear markets for bonds. Although certain asset classes may not move in the same direction over shorter periods of time, some of them are affected similarly over longer periods by general economic factors.

The Popularity Contest

Why is the traditional asset class investment approach more popular than absolute return investing? There are many reasons for the greater popularity of relative return investing, though most would relate to the Wall Street sales engine, training, reports from the traditional pundits, securities regulations, and the secular bull market that started in the early 1980s.

The Wall Street sales engine is fueled by commissions and asset management fees. As a result, the long-term, buy-and-hold philosophy was easy to adapt to their sales model. The pitch encouraged investors to remain invested in stocks at all times and allowed for sector rotations and portfolio adjustments to allow for some turnover in the portfolio. The scholarly research, which generally includes theories based on the long term, has been used to train the young professionals entering the investment industry. As they matriculated into roles advising and assisting investors, MPT, EMH, and CAPM became useful, simple tools for working with their clients. As investment philosophies evolved, the press looked to the experts—Wall Street executives and scholarly researchers—for insights to include in articles about the markets and investing.

At the same time, securities laws and regulations were developed that encouraged the average investor to use traditional Wall Street products and prevented many from accessing the skill-based partnerships. The traditional approach was further reinforced by its success during the great secular bull market of the 1980s and 1990s. In a secular bull market, the demand for skill-based investing is quite low, since the market's winds blow so strongly into investors' sails. As a result, an entire generation has come to see the notion of market-dependent returns as being traditional, while skill-dependent and risk-controlled returns are seen as non-traditional.

Big-Money Dilemma

There are other reasons that the market-dependent approach is the method of choice of Wall Street's largest firms. They have become such a large force in the markets that they do not have the flexibility to make significant changes in their asset class allocations when market conditions change. If you have $10,000, $1 million, or even $1 billion to invest, your job is much easier than the task confronting the market strategists of Wall Street's largest firms. With relatively smaller portfolios, you can make decisions about which investments to emphasize in your portfolio.

Imagine the dilemma of overseeing more than $1 trillion across an extensive base of clients. That is the charter of Wall Street's largest firms. The dilemma is that even if you believe that the market is set for an extended setback, there is little you can do to get out of the way. If you try to sell your positions, the result could accelerate the decline—a self-fulfilling prophecy. When you become so large that you nearly become the market, you have no alternative but to stay invested.

When you are recognized for a long-term, supposedly conservative, buy-and-hold approach, there is considerable risk in being a maverick against the general industry position. During the 1980s, when computers were proliferating throughout companies across America, IBM was recognized as the industry leader and a stable choice for equipment. The old saying among computer department managers was, "No one ever got fired for buying IBM." By that they meant that the widely believed safe decision had great benefits in job security. Even if the equipment did not function well, it would not be the fault of the decision maker. Likewise in the field of investments, not only is it easier to rely on long-term history and emphasize patience, but also it may be the only practical choice for the largest firms.

The uncertain and choppy markets of the past few years have investors questioning the wisdom of the traditional approach. In addition, there are many more investment vehicles and risk management tools available today than in the past. Lastly, the revelations of various Wall Street scandals and questionable practices have unveiled the conflicts of interest in the industry and have awakened investors to a renewed sense of personal responsibility for their investments. As a result, a trend is emerging to put the objective of consistent profits back into investment philosophy.

The next chapter presents a philosophy of investing that recognizes that different investment approaches are needed based on the conditions in the financial markets. There are times when the traditional asset class approach is appropriate and other times when a more progressive approach is needed. In addition, the next chapter will help to develop an investment plan that can adjust to the current conditions to position a portfolio for potentially more consistent profits.

CHAPTER 10

ROW, NOT SAIL

The earliest images of boats appear on Egyptian rock drawings dating back to 6000 BC. The boatmen powered and directed these maiden vessels by shoving long sticks against the river bottom or paddling the water with planks; their active efforts propelled the craft. The first record of a ship under sail appears much later, on an Egyptian pot dating to 3200 BC. The addition of the sail to the vessel enables it to receive power from the wind; as a result, the boatman's primary roles are now to direct the ship and enjoy the ride.

Even after harnessing the power of the wind, however, the Egyptians, and all civilizations since then, retain both modes of travel—rowing and sailing. The early Egyptians, for their part, passed down the knowledge that sailboats do not work very well in certain environments; when there is no wind, the only way to make progress is to row. Even today, many sailboats carry at least a paddle or other means of power in case the weather changes. Likewise, every investor should be prepared with investment strategies that row when favorable secular bull market winds either become unfavorable or shift into a secular bear market stall. By further exploring the concepts of rowing and sailing as they apply to investing, this chapter helps investors develop the appropriate investment philosophy and strategy based on their assessment of the future market environment.

Sailing and Rowing

Most investors, especially those with traditional stock and bond portfolios, profit when the market rises, and lose money when the market declines. They are at the mercy of the market, and their portfolios prosper or shrink as the market's winds blow favorably or unfavorably. They are, in effect, simple sailors in market waters, getting blown wherever the wind takes them.

And yet, as chapter 9 demonstrates, there is another, more consistent, way. The absolute return approach seeks consistent profitability, even under unfavorable market conditions. The absolute return approach works to reduce volatility and risk in the pursuit of steady returns.

Sailing

In sailing with a fixed sail, the boat moves because it grabs the wind; it grabs the environment and advances or retreats because of the environment. Relative return investing corresponds to this fixed-sail approach to sailing. When market winds are favorable, portfolios can increase in value rapidly. When the winds turn unfavorable, losses can accumulate quickly. Bull markets are the friends of relative return sailors, and catching the favorable bull market winds and continuing to ride them are the secrets to making money in a bull market.

The traditional approach to investing in stocks and bonds is known as asset class investing. An asset class is a series of securities whose price tends to move in a similar direction based on external market conditions. For example, stocks and bonds each are individual asset classes. Harry Markowitz's Modern Portfolio Theory (MPT) encourages investors to hold diversified portfolios of stocks and bonds to realize the general trend of the market. Over longer periods of time, both stocks and bonds have produced solid investment returns for investors who held onto the portfolios and rode the trend in the market.

As discussed in chapter 5, those returns tend to come over intermediate periods characterized by secular bull or secular bear markets. During the periods of secular bull markets, an investor can enjoy the plentiful gains in the market simply by holding portfolios of the rising asset classes. Much like the sailor, the investor does some directing and generally enjoys the ride. MPT and the traditional approach to investing provide a few simple rules about diversification and patience, which, in the long term, should provide success.

Rowing

Rowing, as an action-based approach to boating, is analogous to the absolute return approach to investing. The progress of the boat occurs because of the action of the person doing the rowing. Similarly, in absolute return investing, the progress and profits of the portfolio derive from the activities of the investment manager, rather than from broad market movements.

When the secular bull market changes into a secular bear market, the investor can either wait for the next secular surge or grab the paddle. Without rowing, the boat would eventually achieve the historical progress that investors expect over the long run. By its definition, the long-run average is the average of periods of secular bull markets and secular bear markets. Historically, however, the secular bear markets have lasted for five, ten, and as much as twenty-year periods. For investors with shorter horizons of *only* a decade or two, a strategy of patiently watching a flapping sail during a stalled market may not be satisfactory. Further, in some secular bear cycles, there are periods of being pushed backwards into investment losses. At times, investors who desire to avoid losses or generate gains may need to grab the paddle. Examples of rowing strategies can include buying undervalued securities while selling overvalued securities short, exploiting temporary mispricings or market inefficiencies, investing in producing assets such as royalty trusts or timber, and selling options on core investment positions. As Alexander Ineichen writes in his book, *Absolute Returns:*

> Absolute return managers want to make profits not only when the wind is at their back but also when it changes and becomes a headwind. Absolute return managers will therefore use risk management and hedging techniques.... From the point of view of absolute return managers, relative return mangers do not use risk management, and do not manage assets as they follow benchmarks.

Ineichen further contrasts absolute return and relative return investing:

Orthodox financial theory suggests that investors should focus on the long term. It also suggests that investors will generate satisfactory returns if they have a long enough time horizon when they buy equities.

Ineichen emphasizes the assumption of long-term horizons under modern financial theory. One of the challenges facing relative return investors is that they might not live long enough to experience the long term. Absolute return investors, on the other hand, seek consistent performance along the way as well as end-of-period wealth.

Should Today's Investors Row or Sail?

In the first eight chapters, the concepts of secular bull and bear periods were identified and explained. In secular bull markets, the wind is at your back as stock and bond valuations are rising. The value of the stock market increases faster than the growth in earnings as P/E ratios increase, and bond prices increase, providing returns that are greater than the interest payments. These are periods when inflation is declining and interest rates are trending lower. In those times, just open the sail by investing in the asset classes that are best positioned for gains.

When conditions are positioned for a bull market of the magnitude that was experienced in the 1980s and 1990s, when price/earnings ratios (P/Es) started near 7, open the sail even more by using leverage or over-weighting in stocks and enhance the benefits. The more the sail is open, the better the overall performance from the portfolio. As reflected in figure 10.1, stocks soared in the 1980s and 1990s, with almost every year well into positive territory as P/Es rose from near 7 to more than 25.

As the past hundred years have shown, there are periods where investors do not have the wind at their back—times when they do not have the benefit of rising valuations. And when valuations are declining or only flat, rowing becomes an important means of generating profits and avoiding losses. As reflected in figure 10.2, the most recent secular bear market included the typical, volatile choppiness as P/Es declined from well over 20 to near 7. The annual changes in the stock market from 1965 to 1981 reflect the typically

Figure 10.1. Secular Bull Market Chart

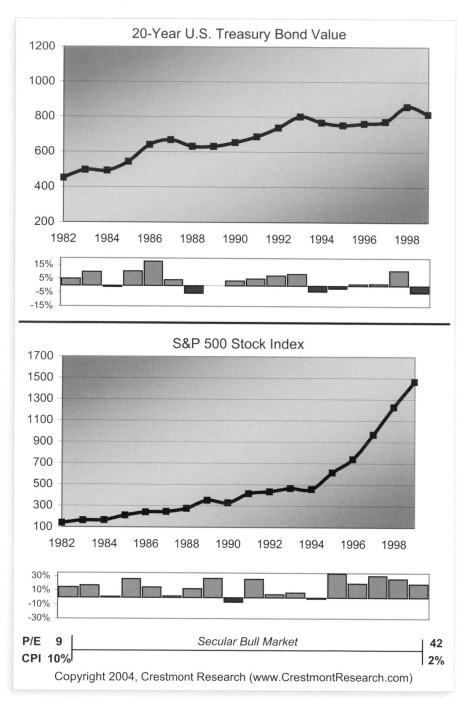

Figure 10.2. Secular Bear Market Chart

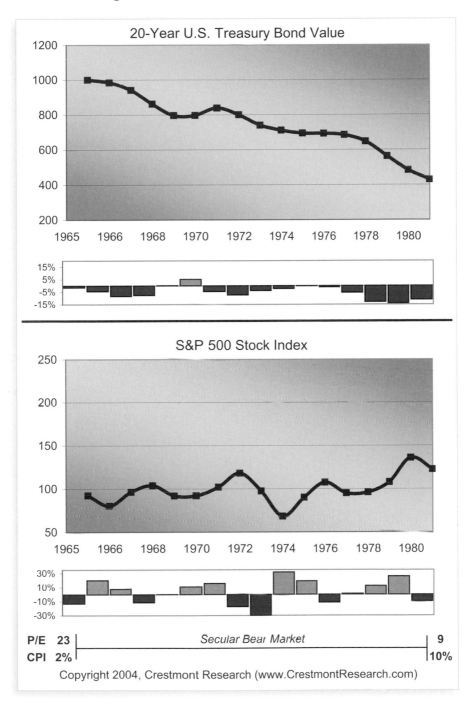

Copyright 2004, Crestmont Research (www.CrestmontResearch.com)

erratic series of intermittent gains and losses, the cumulative effect
of which resulted in little change from beginning to end. For bonds,
the annual results were more consistent, yet negative, as a generally
rising interest rate depleted the value of bonds and more than offset
the annual interest payments.

In periods of declining or flat valuations, the objective is to generate profits through skill-based activities. Although it is possible that
inflation could be maintained near price stability and valuations may
stay up at current levels, note that there has never been an extended
period where inflation and P/Es remained steady for a long period
of time.

Current Forecast

History provides perspective, but the central question investors are
asking is, "What should we do today? Should we grab the oars and
prepare to row, or should we open the sail in expectation of a favorable wind?" Deciding whether to row or to sail involves assessing the current market season and asking whether it is favorable or
unfavorable.

What are the characteristics of the current period, and are they
favorable? Two measures of stock market valuations, the P/E ratio
and the dividend yield, are presented in figures 10.3 and 10.4. Both
measures are reflecting relatively high valuation levels. The P/E ratio of 23 is close to its historical highs, excluding the bubble of the
late 1990s, and near the levels reached at the end of past secular bull
markets. The current P/E ratio is very much in line with valuations
normally found at the beginning of secular bear markets.

In addition, the other valuation measure shown in figure 10.4 is
the dividend yield for the S&P 500. It is near the lowest level of the
past hundred years. As discussed in chapter 5, low dividend yields
correspond to high stock market valuations. As a result, the current
low dividend yield of 1.8% indicates that conditions are similar to
the levels at the end of past secular bull markets and the beginning
of past secular bear markets.

Since 1900, as seen in figure 10.5, periods of rising inflation (or
declines into deflation) have corresponded with bear markets for
stocks, and periods of declining inflation (or moves out of deflation)

Figure 10.3. Historical Price / Earnings Ratio

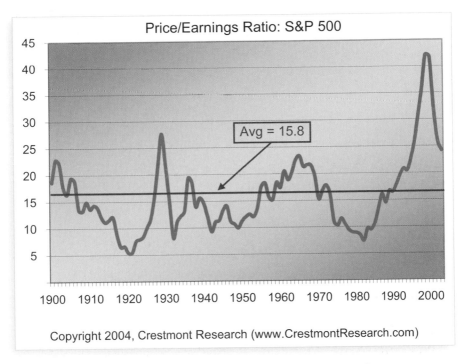

Copyright 2004, Crestmont Research (www.CrestmontResearch.com)

Figure 10.4. Dividend Yield vs. P/E Ratio

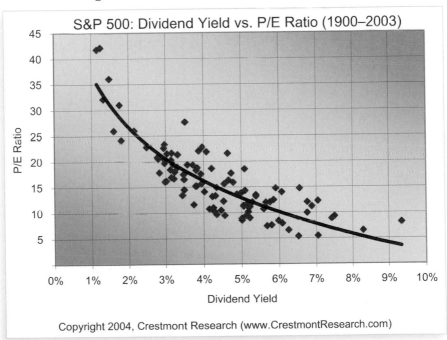

Copyright 2004, Crestmont Research (www.CrestmontResearch.com)

Figure 10.5. Inflation and P/E Ratios

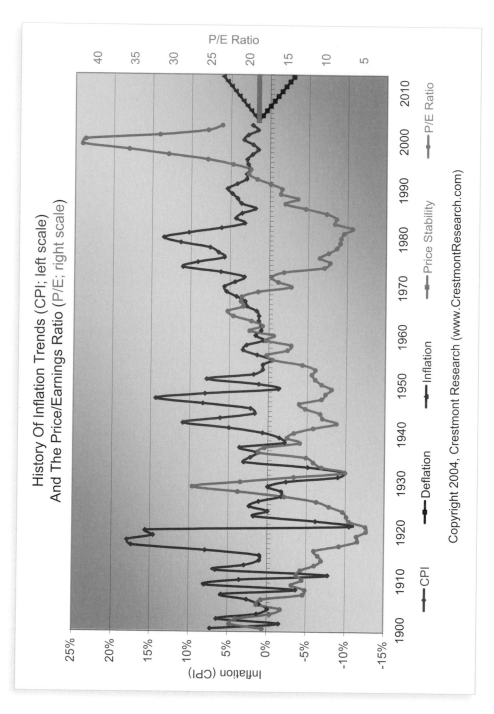

History Of Inflation Trends (CPI; left scale)
And The Price/Earnings Ratio (P/E; right scale)

Copyright 2004, Crestmont Research (www.CrestmontResearch.com)

have corresponded with long-term bull markets for stocks. As *Financial Physics* illustrated in chapter 7, the prime driver of secular bull and secular bear markets has been the trend in inflation either moving toward or away from price stability. As presented in figure 10.5, there are three potential scenarios. The first, designated in purple, reflects an increase in inflation over the next five years. The second, presented in green, reflects an extended period of low inflation and price stability. The third, represented in red, reflects a continued decline into deflation. As the chart shows, there has not been an extended period of stable low inflation during the past century. Also, the magnitude of the swings over the past 104 years has been less dramatic during the second half of the century compared to the first half. Although there appears to be the possibility of landing inflation on the runway of price stability, many economic forces could drive the future trend in inflation either higher or lower. Experts in economics and the financial markets have a wide range of opinions about the future of inflation.

The three factors, high P/E ratios, low dividend yields, and low inflation, reflect an environment similar to the early stages of secular bear markets. They are certainly the opposite of the conditions that provide the potential for a secular bull market. If inflation remains stable, P/Es could sustain their existing heights. Although that has not happened for extended periods historically, it would create a different secular market: one marked by relatively stable interest rates and a stock market driven only by earnings growth. Stock market gains would be well below average, yet not as poor as secular bear markets deliver. Crestmont refers to that hypothetical, yet potential, environment as a secular hybrid market or a secular bear in hibernation.

Of the three alternatives for the stock market environment—secular bull, secular bear, and secular hybrid—the most likely based on history is the secular bear market. A trend in inflation away from price stability would drive P/Es lower and advance the conditions of a secular bear market. Inflation has cycled continuously over the past century and longer—a condition that is more likely to persist rather than change. A change in the cycle and an extended period of price stability would create the new conditions of the secular hybrid market. Given all of the inflationary and deflationary pressures on monetary inflation in the economy, it would take an optimist to believe that those forces can be controlled for an extended period. The last alternative, the secular bull market, is hardly possible under the laws of modern economics and finance. Therefore, the most likely alternative is a secular bear market, and the most hopeful alternative is the secular hybrid market.

Alternating Strategies

The combination of high stock market valuations, low inflation, and low interest rates suggests strongly that the stock market is in the early stages of a secular bear market. Alternatively, while a secular hybrid market would present investors with less drastic conditions, it would still provide investors with below-average returns. Under either the secular bear or secular hybrid market condition, a relative return approach invites high volatility and low, or negative, potential returns. In such an environment, risk is high and return potential is low for relative return investors.

By contrast, well-designed absolute return strategies would dampen portfolio volatility and provide the potential for consistent returns, even during these unfavorable market conditions. As the Egyptian sailors knew, rowing during the stalls advances the ship and enables it to cover greater distances in less time. Although it may have been acceptable to take a long-term perspective and accept the average progress provided by using only the intermittent wind to power the ship, rowing during the stalls would have increased the progress of the trip.

Likewise for investors, investment strategies that increase the value of your portfolio during the choppy, low-progress periods of secular bear markets serve to increase the total value of your portfolio over time. In particular, during the extended multi-decade periods, like the 1965–1981 secular bear, rowing strategies are essential. Even during a possible secular hybrid market, absolute return strategies are needed to better the below-average returns and dampen the effects of market volatility. This does not say that it is time to tear down the mast and sell the sail, though it does indicate that you can pack it away for a while.

Historical Note

If this chapter were being written in the early 1980s, the data would reflect all of the history and information about secular market conditions except the last secular bull; it would still profile secular markets in the same way. The sailing and rowing metaphor would be just as applicable. Yet, the financial market conditions would reflect high inflation, high interest rates, and low P/E ratio valuations. As a result, this chapter would have a strong emphasis on the potential for a strong secular bull market. Without high valuations, the chapter could not talk about a potential secular bear market. The message would be, "Sail, Not Row: Prepare your sails and enjoy the ride."

That was then, this is now, and the conditions are the opposite of those found at the beginning of a secular bull market. Fortunately, you do not need to be optimistic about the market to be confident about the profit potential for your portfolio—if you use the appropriate absolute return strategies. The proliferation of investment alternatives since Markowitz first introduced Modern Portfolio Theory in 1952 has put powerful all-season tools in the hands of today's investors.

Today's strategy? "Row and prosper." Savvy investors will use absolute return tools to lower risk, reduce volatility, and generate more consistent returns. The absolute return tools effectively help investors prosper in a challenging environment.

Drowning in Averages

A story illustrates a key point about one of the most frequently used statistics, the average. One day a civil engineer arrives at a riverbank to determine the amount of water flowing downstream for an upcoming environmental project. Not wanting to get wet, he asks a nearby fisherman about the depth of the river. "It averages about three feet," replies the man. After taking a few estimates of width and flow, the engineer departs to make his calculations. He had exactly what he needed to be accurate in estimating the water flow.

Later that day, a hiker arrives at the riverbank. He too asks the fisherman about the depth of the river. "It averages about three feet," was the reply. The hiker rolls up his pants legs and decides to walk across. Just before midstream he is swept into the current and begins to swim. Responding to the hiker's shocked look, the fisherman continues: "It's really shallow on both banks and six feet or so in the middle."

Beware the use of averages. Whereas some situations permit the use of aggregate averages, others require specific details. For the engineer, the average worked just fine. For the hiker crossing the river, the details were critical. For a fisherman at the banks, the average shallow water depth is most important. For a boat, the midstream depth is a necessity to avoid running aground.

Since the markets resemble rivers with periods of shallow returns and periods of high results, the average is rarely relevant for making decisions about specific periods. The key is to determine the relevant market conditions and reasonably assess the likely return expectations. Investors would be wise to consider whether the next twenty years could experience the dismal returns that would restore the last twenty years to the average. If so, sailing-related investment strategies will not be successful, and rowing-related investment strategies will be required.

The chapters that follow provide examples of specific techniques that can be used to address the current market environment. These power tools can provide additional value and risk control to traditional portfolios. In addition, the last chapter explains hedge funds and similar progressive investment strategies, and concludes with a perspective on the ongoing evolution in investment management and the implications for you as an investor.

Key Concepts for This Section: Investment Philosophy

1. The progressive strategies of absolute return investing rely on skill for seeking consistent returns, and the traditional strategies of relative return investing rely on taking a long-term view of market risk for return.

2. During secular bull markets, the investment strategy of "sailing" by buying and holding stocks and bonds can be very effective; during secular bear markets, the strategy of "rowing" with absolute return strategies can be very effective.

SECTION VI

INVESTMENT STRATEGY

CHAPTER 11

TECHNIQUES FOR TRADITIONAL INVESTORS

Once you have established a perspective on the current and upcoming market climate and have developed a high-level investment philosophy, the next step is to apply effective techniques to your portfolio. There are many good books and experienced investment advisors that can help you, depending on the scope and nature of your investments. The previous chapters have provided perspectives on historical market conditions, current market climate, fundamental factors that drive financial markets, and the relative return and absolute return investment approaches.

The current financial market conditions differ significantly from those in the 1980s and 1990s. The strategies that were most successful during those two decades are not the most effective for today's market environment. Investors have begun to adjust their strategies to include techniques of risk management and return enhancement. Further, investors are increasingly including absolute return strategies in their portfolios.

A number of active techniques can improve the portfolios of traditional investors. In effect, these techniques bring some of the risk management and return-enhancing benefits to relative return investors who may not have access to progressive absolute return strategies. This chapter presents examples of techniques for bond and stock portfolios—techniques that add active risk management and work to enhance returns in unfavorable market conditions.

This section concludes in the next chapter with commentary on the evolving field of investments, including the growing field of risk-controlled investing through hedge funds. The demand from investors for more consistent returns across all market conditions, as well as the availability of risk management tools to reduce the potential for losses, is furthering a convergence between traditional and progressive investing. Soon that convergence will drive the inclusion of risk management techniques and return enhancement into traditional stock and bond asset management.

Power Tools for All Investors

In this chapter, there are a few basic examples of active techniques that can improve the return performance and risk management of a traditional bond or stock portfolio. These techniques do not bring the sophistication or full benefits of absolute return strategies. They are, however, tools that almost all relative return investors can use to add active techniques of return enhancement and risk management to traditional stock and bond market investing. This discussion is not a complete user manual; rather it serves to provide illustrations or examples of the types of techniques that are available. Please review other texts and consult professional advisors for assistance with these and other strategies.

Effective Bond Portfolios

The two largest components in most investors' portfolios are stocks and bonds. Chapter 10 explored the risks associated with large concentrations by investors in these two asset classes. For investors with bond portfolios, or for those considering an effective way to use bonds in the current environment, there are techniques for managing risk and increasing return in bond portfolios. One technique is known as a "bond ladder." For those already familiar with bond ladders, this section explains why they work and how effective bond ladders have been over the past century. First, an explanation of a few bond market basics.

The Yield Curve

The yield curve is a graphical picture of the current rate of interest for all investment periods; it presents the interest rate for short-term notes as well as long-term bonds. Generally, longer-term interest rates will be higher than short-term rates; therefore, the curve is generally sloping upward. Experienced investors keep an eye on the yield curve as one of the most efficient means of tracking the relationships between fixed income securities of varying maturities.

Figure 11.1 shows the yield curve for U.S. Treasury debt, including short-term Treasury bills, intermediate-term Treasury notes, and long-term Treasury bonds. This yield curve example illustrates the typical relationship between bonds of different maturities and the interest rates those bonds pay. With U.S. government debt, short-term securities are known as Treasury bills (Bills), intermediate-term securities are known as Treasury notes (Notes), and long-term securities are known as Treasury bonds (Bonds). In the yield curve example in figure 11.1, 1-year Bills pay slightly over 1%, while 5-year Notes pay a little over 3%, 10-year Notes yield 4.25%, and 30-year Bonds yield near 5%. Although the shape of the curve reflects the normal upward slope, the steepness is much greater than the historical average of nearly 100 basis points discussed in chapter 8.

The Basic Law of Bond Prices and Interest Rates

A basic principle of the bond market is that the prices of existing bonds decline when market interest rates rise. For example, a bond that matures in ten years and has a stated interest rate of 4.25% will decline from a price of $1,000 to a price of approximately $870 if the market interest rate on 10-year bonds rises immediately to 6%. While the bond will recover its face value at maturity, the wait can be long and uncomfortable for holders of long-term bonds. In the early 1980s, for instance, the 30-year U.S. Treasury bond fell in value by more than half during a period of sharply rising interest rates.

Clearly, though, bonds can both rise and fall in value. The inverse relationship between bond prices and interest rates works in both directions, and bond prices rise when interest rates decline. In the example above, had market interest rates declined to 3% immediately,

Figure 11.1. Yield Curve Example

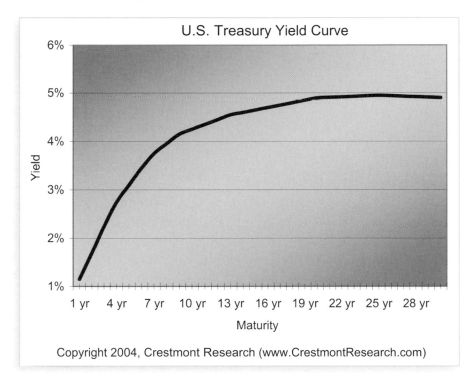

U.S. Treasury Yield Curve

Yield

1 yr   4 yr   7 yr   10 yr   13 yr   16 yr   19 yr   22 yr   25 yr   28 yr

Maturity

Copyright 2004, Crestmont Research (www.CrestmontResearch.com)

the value of that bond with payments of $42.50 annually would rise to approximately $1,110. New bonds being issued in a 3% interest rate market would have interest payments of $30.00, so the higher interest payments of the original bond would be more valuable to an investor.

This is an important concept to understand, since the original investor cannot sell the original bond at a gain *and* reinvest at the old interest rate. Interest rates are now 3%; the original investor will have the principal and gains to reinvest, albeit at the lower interest rate. As a result, the original investor will realize the original yield of 4.25%.

The new buyer of the bond, however, will pay $1,110 to receive a total of $42.50 each year until maturity. The extra annual payments (i.e., $42.50 when new bonds pay $30.00) will be partially offset by the principal loss of $110 at maturity (i.e., $1,110 paid for the face value of $1,000). As a result, the new buyer will realize the new market yield of 3%.

The key concept from these examples is that bond prices change inversely to the change in interest rates. The change in the value of the bond occurs when it has a fixed interest rate and the market interest rate changes.

Surfing the Roll

The second key dynamic with bonds is the effect of time—the impact of getting older. Several effects occur as bonds age toward maturity. Since the yield curve typically has an upward slope, financial professionals refer to the concept of holding bonds as they move toward maturity as "rolling down the curve" or "riding the yield curve." To highlight the powerful effects in an aging bond portfolio, Crestmont has named the impact of aging "Surfing the Roll."

The key to surfing the roll is found in the normally shaped yield curve, as reflected in figure 11.1. In the normal yield curve, bonds with more distant maturities carry higher yields than do shorter-term bonds. So, a 10-year bond pays a higher interest rate than does a 9-year bond. In this case, the 10-year bond pays 4.25% interest, while a 9-year bond pays 4.15%.

Assume you buy a 10-year bond for $1,000. It pays $42.50 per year in interest, or 4.25%. It will continue to pay the same $42.50 in interest each year until it matures, regardless of whether market interest rates rise or fall. Interest payments are an island of consistency in a sea of market volatility.

After one year, if market interest rates have not changed, new 10-year bonds will still pay 4.25% interest and new 9-year bonds will still pay 4.15% interest, just as they did during the preceding year. Further, your bond still pays $42.50 or 4.25% in interest, the same rate as 10-year bonds. But since a year has passed, your bond now has only nine years until maturity. In other words, your bond has rolled from a 10-year maturity down to a 9-year maturity. Your bond, with nine years now left to maturity, carries a higher yield (4.25%) than new 9-year bonds with interest payments of only 4.15%. Because your bond pays a higher interest rate and has the same maturity as 9-year bonds, it has extra value, and the price of your bond increases accordingly. In this example, your bond would increase in value to $1,007 from $1,000. The increase in value of the 10-year bond rolling down to a 9-year maturity is an example of the gain that comes from surfing the roll.

Your total return consists of the interest payment plus the gain in the value of your bond. The interest payment provides 4.25% of the total return. The increase in value of $7 on your original investment of $1,000 adds slightly over 0.7% to toward the total return. Therefore, the impact of the roll is to increase the total return from your bond for the year from 4.25% to 4.99%, a significant increase.

As the bond nears maturity, the value peaks and begins to decline in the last few years back toward its original principal, or par, value. That decline adversely affects the price, but not the value of the bond at maturity. A net benefit still occurs; it is only masked somewhat by the declining price. Keep in mind that the bond's value is both the change in price and the cash received from the interest payment. Although the price peaked and is declining, the interest payment is more than making up for the decline, and the effect of the roll is still occurring; it works as long as the yield curve has a positive slope. In fact, the impact of the roll is often greatest near maturity, as that can be the steepest part of the yield curve.

It is beyond the scope of this discussion to present the equations that quantify these effects. But the next time someone suggests that you sell your bond as it nears maturity to avoid the price decline, remember that you will only be reinvesting at lower interest rates and will not increase your return. In addition, you will pay taxes on the gain and will have less to reinvest. Taxes are due on gains realized from tax-exempt municipal bonds as well; only the interest payments are tax-exempt. Finally, if you sell the shorter maturity bond and buy a longer maturity, you will be increasing your exposure to interest rate risk by lengthening the overall term of your portfolio, and you will incur additional transaction costs.

The gain in total return that comes as longer maturity bonds roll down to shorter maturities positively impacts every bond in a portfolio until the bonds near maturity. At that point, the bond's premium begins to return to the original face value, usually $1,000. Keep in mind that the previously discussed effect of interest rate changes also affects the value of the bonds in your portfolio. The combination of both effects will be discussed shortly. For now, the key concept to understand about the roll is that if the yield curve is positively sloped and interest rates remain the same, bond values increase as they roll toward maturity.

Bond Investor Dilemma: Wait to Invest, or Act Now

Periods of rising interest rates, which drive bond prices down, freeze many investors into inaction and keep them on the sideline waiting for higher rates. They postpone buying bonds and sit instead in money market funds. In many cases, they are advised to sell their bonds, often paying taxes on the gains, and move into shorter maturities. By waiting on the sidelines or moving into short-term maturities, however, investors forgo two significant opportunities: first, they lose out on the higher interest rates they could be earning currently, since bond yields typically exceed money market rates; secondly, they miss out on the total return benefits offered by surfing the roll.

How can bond investors assess the advantages and disadvantages of investing in bonds now versus waiting for the possibility of higher interest rates later? The Breakeven Yield Curve (BYC) methodology represented by figure 11.2 provides the tool for the task. It shows the amount that interest rates would have to rise in the future for a bond investor to be in a worse financial position than a money market investor over the next few years. In addition, the explanation of the BYC will help explain why bond ladders work so effectively. For this discussion, the term "bond" will represent bonds or notes of any maturity.

The BYC combines several effects into a single graph to help investors determine their perspective on the risk or benefit from buying bonds immediately rather than waiting for potentially higher rates in the future. It primarily focuses on assessing interest rate risk by determining the interest rate level that would cause a bond investor to be in a less favorable position than if he had waited for higher rates. The BYC primarily focuses on the breakeven point if interest rates rise; it does not present all of the benefits of investing in bonds if interest rates decline after the bond is purchased.

Two components relate to the BYC: opportunity costs and the effect of surfing the roll. Opportunity costs are the forgone benefits that are lost by an investor who stays in a short-term cash investment rather than investing in a bond with a higher yield. Since longer-term rates are typically higher than shorter-term rates, there is a benefit to owning the longer-term bond. The effect of surfing the roll, as previously discussed, relates to the benefit of having the higher interest rate of the longer-term bond as it becomes a shorter-term bond. When the two components are combined, they provide a threshold of the level of interest rates that would have to occur for the investor to be in a worse financial position compared to staying in a short-term cash investment. As a threshold, any interest rate level below that point is favorable to the investor who purchased the bond.

For example, assume an investor has a choice of earning 1% in a money market fund or buying a $1,000 10-year bond yielding 4.25%. An investor who buys a $1,000 10-year U.S. Treasury bond would receive 4.25%, or $42.50 in interest, over the first year. If he had stayed in the money market fund, he would have earned only 1%, or $10 interest, during the year.

The extra $32.50 received is the opportunity benefit from owning the higher-yielding bond. It serves as a cushion against a possible decline in bond prices. The $32.50 of extra income means that the $1,000 bond could fall to $967.50 before the investor would start to be in a worse financial position than if he had just stayed in the 1% money market fund.

For the bond to fall to $967.50 by the end of the first year, the interest rate on 9-year bonds would have to rise to 4.7%. After a year, the 10-year bond that was purchased initially will have nine years remaining. The effect of the roll means that the higher coupon of the original 10-year bond will be valued based on the 9-year interest rate. Therefore, including the opportunity benefit of the higher yield and the effect of surfing the roll, the breakeven point for the 9-year interest rate one year later is 4.7%, reflected as the purple line in figure 11.2.

Consider another example, which involves holding the same bond for three years. The 10-year bond is purchased in 2004. After three years, in 2007, the bond will have seven years of remaining life. The key question: "What level of interest rate on 7-year bonds in 2007 will cause the 10-year, 4.25% bond purchased in 2004 to be in a worse financial position than if the money had remained in a money market fund?

To answer the question, look at the green line in figure 11.2. The green line represents the BYC for 2007. Now look at the portion of that line that corresponds to a 7-year bond—the time remaining to maturity on the 10-year bond in 2007. The value presented is 6%. So, 7-year bond yields, currently less than 4%, would have to rise to over 6% by 2007 for the originally purchased 10-year bond to be in a worse financial position than if an investor had stayed in a money market fund. Such a large increase in interest rates is certainly possible, but it may not be likely.

Figure 11.2. Breakeven Yield Curve

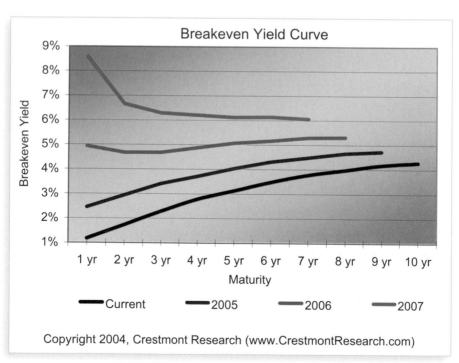

Bond Ladders

The power tool for bond investors, especially in steady or rising interest rate environments, is the bond ladder, which harvests the beneficial effects of the roll and provides substantial protection against rising interest rates, as reflected by the Breakeven Yield Curve methodology discussed previously. In addition, bond ladders are easy to use; all investors can construct them.

A bond ladder is a portfolio of bonds with a portion of the portfolio maturing each year. Often the ladder is designed so equal amounts mature each year over the life of the ladder. A ten-year ladder, for example, might have 10 percent of the bond portfolio maturing each year over the next ten years. If $120,000 were invested, $12,000 would be used to buy bonds maturing in one year; $12,000 would be used to buy bonds maturing in two years; and $12,000 would be used to buy bonds maturing in each of the next eight successive years.

As the nearest-dated bond matures, the cash is used to buy new bonds with a 10-year maturity, and in each succeeding year, new 10-year bonds are bought with the cash from maturing bonds. The simple process can be continued indefinitely. While intermediate-term bond ladders of seven to ten years are common, ladders can be tailored to the preferences of the investor. Some ladders are as short as two years, while others stretch out as long as thirty or more. In summary, bond ladders combine safety, flexibility, and ease of use to become a particularly robust tool for investors.

Remarkable Bond Ladder Track Record: Positive Returns Over a Century

The analysis in figure 11.3 presents the total return, including interest payments and price changes, for various lengths of bond ladders since 1900. Interestingly, the total returns have been positive each year over the past 100 years for seasoned bond ladders with lengths of ten years or less. Seasoned ladders are those whose next maturity started in the longest maturity position. This occurs, for example, in the seventh year for a seven-year bond ladder.

Figure 11.3 illustrates the consistently positive returns bond ladders have generated over the past 104 years. In addition, the tables

Figure 11.3. Bond Ladder Returns

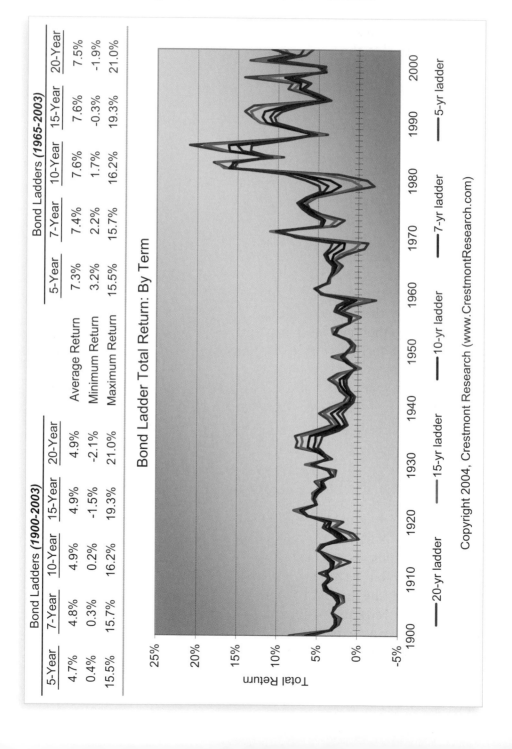

Bond Ladders (1900-2003)						Bond Ladders (1965-2003)				
5-Year	7-Year	10-Year	15-Year	20-Year		5-Year	7-Year	10-Year	15-Year	20-Year
4.7%	4.8%	4.9%	4.9%	4.9%	Average Return	7.3%	7.4%	7.6%	7.6%	7.5%
0.4%	0.3%	0.2%	-1.5%	-2.1%	Minimum Return	3.2%	2.2%	1.7%	-0.3%	-1.9%
15.5%	15.7%	16.2%	19.3%	21.0%	Maximum Return	15.5%	15.7%	16.2%	19.3%	21.0%

Bond Ladder Total Return: By Term

— 20-yr ladder   — 15-yr ladder   — 10-yr ladder   — 7-yr ladder   — 5-yr ladder

Copyright 2004, Crestmont Research (www.CrestmontResearch.com)

at the top of the figure uncover insights into the performance of bond ladders. The long-term average return of intermediate-term bond ladders — those with a maximum maturity of seven to ten years — is virtually identical to the long-term average return of much longer-term bond ladders with maximum maturities of fifteen to twenty years. Thus bond ladder investors can employ intermediate-term bond ladders and enjoy good returns without taking the risks inherent in owning the longest-term bonds.

Why Bond Ladders Work Well

Bond ladders work well for a number of reasons. Bonds mature on schedule, and investors receive their money back (as long as the bonds do not default) at a specific date, plus they receive interest payments along the way. Further, the interest received is almost always higher from longer-term bonds than for short-term money market investments. Also, bond ladders are less volatile and more stable than are longer-term bonds.

In summary, the simple discipline of the bond ladder strategy helps investors keep their money productively invested, while avoiding poor market-timing decisions and the stress of deciding what to do next. The interest payments and the roll (the dynamic in a bond that enhances its value each year until it nears maturity) have buffered bond ladder performance even during periods of rising interest rates, and provide solid returns during periods of stable or declining interest rates.

Current Trend for Interest Rates

Short-term interest rates during 2004 and 2005, as emphasized repeatedly by Alan Greenspan, are expected to trend higher. The fear of rising interest rates has paralyzed many fixed income investors; they fear a decline in the value of bonds if long-term interest rates rise as well. As a result, they stand on the sidelines holding money market funds that have been paying microscopic interest.

In chapter 4, the dichotomy between short-term interest rates (controlled by the Fed) and long-term interest rates (driven by inflation expectations) was explored. In chapter 8, the normal yield curve slope of approximately 100 basis points (1%) was presented. During the first half of 2004, the yield curve slope was well over 300 basis points and sometimes close to 400. Toward the last half of 2004, the slope began to flatten somewhat.

Going forward, even if short-term interest rates rise to 3%, as many Fed watchers and financial market spectators expect, long-term interest rates can remain unchanged and the slope of the yield curve will still be above the historical average. As the Fed emphasizes its commitment to low inflation and price stability, long-term interest rates may even decline in the face of rising short-term interest rates. Unforeseen circumstances outside the Fed's control, however, could result in rising long-term interest rates. As has always been the case — it is not a modern phenomenon — there is significant uncertainty and volatility in the financial markets.

Summary

Bond ladders are an effective technique for actively managing a portfolio of fixed income securities, including bonds. The analysis suggests that investors who invest in intermediate-term bond ladders are likely to outperform those who stay in cash or money markets, fearfully or hopefully awaiting higher rates. The strategy of buying long-dated bonds and holding them as interest rates declined was an effective "sail" strategy during the recent secular bull market in bonds. From relatively low levels of interest rates with a positively-sloped yield curve, bond ladders can be an effective "row" technique to enhance returns and hedge some of the risk of potentially rising interest rates while maintaining good potential for returns.

Rebalancing Stock Market Portfolios

Most investors have both stocks and bonds in their portfolios. Some are also familiar with the mutual funds that include both stocks and bonds and are known as "balanced funds." Which asset class, stocks or bonds, would you rather have more heavily weighted in your portfolio? Of course, you say, the one that is expected to have the greatest increase in value.

Investments in a portfolio have an interesting effect that can work to your benefit or detriment depending on the trend or choppiness of the market. Crestmont calls that effect "auto-resizing." The term refers to the fact that investments that increase in value become a greater portion of your portfolio, and investments that go down become a smaller portion of your portfolio. In other words, your winners work harder and your losers hurt you less. Both situations automatically resize within the portfolio to your benefit.

Although that effect may seem ideal, it also creates a latent risk in your portfolio—the risk that your portfolio will lose its balance and diversification. When a winner becomes a disproportionately large position, any further gains or losses have a greater impact than if the position were its original size. Although there is a benefit to having a heavily weighted position that continues to appreciate, a heavily weighted position that declines in value will have a disproportionately negative impact on your overall returns.

Likewise, an investment that has fallen and becomes a small part of the portfolio will not have much impact if it reverses and begins to climb. The concept of periodically shifting funds from over-weighted positions to under-weighted positions to restore the original or desired balance is known as rebalancing. Once rebalanced, an over-weighted position will not have a disproportionate impact on your returns.

Rebalancing

By definition, rebalancing is the active management technique that capitalizes on short-term cycles in the financial markets. Over-performance in one category or asset class is shifted to another category to benefit from the second category's later good performance, or to hedge against the first category's later poor performance. Rebalancing thus provides a disciplined and effective means of benefiting from short-term market volatility.

Suppose, for example, that you had decided to keep half your money in stocks and half in a bond ladder. If you started with $100,000, you would put $50,000 into stocks and $50,000 into the ladder. Assume that over time the stock portion grows to $95,000, while the bond ladder grows to $55,000. Although the two positions started with equal weights and equal impact on the portfolio, stocks now have significantly greater impact than the bonds. If stocks continue to perform well, the portfolio will benefit from the over-weighting in stocks. If there is a reversal and stocks do poorly, the over-weighting in stocks will cause the negative impact to be greater than it would have been had stocks and bonds been evenly weighted.

Through rebalancing the portfolio, you would reestablish your initial 50/50 balance. You would move $20,000 from the outperforming stock class to the bond ladder and be balanced again with $75,000 in each asset class. You would have locked in some gains from the outperforming stock class, and by adding those funds to the bond ladder, you would be positioned to have the original exposures to stocks and bonds, in case stocks do not perform as well or bonds do perform well. Although this simple example uses only two asset classes out of many that are possible, and the money is evenly divided between the asset classes, the principles work similarly under other scenarios and weightings due to the power of auto-resizing.

David Swensen, Chief Investment Officer with Yale University, relates in his book, *Pioneering Portfolio Management:*

> The alternative of not rebalancing to policy target causes portfolio managers to engage in a peculiar trend-following market-timing strategy. Like many other contrarian pursuits, rebalancing frequently appears foolish as momentum players reap short-term rewards from going with the flow. Regardless of potentially negative reputational consequences, serious investors maintain portfolio risk profiles through disciplined rebalancing policies, avoiding the sometimes expedient appeal of market timing strategies.

With the previous example, note that continued strong gains by stocks — as are often seen in secular bull markets — would yield greater results if the portfolio were over-weighted in stocks. Yet, in choppy, secular bear markets, rebalancing repositions the portfolio for the ups and down in the market. There is an appeal to over-weighted trend following, especially in secular bull markets, yet secular bear markets seem to present ideal conditions for disciplined rebalancing. What, then, is the overall impact of rebalancing across full market cycles that include both bull and bear markets?

Impact of Rebalancing Across Market Cycles

In strong trending markets, like secular bull markets, the best strategy is to get fully invested in stocks and remain so. Being fully invested means holding the highest stock allocation that is appropriate for a particular investor. As a result, when there are profits, which has occurred most years during secular bull markets, the over-allocation in equities compounds to your benefit. In directionally trending markets, less frequent rebalancing is more desirable, as it enables the best-performing investment (stocks, for example) to become a larger part of the portfolio.

In choppy and volatile markets, like secular bear markets, a more frequent rebalancing approach can add significant additional return to an investor's portfolio. It enables the soon-to-be-better-performing investment to be increased to a larger part of the portfolio as capital is reallocated from the investment that has begun to peak, into the investment that is expected to increase. In addition, rebalancing also harvests some profits from the currently outperforming asset classes, thereby reducing the risk of giving back profits in a subsequent decline.

Figure 11.4 illustrates the impact of less frequent rebalancing during secular bull markets, and figure 11.5 illustrates the impact of more frequent rebalancing during secular bear markets. As the figures reflect, to enhance returns optimally, one should rebalance portfolios more frequently in secular bear markets and less frequently in bull markets.

The charts also answer the question of many investors, "What should I do if I want to adopt a consistent strategy and not try to determine whether I'm in a bull or a bear market?" The answer: rebalance more frequently. As this analysis indicates, based on its assumptions, the benefits of rebalancing more often in bear markets outweigh the cost of rebalancing more often in bull markets. In addition, the overall volatility of equity swings to the portfolio can be reduced by increasing the frequency of rebalancing in the portfolio.

Figure 11.4. Rebalancing in Secular Bull Markets

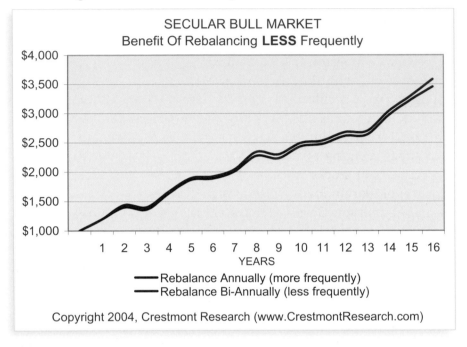

Figure 11.5. Rebalancing in Secular Bear Markets

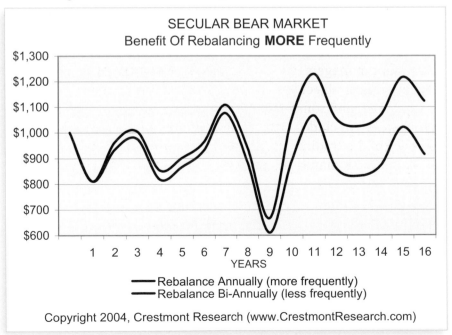

Summary

Rebalancing is an effective technique for actively managing a portfolio of equity securities in diversified portfolios. The analysis above suggests that investors who rebalance more often are likely to outperform those who do not rebalance or rebalance less often, particularly during secular bear markets. The strategy of buying stocks and holding them as price/earnings ratios (P/Es) rose was an effective "sail" strategy during the past secular bull markets in stocks. In fact, supplementing the buy-and-hold "sail" strategy with additional purchases of stocks on dips, or buying additional stock using the leverage of margin loans, further opened the sail to the wind of the rising bull market. Given a relatively high level of P/E ratios in the stock market, especially with the risk of a trend in inflation away from price stability, rebalancing can be an effective "row" technique to increase returns and position the portfolio against the risks of a potentially choppy market environment.

Early chapters focused on historical perspectives about the financial markets and identifying lessons learned from observing their cycles and trends. The journey continued through the *Financial Physics* model and other methods of explaining the underlying reasons for secular market cycles. The past few chapters have discussed strategies and techniques for investing based on the particular market environment. In the next chapter, the journey continues into the evolution of investment management and the inclusion of risk management and absolute return objectives. To provide an example, hedge funds will be explained, and some of the common myths about them dispelled. The chapter concludes with a look toward the future and the convergence of the traditional risk-based approach with the progressive, skill-based, risk-managed approach to investment management.

CHAPTER 12

INVESTMENT MANAGEMENT EVOLUTION

When the first caveman used a large stone to block the entrance to his cave each night, he was practicing investment management. While he lacked the mathematical sophistication of today's investors, he had the right idea. He was maintaining his wealth and protecting his assets from harm.

A Brief History

In about 1800 BC, King Hammurabi of Babylon established laws governing credit, collateral, and permissible interest rates. A little over a thousand years later, free trade and an active marketplace—but no stock exchange—could be found in the Greek *agora*. By the first century AD, Greek dominance had given way to both Roman ascendancy and financial high jinks. Nero not only played the fiddle, he debased the value of Roman coins and thereby created inflation.

The world's first stock exchange, though, was still more than 1,000 years in the future. It developed in the picturesque city of Bruges, Flanders, in the early 1300s. And hard on its heels, less than fifty years later, came a flourishing debt market—an active secondary market in long-term municipal debt in Florence.

By 1602, shares of the East India Company were being traded under the Amstel Bridge in Amsterdam, the same location where the

Pilgrims obtained financing for their journey to America. Within two generations, tulip mania broke out, and formerly taciturn Dutchmen exchanged entire estates for single tulip bulbs. In retrospect, they would have done well to have held on to their estates. Meanwhile, across the English Channel and roughly eighty years later, Englishmen caught the speculative fever and created the South Sea Island Bubble. Almost simultaneously, John Law and the French were enjoying the famed Mississippi Bubble. Both bubbles, of course, eventually burst, enormous wealth vanishing in the process.

According to *Smart Investing,* The Stock Exchange in London, which got its name in 1773, grew up inside the walls of an early-day Starbucks named Jonathon's Coffee House. An ad of the time by a broker named John Taylor proclaimed *"Buyeth and selleth new lottery tickets, Navy victualling bills, East India bonds, and other publick securities."*

Within only three years, in 1776, the United States announced its Declaration of Independence, and Adam Smith published *The Wealth of Nations,* a widely read volume promoting free trade. By 1790, the first stock exchange in America opened in Philadelphia. Not to be outdone by their Philadelphia brethren, New York brokers met only two years later under a buttonwood tree to establish a securities exchange, which eventually became the New York Stock Exchange. Competing with the buttonwood tree brokers were a group known as the Curbstone Brokers, who, remarkably, conducted their business outdoors, regardless of the weather, for over a hundred years. They moved indoors only after World War I, eventually taking the name The American Stock Exchange.

But major developments had occurred while the Curbstone Brokers were standing in the rain. The telegraph, invented in 1844, transformed stock market activity by providing information at the speed of electricity across vast distances. Likewise, the first ticker tape made its appearance in 1863, and by 1896, the first Dow Jones Industrial Average was born, the child of publisher Charles H. Dow. By then, over 150 companies were traded on the New York Stock Exchange, the very first having been the Bank of New York. In 1913, two other major developments affecting the financial markets were established: the Federal Reserve Bank and the personal income tax.

In the meantime, bull markets came and went, a notable one quadrupling the market between 1925 and 1929. The crash of 1929 followed, eventually taking the Dow down by nearly 90 percent. While some rules were written to reduce market manipulation following the crash and the subsequent period of depression, the playing field remained far from level for many years, with insider trading being outlawed only as late as 1961. By then, however, several disciplined forms of investing, including value investing, were already giving ordinary investors a better chance at success.

Value Investing

Early investors bought stocks they liked without too much regard for the composition of the overall portfolio. Bonds, for their part, were purchased to provide portfolio stability and income. Investor sophistication was limited at best.

According to the Heilbrunn Center for Graham & Dodd at Columbia Business School in New York:

> In the early 20th century, investors were guided mostly by speculation and insider information. Graham believed, however, that the true value of a stock could be determined through research. He worked with Dodd to develop value investing—a methodology to identify and buy securities priced well below their true value. Graham and Dodd's security analysis principles provided the first rational basis for investment decisions.

Benjamin Graham and David Dodd were finance professors at the Columbia Business School in the 1920s. As a result of their work, investors began to see stocks as an instrument for participating in the future earnings of companies. Investors thus needed to assess the business prospects of these enterprises to develop a fair value for the stock.

Graham and Dodd provided a means of mathematically analyzing whether stocks were undervalued. They focused, as might be expected, on rigorous analysis of fundamental corporate data. While some of the techniques of analysis they advocated were new, or at least not widely known, the principles they espoused extended far back in time, having been colorfully enunciated in an earlier era by Baron Rothschild when he reportedly said, "Buy when the cannons are firing and sell when the clarions of victory sound."

Until the second half of the twentieth century, the financial markets, including both stock and bond markets, were relatively unsophisticated and inefficient. Even today, some would say that the markets remain inefficient and full of opportunities! As discussed in chapter 4, before the 1960s, interest rates were relatively disconnected from inflation—a relationship that changed several decades ago and is now recognized as a relationship fundamental to the financial markets. Bond market investors received a relatively similar rate of interest for many decades, despite the fact that inflation was quite volatile. As a result, bond investors at times were grossly under-compensated for inflation and at other times received excessive real rates of return.

During the 1950s and 1960s, investment management further evolved with groundbreaking research by such Nobel laureates as Harry Markowitz, Eugene Fama, and William Sharpe. Their investment theories—Modern Portfolio Theory, Efficient Markets Hypothesis, and the Capital Asset Pricing Model—advanced investment management and introduced a sophisticated concept of risk to the field. As a result, investors were taught how to use the available tools and information to construct investment portfolios that provided more efficient returns based on the associated risk profile.

Following the introduction of Modern Portfolio Theory in 1952, institutional investors began thinking of stocks as an asset class that should be owned as a category within the overall portfolio. Ownership of a widely diversified group of stocks then enabled the investor to participate in the long-term growth of the economy. And combining a belief in the desirability of asset class ownership with a long time horizon set the stage for the growth of the relative return approach to investing.

In the 1950s, most households held their direct stock market investments in individual accounts. Even into the 1970s, with fewer than 300 mutual funds available, investors continued to be active managers who selected securities within their portfolios. Investors and their advisors were stock hunters who had to do their work directly through stock selection rather than indirectly through mutual funds.

Parsing Risk

The next step for investment management evolution related to the growth in pooling securities, including the growth in mutual funds. These funds provided liquidity and elements of risk management. Pools of similar assets were created to allow more investors greater diversification in their holdings, and, as a result, to reduce individual security risk. And since the pools were tradable, investors had the efficiency of liquidity. In the fixed income sector, the first mortgage-backed security was issued in the 1970s. By 1980, there were approximately 500 mutual funds for both stocks and bonds.

Investors ascended to a more advanced level of investment management. They began to orchestrate the process by hiring the hunters—the investment managers in the mutual funds, who were charged with managing the portfolio. Further, investors could hire and fire these managers at will by buying or selling their holdings and replacing them with other funds. Armed with these tools and their new role, investors began to demand more specialized pools of stocks and bonds; thus the number of mutual funds exploded. Today there are more than 10,000 mutual funds available across a wide range of asset subclasses.

During the 1980s and 1990s, the combination of improved technology and a bull market facilitated another group of investors—the day traders. Previously, day trading was an activity primarily available to larger institutions and investment partnerships. Online trading and low commission costs enabled small investors to participate. The additional participation increased the volume and liquidity of the markets. More investors and investment organizations were becoming increasingly sophisticated.

Over time, individual investors began to take a more sophisticated role as asset allocators or active market traders. The more specialized mutual funds enabled investors to segment the market in structuring their portfolios. As a result, many investors began subdividing their portfolios among large-cap, small-cap, value, growth, and international stocks, as well as among other sectors and styles.

Meanwhile, the seemingly unending bull market encouraged almost all investors to believe that their allocation strategies were solid and sufficient. As the rising tide carried all boats higher, many brokers, clients, advisors, and pundits forgot the sign on a veteran trader's wall: DON'T CONFUSE BRAINS WITH A BULL MARKET. But as long as profits rolled in, most investors did not question their strategies.

Yet, while bull market complacency and contentment ruled the day in much of the relative return investment world, striking developments were revolutionizing the realm of absolute return investments. Extraordinary tools for risk management and control were being developed. Investment sophistication was evolving rapidly and becoming available to a wider range of investors.

During the 1980s and 1990s, additional tools were developed to parse risk. In 1986, mortgage strips were introduced. In mortgage strips, the cash flows from mortgage-backed securities are separated into securities that represent either the principal payments or the interest payments. These individual securities allowed investors to accept or hedge specific risks. Also in the 1980s, standardized swap contracts were introduced that allowed a new market to evolve for exchanging risks. Swap contracts let people hedge risks by exchanging an undesirable risk for a desirable risk. For example, corporate treasurers can use swaps to hedge interest rate risk by exchanging a short-term interest rate for a long-term rate. Certain investors use swaps to hedge credit risk on investment positions. In addition, both strips and swaps can be used as speculative investments by traders who want to take a position on the outcome of a risk.

Strips and swaps are only two of the many derivative securities that have become widespread during the past two decades. In addition, there are Exchange Traded Funds (ETFs), Treasury Inflation Protected Securities (TIPS), and Collateralized Debt Obligations (CDOs), to name a few.

The purpose of introducing the concept of derivatives is to highlight the significant changes in the financial markets and investing that have occurred over the past two decades—and certainly since the formulation of the traditional investment theories almost five decades ago. Recognizing the dramatic changes that have occurred up to now emphasizes an accelerating trend that is propelling the sophistication of investment management and risk management. Since derivatives are less familiar than stocks and bonds to many investors, advisors, and writers, they are often misunderstood. Used properly, however, derivatives become powerful tools for sophisticated investors to limit risk or enhance their participation in a range of markets.

Derivatives

Derivatives are securities or contracts that are *derived* from other securities or relationships. As a result, they can represent one or more of the risk elements associated with a security or situation. Thus derivatives are sometimes believed to be risky. They should not, however, be considered inherently risky; rather their risk should be carefully evaluated as a function of their use. For example, the swap contract used by a corporate treasurer to hedge a loan with a variable interest rate actually reduces the interest rate risk to his company. Yet, the same swap contract would be a risky speculation to someone who did not have a debt to hedge. For the speculator, if interest rates changed adversely, the swap could become very unprofitable. Likewise, a change in the right direction would create great profits. Nonetheless, for the corporate treasurer, the swap hedged the company's debt and made certain the rate of interest that it would have to pay. So, for the corporation that uses the derivative as a hedge, the derivative *reduces* risk.

Summary

Early investment management was largely speculative, and the financial markets were not sophisticated. Eventually, pioneer researchers helped bring rational approaches to security valuation and portfolio construction. The early investors were hands-on managers of their portfolios. Later, academic research provided the insights and technology to address the elements of risk and risk management through diversification. Ultimately, a significant growth in mutual funds enabled investors to evolve into portfolio managers, who could hire numerous underlying specialists to perform securities selection. More recently, the emergence over the past two decades of readily available risk management tools and the expanding awareness of risk is driving further evolution for investment management.

Hedge Fund Investing

A significant development over the past twenty years has been the proliferation of private investment partnerships known as hedge funds. Some question whether the evolution of an investor into a hedge fund manager requires the development of a larger or a smaller brain. Certainly, the stress of the job seems to add a little furrow to the brow.

In reality, many hedge fund managers are among the best and brightest in the investment field. Their objective of absolute return investing requires techniques of ambidextrous investment management. As a result, hedge fund managers are required to have the tools of returns in one hand and the instruments of risk control in the other.

To understand hedge funds clearly, it may be helpful to first demystify hedge fund investing, and then develop an understanding of the approaches hedge fund managers use. As a result, you will be able to identify or implement progressive investment strategies for today's more challenging environment. Further, many of the elements that are included in the structure and investment management of hedge funds will be more commonly used in the future as the convergence continues between the traditional and progressive approaches to investment management.

Hedge Funds Defined

Hedge funds are private pools of capital that use a wide range of unique approaches and sophisticated investment strategies to seek positive returns regardless of the general direction of the financial markets. They are essentially businesses that use financial securities as their inventory to generate profits from inefficiencies in the markets, mispriced securities, better information, or prudent risk management. Although there are certain similarities among many hedge funds, they can have a wide range of differences in structural terms, investment strategy, and risk profile. For this overview of hedge funds, the discussion will relate to typical elements found in hedge funds.

One of the first questions that many people ask is, "Why are they called hedge funds; what do they hedge?" The first hedge fund is attributed to Alfred W. Jones in 1952. He referred to his fund as a "hedged fund" since he included stocks that were purchased (the "longs") with stocks that were sold short (the "shorts"). The combination of longs and shorts in the portfolio was intended to hedge the portfolio from some of the volatility of stock market swings. When his strategy was reported in the press, the term was shortened to "hedge fund."

Today hedge funds use many strategies, well beyond the original equity long/short approach that combines long and short stock positions in the portfolio to manage risk and generate returns. Yet, virtually all hedge funds share those two objectives in common. The first is hedging or managing risk, with risk defined as being the possibility of a loss; the second is maintaining an absolute return goal, one that seeks profits each year regardless of the general direction of the markets.

Hedge funds use investment strategies that wealthy families and brokerage firms have employed for many years. When a brokerage firm has an internal unit that trades the firm's own proprietary capital, that unit is known as a proprietary trading desk, or "prop desk." Examples of some strategies used by hedge funds are convertible bond arbitrage, merger arbitrage, fixed income arbitrage, pairs trading, statistical arbitrage, equity long/short, distressed securities trading, and many other styles or variations on these styles. It is beyond the scope of this overview to explain each style; the introduction of the style descriptions is intended to reveal the breadth of hedge fund investing.

During the last decade or two, there has been a rapid rise in the number of individual hedge fund partnerships using these approaches, as both investors and investment managers have begun to seek profits from the markets using absolute return strategies. This change has also been facilitated by technological advances that have allowed small partnerships a platform for executing sophisticated strategies, as well as by the further development of derivatives as risk management tools.

Importantly, hedge fund investing reflects an investment style, approach, and a philosophy of absolute return investing. Hedge funds are not an asset class that move in unison. Rather, hedge funds seek returns from their activity in the markets based on the skills of the manager. And the skills employed, as well as the actions taken, drive both return and risk management as the hedge fund seeks to generate active returns regardless of the market's overall direction.

Artistry of Design

Beyond the similarities in the approach of hedge funds, there are similarities in their structural terms. The terms are based on rational principles of aligning the interests of the investor and the hedge fund manager. There is an artistry of design to the typical hedge fund structure.

To help illustrate some of the elements of hedge fund design, take a clean sheet of paper. If your objective is to consistently increase your wealth, how would you structure the relationship with a manager who will manage your money? As with most businesses, the objective is to align the interests of the shareholders and the employees toward a common goal.

First, you would probably want the manager to have a businesslike goal of making money, not just participating in asset class trends. So, philosophically, you would start with an absolute return approach. Secondly, people are generally driven by incentives, whether in the form of bonuses or profit sharing. In this case, you would want the structure to include bonuses based on performance—through participation in the profitability.

Further, you would want to structure the investment management to include risk controls. Often, the best way to protect your own capital is to make sure that the manager invests his own capital side by side with you. To further control risk, you might structure the fund so you can withdraw your capital if you sense that the fund will not be profitable.

The design of most hedge funds reflects the elements outlined in the clean-sheet exercise. Many hedge funds are absolute return focused, the compensation structure emphasizes performance, and most hedge fund managers have a significant amount of their own personal net worth in their funds. Figure 12.1, Artistry of Design, sums up the key ingredients of hedge fund design.

Two elements of hedge fund design that have not been discussed so far are liquidity frequency and tax efficiency. Liquidity provisions provide investors an ability to withdraw all or part of their capital upon advance notice to the hedge fund. Most hedge funds are designed with at least quarterly liquidity, though some are structured with monthly, semiannual, or annual provisions. In fact, hedge funds are one of the few alternative investments that provide relatively frequent liquidity. Real estate, energy, and private equity funds typically provide little, if any, opportunity for investors to withdraw their capital on relatively short notice.

Figure 12.1. Hedge Fund Structure: Artistry of Design

RETURNS	**Orientation Toward Absolute Returns**
INCENTIVES	**Fees Based Upon Performance**
RISK CONTROLS	**Significant Investment By Manager; Business Closure If Significant Drawdown**
CONSISTENCY	**Monthly Focus On Returns & Risk Control**
LIQUIDITY	**Reasonable Liquidity**
TAX EFFICIENT	**Pass-Through Taxation**

Regarding taxes, hedge funds offer tax efficiency by providing pass-through taxation. In contrast, stock market investments are subject to double taxation. Stocks are investments in corporations that pay taxes on their profits before the profits are distributed. Those profits are again subject to taxes when dividends are distributed or when capital gains are realized. Hedge funds, however, are companies that generally are structured as partnerships. As a result, their gains are not taxed before being distributed to the investors.

This design is in contrast to the traditional approach. Mutual funds, for example, have a relative return approach, in which the returns are dependent on the market, have fees based on assets with no incentive for profitability, measure risk against benchmarks, and generally have a modest investment (if any) by the portfolio manager. On the favorable side, they provide greater liquidity than hedge funds and share the same characteristic of pass-through taxation.

Hedge Funds: Common Elements

Figure 12.2, Hedge Funds: Common Elements, summarizes typical features and terms for many hedge funds. The terms of hedge funds in the United States are affected by securities laws. Despite the general perception to the contrary, hedge funds must follow all regulations and laws relating to the trading of securities by the funds and the offering of securities to potential investors in hedge funds. Hedge funds are subject to the same laws of securities trading and ownership as other investments. They do, however, rely on certain exemptions to registration that avoid the limitations and disclosures required for securities that are readily traded in the markets. Registration is the process by which securities become eligible to be readily sold and traded.

Under the permitted exemption from registration, a provision that private businesses commonly use to raise capital for formation or growth, hedge funds are limited in the number and qualifications of investors that they can accept. Generally, private placements of unregistered securities are limited to one hundred investors. In addition, the investors generally must meet a standard of sophistication. That standard, relating to what is known as "accredited investor status," currently requires that investors have a minimum net worth of $1 million or $200,000 of annual income. The financial requirements—imposed by law—are the reasons that hedge funds are reported to be investment funds for the wealthy.

The limitation on the number of investors also impacts the minimum investment thresholds that most hedge funds impose. Since hedge funds are generally limited to one hundred investors, they must set a minimum size to enable the fund to be large enough to keep costs and fees at a reasonable level. Therefore, the typical hedge fund has an investment minimum of $500,000 to $1 million. There are further exceptions that allow hedge funds to increase the number of permitted investors, though they require that investors be super-accredited and meet a much higher net-worth standard.

Figure 12.2. Hedge Funds: Common Elements

MINIMUM INVESTMENT	**$500,000 - $1,000,000**
ADDITIONS/WITHDRAWALS	**Quarterly; 30-60 Days Notice**
LOCKUP	**One Year**
FEES	**1%-2% Management; 20% Of Profits**
HIGH-WATER MARK	**Fees Paid On Gains Only Once**
ACCREDITED INVESTORS	**$1 Million Net Worth or $200,000 Annual Income**
MASTER/FEEDER	**Aggregates Funds From Domestic And Tax-Exempt Or Foreign Investors**

For tax and accounting reasons, hedge funds generally accept new investments and permit withdrawals at month's end, generally on a quarterly schedule. Initial investments, though, are typically required to remain for one year. This is known as the lock-up period.

Typically, the fees are structured to provide a management fee of 1%–2% of assets and a performance incentive of 20 percent (one-fifth) of the net cumulative profits. In addition, the compensation agreement typically contains a high-water mark provision, which means that performance incentives are paid on gains only once. For example, if your investment of $1 million grows to $1.2 million over the first year, the hedge fund receives a $40,000 performance incentive (20% of the $200,000 profit). In the next year, assume your balance falls to $1.1 million. Even if the market is down that year, there is no performance incentive, since the incentives are based only on actual gains. The hedge fund will not receive another performance incentive until your balance exceeds the previous high value (i.e., the high-water mark).

Those outside the industry often criticize hedge fund compensation. The critics may not understand that the typical hedge fund averages approximately $35 million under management. That provides the hedge fund manager $350,000 to pay rents, salaries, accounting, overhead, regulatory costs, travel, and other operating expenses. As a result, hedge fund managers are highly dependent on the performance incentive. And that incentive can be significant if the fund is successful. For example, an average-size hedge fund that returns 15% before incentives would generate profits of almost $5.3 million for its investors. Therefore, the fund manager and team will receive an incentive of over $1 million. The investor, for his part, will have realized a return of 12% net of all fees and expenses. Keep in mind, however, that the investor only pays the incentive if there is investment success.

Few other professions are willing to include such a performance requirement on compensation. Some law firms will take the risk of not being paid unless they win certain lawsuits, known as contingency-fee cases, but they typically charge 33 percent or more of recoveries. Surgeons and doctors are certainly not willing to risk 75 percent of their fees on your successful recovery. In the previous example, the performance incentive represented 75 percent of the compensation to the hedge fund. Further, almost everyone has paid a repairman for working on a problem that ultimately could not be fixed or required further attention — which is pay for effort rather than for successful performance. These comments will hit closest to home for many salespeople; you, and others in similar positions, appreciate what it means to say "You only get to eat from what you reap."

In a similar vein, there is another saying in the hedge fund industry. It relates to the fact that most hedge fund managers have substantial investments in their own funds — a fact that aligns the interests of the manager directly with the interests of the investors and drives much of the decision making. In the industry, it is called "eating your own cooking."

Hedge Funds as Businesses

Hedge funds are businesses that use financial securities as their inventory to generate profits from the mispricings or inefficiencies in the financial markets. This concept can be emphasized with a story that contrasts the cotton brokerage business and hedge fund investing.

The story relates to one the largest cotton brokers in the United States. The company was a distributor, whose business was to buy cotton from farmers and suppliers and to sell it to numerous mills and other users. They used a variety of methods to hedge their inventory to ensure that they did not take excessive risk that cotton prices might change from the time of purchase to the time of sale. With some suppliers or customers, they would agree to a set price well in advance. To hedge one of the greatest risks to price — weather, which can affect both the supply and the price of cotton — they would use weather hedges. Since the company wanted to be profitable regardless of the direction of cotton prices, they used a variety of risk-control methods.

The company is a good, stable business with solid management and a strong niche in its industry. Although it did not make money every month, it was generally very profitable from year to year. Management certainly started every year expecting to make money; the company's business objective was to be profitable.

The purpose of the story is to relate a key concept. Had the words "stock" or "bond" been substituted for the word "cotton" in this story, you may have perceived a company that is widely recognized as a successful business to be a speculative activity.

Hedge funds buy and sell financial securities, believing that there will be a profitable spread between the underpriced assets that are bought and the overpriced assets that are sold. They receive a profit for having the skill to have better information, insight, risk management, or access to finding securities that are expected to generate relatively near-term profits. Some hedge funds have very short-term holding periods, while others hold the positions for years. As with the cotton brokerage company, they share the mandate to seek profits each year from their activity, rather than from the direction of the market.

In sharp contrast to the activity-based profits of hedge funds, relative return investing applies a passive approach to investing, in which eventual profitability is predicated on the hope of gains over the long term. For stocks, the gains are anticipated to come from participating in the long-term growth of the economy. For bonds, returns come from lending money and receiving interest payments and a return of principal at maturity. Such asset class investing is the opposite of hedge fund investing, where managers hedge the undesirable swings of the market and concentrate their skills on selecting profitable positions.

Lastly, it may have previously seemed surprising to hear that many hedge fund managers have a majority of their net worth committed to their funds. Yet, their actions are in line with many entrepreneurs and business owners who have nearly all of their net worth committed to their companies. Hedge fund managers are entrepreneurs whose personal success often depends on the success of their enterprise.

Advantages of a Diversified Portfolio of Hedge Funds

Despite the fact that hedge funds function as businesses that seek to manage risk in the pursuit of returns, they have a variety of individual risks. In traditional asset management, diversification can work to mitigate certain risks while maintaining others. In the hedge fund industry, a portfolio of hedge funds can provide desirable diversification.

In fact, a diversified portfolio of hedge funds offers a range of significant advantages to investors. First, diversification reduces the risks associated with individual hedge funds. If one fund loses its edge or has an unsuccessful year, positive performance from other funds in the portfolio can help make the year successful, in the aggregate, for the investor. Secondly, investing in a well-selected portfolio of hedge funds reduces the overall variability of returns. If the funds are generally uncorrelated, with returns that do not follow the returns of other funds in the portfolio, some funds will zig while other zag. The effect will be a smoother return pattern. Finally, the diversified-portfolio approach to investing in hedge funds increases the portfolio's reward-to-risk relationship.

Hedge funds can be used as a core strategy for investors, or can supplement a traditional portfolio. When used in a more traditional portfolio, they provide a component that is not correlated with traditional asset classes such as stocks and bonds. The lack of correlation can lower the portfolio's overall volatility and increase the returns.

As a result of these advantages, a diversified portfolio of hedge funds can offer the potential for returns that are comparable to traditional asset classes but with greater consistency of returns. Historical returns have been similar to or greater than the returns from equities over the long term, but with less of the roller-coaster ride that equities have faced along the way. In addition, a diversified hedge fund portfolio can be a reasonable complement to bonds in environments of low bond yields, or when rising interest rates pose a principal risk to bonds.

Figure 12.3, Portfolio of Hedge Funds, illustrates the strength and consistency that can be achieved by combining a diversified group of hedge funds into a portfolio. Each mark represents the return from a fund in the portfolio for a given month. The black dashed mark, connected by a line, represents the return for the total portfolio. Note the variability among the portfolio's individual components, yet the consistency of the total composite. Conceptually, the portfolio can be viewed as a diversified group of independently robust absolute return strategies, rather than as a traditional combination of stocks or asset classes. The process of combining uncorrelated absolute return strategies provides the benefit of lowering the variability of returns without necessarily compromising the ultimate total return.

Hedge Fund Caveat

The label "hedge fund" carries little meaning; the term refers to a broad range of investment pools. As always, it is the reality that matters—the reality of the strategies, the risk management tools, the management skills, and the goals of a particular fund. Investors who are not prepared to assess the detailed elements of hedge funds accurately and diligently should seek competent assistance before investing in them. This chapter focuses on the broader category of hedge funds that operate as risk-averse businesses, rather than on the more speculative, intuitive style of funds. Be aware that funds labeled as hedge funds may not actually represent disciplined businesses. A careful review of how the manager implements each concept discussed in this section can serve as a key part of due diligence.

Figure 12.3. Portfolio of Hedge Funds

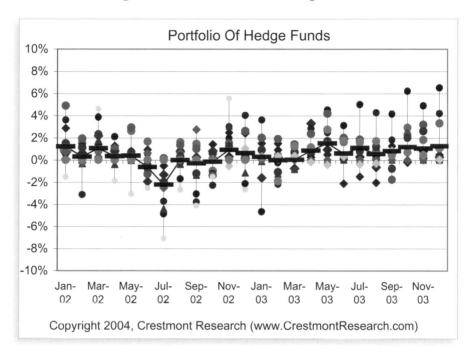

Copyright 2004, Crestmont Research (www.CrestmontResearch.com)

Vision of Future Investment Management

The traditional approach to investing can be characterized as asset class oriented and relative return directed. It approaches risk management through diversification and disclosure, but it remains vulnerable to the market's direction within each asset class. The traditional approach relies heavily on a very long-term perspective and remains invested through the cycles that often deliver returns or losses in spurts. Keep in mind that the lengths of these cycles have often exceeded the relevant time frames for many individual investors.

The progressive approach to investing can be characterized as skill based and absolute return directed. Active risk management is integral to the approach. In addition, the objective is to achieve long-term return through consistent short-term profitability, rather than through waiting for profits to emerge from the long-term averages of generally rising cycles. Unfortunately, at least at this point, access to many of the complex techniques is restricted by law to sophisticated and accredited investors.

Convergence of Traditional and Evolving Approaches

Moving forward, as the investment industry evolves in sophistication, it will begin to develop further tools and techniques of risk management that will become available to all investors. As a result, absolute return investing will be accepted and practiced by a much wider range of investors. The expected secular bear market will accelerate this evolution in the same way that the secular bull market encouraged the rise of the mutual fund industry and relative return investing.

Peter L. Bernstein, author of the bestseller *Against The Gods: The Remarkable Story Of Risk,* reinforced this convergence when he wrote:

> The notion of uncorrelated returns—especially, absolute return— has a compelling attraction. If adding short selling to the arsenal of portfolio management tools can improve the optimization process, then investors will move in that direction.

The end result will not open the existing hedge fund structure to all investors, or mutate mutual funds into hedge funds. Rather, it will create a new type of investment vehicle with many of the benefits of both, particularly an absolute return and risk management orientation.

Business consultants often say, "If you can measure it, you can manage it." As risk measures are adopted as a component of total performance, investment professionals will be seeking the tools and investment funds that enhance the return and risk relationship. For mutual funds, performance is currently based on one-, three-, and five-year returns. For hedge funds, performance is based not only on returns, but also on the consistency of returns and the magnitude of any monthly losses. As risk measures are further integrated into traditional investment management, the number of mutual funds with an absolute return approach will increase. Further, the addition of risk measures will refine the ways in which mutual funds are categorized. The industry can expect that funds will increasingly be evaluated and categorized with a focus on evaluating measures of risk in addition to the history of returns.

Increased Investor Sophistication

During this evolutionary phase of investment sophistication, investors will look for external risk management tools or for funds that internally employ risk management techniques. This focus, on both return and risk, will drive investors to adopt an absolute return philosophy and strategy for their investments. Today, twenty years after mutual funds began to proliferate, it is hard to imagine life without mutual funds — and traditional investing is now synonymous with the relative return approach. Twenty years from now, it will be hard to imagine life without risk-managed investments — and traditional investing will become synonymous with absolute return investing.

Closing the Loop

The journey started by loading your backpack with relevant concepts and principles. Throughout the book, a number of critical findings about the financial markets and investing were explored. First, the financial markets are much more volatile than most investors realize, and volatility can be your friend or your foe. Secondly, market-based returns are substantially determined by the trend in inflation; the inflation trend drives extended secular periods of rewarding bull, and disappointing bear, conditions. Thirdly, the level of valuation in the financial markets significantly affects the potential for future returns. Lastly, the investment approach for secular bull markets is drastically different from the philosophy needed for secular bear periods.

The journey continued through a discussion of two concepts of investing, the traditional relative return approach and the progressive absolute return approach. Both are solid approaches to investing, and perform quite differently depending on the financial market environment. In secular bull markets, when the trends are largely upward, the traditional relative return approach best captures the trends. In secular bear markets, when conditions are choppy and relatively unproductive, the progressive absolute return approach generally outperforms. When an investor is uncertain, a combination of the two within a diversified portfolio can provide a balance of risk and return profiles.

Ten Key Concepts

The journey is nearly over. It has provided ten key concepts, which dispel myths from conventional wisdom, provide insights about the financial markets, explain the factors that drive stock market returns, highlight current conditions and their implications for below-average returns in stocks and bonds for many years, and present ideas for investment strategy and techniques during the current secular bear market.

The list includes ten key concepts:

1. Valuation matters. Over periods of decades, the average rarely happens; above-average returns occur when P/E ratios start low and rise, and below-average returns occur when P/E ratios start high and decline.

2. The financial markets are much more volatile than most investors realize! Volatility matters. Two gremlins can devastate the returns that are actually realized: negative numbers and the dispersion of returns.

3. The stock market experiences extended periods of secular bull markets and secular bear markets based on the trend in P/E ratios, which is driven by the trend in inflation.

4. The Y-Curve Effect reflects the strong relationship between P/E ratios and inflation or deflation.

5. The current financial conditions indicate either low or negative returns from stocks and bonds.

6. Crestmont's *Financial Physics* model aligns the interconnected relationships between the economy and the financial markets that determine the stock market's overall direction.

7. P/E ratios for the market have a sustainable peak or limit in the range of 20–25 when inflation is near price stability—very close to where P/Es were in 2004.

8. The progressive strategies of absolute return investing rely on skill for seeking consistent returns, and the traditional strategies of relative return investing rely on taking a long-term view of market risk for return.

9. During secular bull markets, the investment strategy of "sailing" by buying and holding stocks and bonds can be very effective; during secular bear markets, the investment strategy of "rowing" with absolute return strategies can be very effective.

10. Evolution in the financial markets and investment management is expanding the concept of risk management from use in absolute return strategies to use in traditional portfolio management.

Fork in the Road

The concepts and information throughout this book are intended to help you better understand the wide range of information and advice that you constantly receive. As a result, you should feel a heightened confidence about making rational investment decisions. It is now time to return to the fork in the road first presented in chapter 1. As you approach the fork with the objective of finding your way to the land of truth, you can see the stumpy old troll squatting before you. The troll has acknowledged that he is either from the land of truth or from the land of lies, but you do not know his home village.

You ponder that everyone from the land of truth always tells the truth, and everyone from the land of lies always tells a lie. Since you can ask only one question to know with certainty which way to go, your question has to be absolutely revealing. You ponder the critical issue—what one question can you ask that will clearly reveal which trail to take, if you seek the land of truth. At that moment, *the* question becomes clear: "Which trail leads to your village"?

NOTES

DATA SOURCES AND METHODOLOGIES

Most of the charts and analyses referenced in this book are based on work developed by Crestmont Research, an initiative established by the author in 2001. The mission of Crestmont Research is to provide provocative research on the financial markets to assist investors in their investment planning and execution.

The data employed in Crestmont's research was procured or derived from various sources. For an index of the stock market and related information (earnings per share, price/earnings ratio, etc.), two series of data have been used. The first is the Dow Jones Industrial Average closing prices available from Dow Jones & Company. The second is the S&P 500 Index data series available from Professor Robert Shiller at http://aida.econ.yale.edu/~shiller/. The Shiller series has at least one hundred years of history, has been reviewed extensively, and is generally recognized as valid and credible. The data is based on a methodology less subject to single-point distortions; it represents the average daily price for each month or year. Many analyses use a single period of time (e.g., the close on December 31), which can deliver distorted results by having a price that may not be representative of the price levels in the market during that year. The average daily price is a more consistent means to measure price levels of the year. For a more extensive discussion, please refer to Professor Shiller's website.

The values for earnings per share for the S&P 500 Index were also determined from Professor Shiller's website. The methodology and assumptions are further explained in his books *Market Volatility* and *Irrational Exuberance*. The price/earnings ratio is developed using the current index, generally the daily average price, divided by the trailing ten-year average of the inflation-adjusted, or real, earnings per share. As Professor Shiller explains, this reduces the distortions that can occur during periods when earnings reports are temporarily distorted due to unique corporate or economic events.

Some have noted that the methodology Professor Shiller used for the price/earnings ratio (P/E) understates the ratio as a result of the approach he uses for determining earnings per share (EPS). This results from averaging ten years of historical EPS. It is important to note that he adjusts the EPS to current dollars to reduce the impact of inflation. As a result, the average EPS represents a slightly lagged value in real (i.e., current period) terms. Since the long-term real growth in earnings has averaged less than 3%, the impact of the adjustment is slight. Therefore, this does represent a reasonable approach to adjust for the distortions and variability of EPS due to the business cycle and other periodic factors. For historical analyses, if this methodology is used consistently, Professor Shiller's approach provides a valid and consistent measure for stock market analysis.

When assessing the current P/E value or a value in the future in relation to Professor Shiller's historical data, it is necessary to use an estimate for EPS that is consistent with his methodology to remain comparable. Keep in mind that a P/E ratio based on a currently reported EPS value will be understated when compared to Shiller's historical series. The effect over time will average somewhat over 10% (e.g., 2 multiple points, or $18\times$ versus $20\times$). If a current assessment of the P/E level is based on EPS using the Shiller methodology, then the P/E can be rationally compared to the historical series. Analyses that include future projections can be developed by extrapolating the averaged EPS value into the future at the estimated real growth rate for earnings.

Alternatively, for future estimates and analyses involving EPS, Crestmont Research employs the methodology presented in chapter 7 during the discussion of *Financial Physics*. Future EPS is developed

based on the historical relationship between EPS and GDP and projections of future GDP and inflation. This approach provides a value that adjusts for the variability of EPS around the general growth
trendline of the economy, and provides a value for each year that is
comparable to current and future values of EPS and P/E. Figure N.1
presents a graph of the historical EPS and P/E values as actually reported, as provided by Professor Shiller's methodology and as developed by Crestmont Research. The graphs reflect a strong relationship
between actual history and the Shiller and Crestmont Research series. Further, the Shiller and Crestmont Research series reduce the
actual historical distortions that occur from year to year.

Figure N.1. Historical EPS and P/E

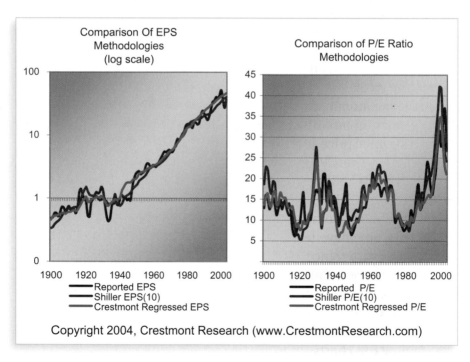

Copyright 2004, Crestmont Research (www.CrestmontResearch.com)

The economic and market data also includes measures of the economy and interest rates. Gross Domestic Product (GDP) is the chosen
measure of overall economic output. There are two series for GDP:
one that includes the effects of inflation, Nominal GDP (GDP-N), and

one that is reduced by inflation, Real GDP (GDP-R). Data subsequent to 1929 was obtained from the Bureau of Economic Analysis. For the series prior to 1929, the data was developed by Balke and Gordon (1989) and presented in the *Journal of Political Economy.*

For interest rates, Crestmont's series was developed based on data in *A History of Interest Rates,* Third Edition, by Sidney Homer and Richard Sylla, to reflect the U.S. Treasury equivalent note with a constant ten-year maturity for periods from 1900–1989. Subsequent data was obtained from the Federal Reserve Bank and other sources.

For the analysis known as "The 6/50 Rule," reflecting interest rate changes over six-month periods, the yield curve was constructed using data available from the H.15 report published by the Federal Reserve. The maturities range from three months to thirty years. The interest rate represents the rate on Friday of each week. The change in interest rates represents either the maximum increase or decrease from the base week across the subsequent six months; five basis points are added to the range to reflect estimated variations during the week.

Another economic variable that is assessed and discussed throughout the book is inflation. Two measures with long-term series are used: consumer price index (CPI) and gross domestic product inflation (GDP-I). The CPI is an index of price changes for a basket of consumer items and the GDP-I is the difference between nominal economic growth (GDP-N) and real economic growth (GDP-R). Although the two measures do not track each other precisely, the changes and trends over time have been relatively consistent. Figure N.2 presents the two measures since 1900. The relative consistency between the two measures of inflation, especially since they are derived differently, provides each of them a degree of validity as reasonable measures of inflation over time.

Some people have said, "Statistics don't lie, but statisticians do." The goal of the charts, graphs, and interpretations included in this book is to organize financial market data into a straightforward, objective, and balanced series of analyses. Although any analysis can be misused out of context, the information throughout this book was developed with rational reasoning and objective standards. Despite the best of intentions, judgment calls and subjective assessments based on professional experience are sometimes required. Please note that a number of the charts and graphs are presented more than once to assist the reader as relevant subjects are addressed.

Figure N.2. Two Measures of Inflation

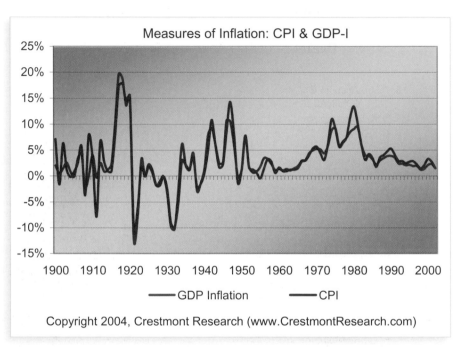

Copyright 2004, Crestmont Research (www.CrestmontResearch.com)

Additional Concepts

Nominal and Log Scale

Crestmont seeks to present charts and graphs that provide a reasonable perspective about their subject. This can be a challenge for long-term series or for series that have high growth rates. For example, consider a graph of your account growing at 10% over 48 years. In figure N.3, the value of your account for each year is represented by a bar. As the balance compounds each year, with gains building on prior gains, the actual dollar amount by which your account increases becomes greater each year. In the first year, $10,000 increasing by

10% adds $1,000 to become $11,000. In the second year, 10% growth represents $1,100. Although the percentage is the same, the actual dollars are greater. The left graph in figure N.3 presents the results in nominal scale. The increases appear to have accelerating growth even though the percentage is the same. If misused, the graph can imply accelerating conditions rather than consistency.

Figure N.3. Example of Nominal and Log Scale Graphs

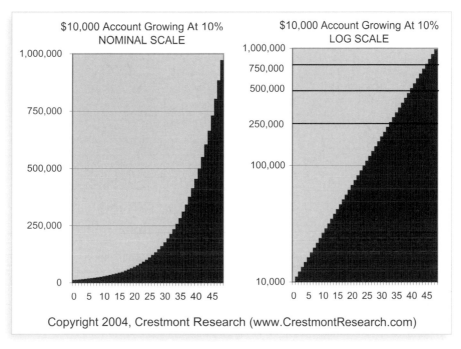

The same account is presented on a logarithmic scale, known as "log scale," in the right side of figure N.3. This adjusts the left-axis values to reflect the same percentage distance between the lines on the scale of the left axis rather than the same dollar change. As a result, the chart reflects the percentage growth and, in the example of your account, reflects a smooth 10% growth rate. By shifting to the log scale, the graph now highlights the consistency of 10% growth.

Sometimes, a graph is more appropriate on a nominal scale, to reflect actual dollar changes. Other times, the graph is more representative using the log scale to reflect percentage changes. For example, if the growth rate is declining over time, the nominal scale may not visually reflect the trend. Yet, the log scale will reflect the decline through an upward-sloping line that begins to reduce its slope by flattening. When the effect of compounding in the series becomes a greater component of growth, typically over longer periods of time, the log scale may provide a more accurate picture. At times in Crestmont's research, you may find both versions in the graphics.

Coincidence and Causality

One key concept in this book is the notion of cycles in the financial markets. Another is the relationship between two unique components of the markets or the economy. Analysts armed with spreadsheets can assess the relationship between any two data series. One of the more popular methods is to calculate the correlation between the numbers. Correlation assesses the similarity between two data series and is represented by a number between 0 and 1. A correlation of 0 indicates that the two series do not move in a similar pattern. A correlation of 1 indicates that the two series move in direct relationship to each other. When the relationship is opposite, and one series zigs while the other zags, the correlation is expressed as a negative. A perfectly inverse relationship is represented as a correlation of –1.

Both concepts — cycles and correlation — can be quantitatively measured. Despite the ability to assess a statistical relationship, the mere existence of a high value does not indicate that the relationship can be expected to continue. High correlations can be driven by causality as well as by coincidence. Causality indicates that one series causes another to move in a certain way. For example, the movements of the stock market directly affect the performance of your stock mutual funds. Since stock mutual funds are composed of stocks contained in the stock market, the relationship is not only high, but also causal.

At other times, the correlation can be coincidental. Some studies relating to historical stock market returns have found high correlation between the stock market direction and the width of men's ties or the length of women's skirts. Other popular relationships include stock market performance and professional football champions. Despite the solid track records and impressive statistics, it is hard to see a fundamental reason for these relationships. When two series act similarly without a fundamental reason, the likely cause is coincidence. The challenge for any reader of investment reports is to assess when correlations and relationships are causal and when they are coincidence. In this book and throughout Crestmont's research, the priority is to determine, and when possible prove, that fundamental relationships exist between components in the research that are used for conclusions.

Purpose

Unexpected Returns is intended to educate investors and should not be construed as investment advice nor a recommendation or solicitation to purchase or sell any security or investment.

Chapter One

1. Dava Sobel, *Longitude: The True Story of a Genius Who Solved the Greatest Scientific Problem of His Time* (United Kingdom: Penguin Books, 1995).
2. Roger Lowenstein, *Buffett: The Making of an American Capitalist* (Main Street Books, 1996).
3. George Santayana, *The Life of Reason* (New York: Scribner's, 1905), 284.
4. Campbell R. Harvey, personal interview, 2004.

Chapter Two

1. Roger Lowenstein, *Buffett: The Making of an American Capitalist* (Main Street Books, 1996).

Chapter Three

1. *The Matrix* (Warner Brothers, 1999).

Chapter Four

1. Robert J. Shiller, *Irrational Exuberance* (New York: Broadway Books, 2000), 3.
2. Sir Reginald McKenna quote, World Newsstand. http://www.worldnewsstand.net.

3. Sydney Homer and Richard Sylla, *A History of Interest Rates 3rd Revised Edition* (Piscataway: Rutgers University Press, 1996), 3.
4. Milton Friedman, "The Role of Monetary Policy," *The American Economic Review,* Vol. LVIII (1), March 1968.
5. Harvey Rosenblum, Business Economics, 2003, 6, 15.
6. Ed Easterling, "Dynamic Interest Rate Presentation," www.crestmo ntresearch.com.

Chapter Five

1. Edwin Lefevre, *Reminiscences of a Stock Operator* (New York: John Wiley & Sons, 1992), 122.
2. William Manchester, *The Last Lion: William Churchill* (New York: Little, Brown and Company, 1983).
3. Mark Twain, www.twainquotes.com.
4. William Proctor, *The Templeton Touch* (Radnor: Templeton Foundation Press, 1983).

Chapter Six

1. Charles D. Ellis, *Winning the Loser's Game,* 4th ed. (New York: McGraw-Hill Trade, 2002), 98.
2. James Grant, *Grant's Interest Rate Observer* (New York: Grant's Financial Publishing,Inc., 2004).
3. Francoise M. Voltaire, *Candide*. Reissue ed. (New York: Penguin Books, 1990).
4. Richard Russell, *Dow Theory Letters*, 2004.

Chapter Nine

1. Alexander M. Ineichen, *Absolute Returns: The Risk and opportunities of Hedge Fund Investing* (New York: John Wiley & Sons, Inc., 2002).
2. Harry Markowitz, "Portfolio Selection," *Journal of Finance,* Vol. VII, No. 1, March 1952.
3. Jonathan Burton, "Revisiting the Capital Asset Pricing Model," http://www.stanford.edu/`wfsharpe/art/djam/djam.htm. Reprinted with permission from Dow Jones Asset Manager. May/June 1998, 20.

Chapter Ten

1. Alexander M. Ineichen, *Absolute Returns: The Risk and Opportunities of Hedge Fund Investing* (New York: John Wiley & Sons, Inc., 2002), 22, 23.

Chapter Eleven

1. David F. Swenson, *Pioneering Portfolio Management: An Unconventional Approach to Institutional Investment* (New York: Free Press, 2000), 73.

Chapter Twelve

1. Christopher Finch, *The Illustrated history of the Financial Markets: In the Market* (New York: Abbeville Press Publishers, 2001), 341–50.
2. "A Short History of Wall Street," *Smart Investing*, 2004.
3. Economist.com, "Buy When You Hear Cannons Roar!" www.economist.com.na., 2001.
4. Heilbrunn Center for Graham and Dodd, Columbia Business School, *Value Investing History*, 2003.
5. Benjamin Graham and David Dodd, *Security Analysis, The 1934 Edition* (New York: McGraw-Hill Trade, 1996).
6. Peter L. Bernstein, "Points of Inflection: Investment Management Tomorrow," *Financial Analysts Journal*, July/August, 2003.

Bibliography

Balke, Nathan S., and Robert J. Gordon. "The Estimation of Prewar Gross National Product: Methodology and New Evidence". *Journal of Political Economy,* 1989, vol. 97, no. 1

Bernstein, Peter L. *Points of Inflection: Investment Management Tomorrow.* Financial Analysts Journal. July/August. 2003.

The Bond Market Association. www.bondmarkets.com

Buffett, Warren E. 2001. *Berkshire Hathaway Annual Report.*

Burton, Jonathan. *Revisiting the Capital Asset Pricing Model.* Reprinted with permission from *Dow Jones Asset Manager.* May/June 1998. http://www.stanford.edu/~wfsharpe/art/djam/djam.htm.

Easterling, Ed. Crestmont Research. www.CrestmontResearch.com, 2004.

Economist.com. "Buy When you Hear Cannons Roar!" www.economist.com.na, 2001.

Ellis, Charles D. *Winning the Loser's Game.* 4th ed. New York: McGraw-Hill Trade, 2002.

Finch, Christopher. *The Illustrated History of the Financial Markets: In the Market.* New York. Abbeville Press Publishers, 2001.

Friedman, Milton. "The Role of Monetary Policy." *The American Economic Review.* Vol. LVIII(1). March 1968.

Friedman, Milton, and Anna Schwartz. *A Monetary History of the United States, 1867–1960.* Princeton: Princeton University Press, 1971.

Graham, Benjamin, and David Dodd. *Security Analysis.* The 1934 Edition. New York: McGraw-Hill Trade, 1996.

Grant, James. *Grant's Interest Rate Observer.* New York. Grant's

Financial Publishing Inc., 2004.

Harvey, Campbell R. Fuqua School of Business, Duke University. Personal Interview, 2004.

Heilbrunn Center for Graham and Dodd. *Value Investing History.* Columbia Business School. 2003. http://www.1.gsb.columbia.edu/valueinvesting/about/history.html

Homer, Sidney, and Richard Eugene Sylla. *A History of Interest Rates.* 3rd rev. edition. Rutgers University Press, 1996.

Ineichen, Alexander M. *Absolute Returns: The Risk and Opportunities of Hedge Fund Investing.* New York: John Wiley and Sons, Inc., 2002.

Keynes, John Maynard. *The General Theory of Employment, Interest and Money.* New York: Harcourt, Brace, and World, 1936.

KingTutShop. 2004. *Ancient Egyptian Boats.* http://www.KingTutShop.com.

Krueger, Alan B. "Economic Scene." *New York Times.* August 22, 2002.

Laise, Eleanor. "Interview with Sir John Templeton." *Smart Money.* April 2004.

Lefevre, Edwin. *Reminiscences of a Stock Operator.* Originally published 1922. New York: John Wiley & Sons, Inc., 1994.

Lowenstein, Roger. *Buffett: The Making of an American Capitalist.* Main Street Books, 1996.

Manchester, William. *The Last Lion: William Churchill.* New York: Little, Brown and Company, 1983.

Markowitz, Harry. "Portfolio Selection." *Journal of Finance,* 1952.

The Matrix. Directors: Andy Wachowski, Larry Wachowski. Producer: Joel Silver. Warner Brothers, 1999.

Mauldin, John. *Bull's Eye Investing: Targeting Real Returns in a Smoke and Mirrors Market.* New York: John Wiley & Sons, Inc., 2004.

National Maritime Museum, 2004. http://www.nmm.sc.uk.

Proctor, William. *The Temple Touch.* Radnor: Templeton Foundation Press, 1983.

Rosenblum, Harvey. *Business Economics*, January 2003.

Santayana, George. *Life of Reason*. New York: Scribner's, 1905.

Russell, Richard. *Dow Theory Letters*, 2004.

Shiller, Robert J. *Irrational Exuberance*. New York: Broadway Books, 2000.

A Short History of Wall Street. Smart Investing, 2004. www.stocks-investing.com/stock-markethistory.html.

Sobel, Dava. *Longitude: The True Story of a Genius Who Solved the Greatest Scientific Problem of His Time*. United Kingdom: Penguin Books, 1995.

Swenson, David F. *Pioneering Portfolio Management: An Unconventional Approach to Institutional Investment*. New York: Free Press, 2000.

Twain, Mark. www.twainquotes.com

Voltaire, Francoise M. *Candide*. Reissue edition. United Kingdom: Penguin Books, 1990.

World Newstand. http://www.worldnewsstand.net

INDEX